THE ISOPLEX METHOD

MUSCULATION PROGRAM FOR AN AESTHETIC AND TRULY ATLETHIC BODY

Isometrics * Plyometrics * Flexiometrics

T̄ime T̄ested – M̄inimal Ēquipment – S̄uitable for Āll

By

Marc De Bremaeker

Fons Sapientiae Publishing

THE ISOPLEX METHOD - MUSCULATION PROGRAM FOR AN AESTHETIC AND TRULY ATLETHIC BODY

Published in 2017 by Fons Sapientiae Publishing, Cambridge, United Kingdom.

Please note that the publisher and author of this instructional book are NOT RESPONSIBLE in any manner whatsoever for any injury that may result from practicing the techniques and/or following the instructions given within. Physical Training can be dangerous, -both to you and others-, if not practiced safely. If you are in doubt as how to proceed or whether your practice is safe, consult with an accredited coach, physical trainer before beginning. Since the physical activities described maybe too strenuous in nature for some readers, it is essential that a physician be consulted prior to any type of training.

Copyright © by Marc De Bremaeker

All rights reserved. No part of this publication may be reproduced or utilized in any form or by any means, electronic or mechanical, without prior written permission from the author and/or the publisher.
martialartkicks@gmail.com

ISBN of Printed version: 978-0-9957952-0-4

Recommended reading, by the same author:

"Plyo-Flex-Plyometrics and Flexibility Training for Explosive Martial Arts Kicks" (2013)

Dedication

This Book was the idea of my son Nimrod. Without his nagging pressure, it would not have been written. I am grateful and wish to dedicate this work to him. His perfectionistic outlook on life is an inspiration.

**Remember that our sons and grandsons are going to do things that would stagger us.
~Daniel Burnham**

Dear Reader,

In this day and age, the life of a serious author has become quite difficult. The proliferation of books and the explosion of internet content has made it nearly impossible to promote work based on extensive research and requiring complex lay-out.
Please enjoy this book. Once you are finished, I would ask kindly that you take a few short minutes to give your honest opinion. A unbiased Amazon review, of even a few words only, would be highly appreciated and encouraging.

Thank You,

Marc

**Kindness in words creates confidence. Kindness in thinking creates profoundness. Kindness in giving creates love.
~Lao Tzu**

ACKNOWLEDGEMENTS

Without the active support of my wife and life companion, *Aviva Giveoni*, this book would not have come to life. Being an athlete in her own right, she understands the meaning of hard work and dedication.

Aviva

Sensei Shlomo Faige

Among many teachers,- and head and shoulders above all-, my late Coach and Sensei, *Sidney (Shlomo) Faige*, should be mentioned with longing thankfulness.

Special Thanks to my life-long friend, athlete emeritus, coach and training partner, *Roy Faige*, for his help and support. Roy is now heading the Shi Heun Martial Arts School is also my co-author of *The Essential Book of Martial Arts Kicks*. His influence and advice is felt in nearly every page of this work and in the books of the 'Kicks' series.

Roy and Marc

The drawings in this book are mine. Everything that I have learned about line art, I have done so from professional Illustrator *Shahar Navot*, who illustrated *The Essential Book of Martial Arts Kicks*. Thanks Shahar!

Strength does not come from winning. Your struggles develop your strengths. When you go through hardships and decide not to surrender, that is strength.
~Arnold Schwarzenegger

Contents

Introduction 11
Chapter One - Isoplex in Brief 17
Chapter Two - Bodybuilding 20
Chapter Three - Plyometrics Theory 23
Chapter Four - Flexiometrics Theory 27
Chapter Five - Isometrics Theory 34
Chapter Six - Isoplex: Putting It All Together 41
Chapter Seven - Nutrition and Sleep 43
Chapter Eight - Plyometric Exercises 46
Chapter Nine - Flexiometric Exercises 84
Chapter Ten - Isometric Drills 118
Chapter Eleven - The Isometric 'Machines' 148
Chapter Twelve - The Programs 152
    The Beginner 154
    The Trainee 175
    The Intermediate 202
    The Advanced 228
    The Partner 251
Afterword 275

> **I question myself every day. That's what I still find motivating about this. I don't have the answers, I don't pretend that I do just because I won the match. Just keep fighting and maybe something good happens.**
> **~Andre Agassi**

Introduction

<u>**Isoplex**</u> stands for **Iso**metrics, **Pl**yometrics and **Flex**iometrics. The well-organized combination of these three training methods will give the serious trainee the most effective path possible to powerful and aesthetic muscles, in a minimum of time. That is what this book is all about.

The author has penned a previous book named '*Plyo-Flex*' on the same general subject, but that book is a specialty work targeted specifically at kicking Martial Artists. The full sub-title of this previous book is: "*Plyometrics and Flexibility Training for Explosive Martial Arts Kicks and Performance Sports*".

Obviously, Plyo-Flex stands for: *Plyometrics* and *Flexiometrics*. But *Plyo-Flex* is for well-trained Martial Artists, is very specific and it does pre-supposes a basis of at least well-trained strong muscles. Moreover, it was written as very focused on kicking power and it presents numerous specific kicking drills that are of no interest to the average and general trainee.

The success of '*Plyo-Flex*' though, together with many enquiries and positive reviews, did lead me to consider a treatise more suitable for the general population: A training method with minimal equipment for all, men or women, beginners or advanced trainees, involved in all possible athletic activities or not, but striving for an athletic and aesthetic body. Based on my long training and coaching experience, I consider that the lacking "muscle-building" tenet from '*Plyo-Flex*' is best- and fastest-achieved by *Isometric* Training. Therefore, we added *Isometrics* to the basic principles exposed in '*Plyo-Flex*' and designed the universal training program hereto described: **ISOPLEX**, quick progress for everyone. *Isometrics, Plyometrics, Flexiometrics…*

<u>**Isometrics**</u> are a very safe, efficient and easy way to build the muscles. *Isometric* simply means: 'same length'; the underlying principle is that the exercised muscle's *length* stays constant during the drill. These exercises are by definition done in **static positions**. Theoretically at least, the angle of the joint and the length of the muscle do not change during the muscle contraction…

... An example of an *Isometric* exercise would be pushing against the wall (**Overcoming isometrics** = you cannot push the wall away) or maintaining the position against a partner's weight (**Yielding isometrics** = you could push the partner away if you wished to). Maintaining a challenging position, like standing with a leg in extended kicking position, is another example of a truly Isometric exercise, well-known in Martial Arts training halls. This leads us to note that, in fact, many *Yoga* balance exercises are also extremely beneficial isometric exercises: maintaining the position and balance requires the static work of many opposing muscle groups. Presented here, just as an illustration are the Chair Pose (*Utkatasana*) and the Warrior 3 Pose (*Virabhadrasana*). Just try to keep the poses for 30 seconds and you'll feel that it only *looks* easy.

Chair Pose

A close relative of *Isometrics*, is **Dynamic Self-Resistance**, in which you use your own muscles against their opposites to develop a very slow and concentrated movement. In this case, the trained muscle length does change, albeit extremely slowly against the resistance of another muscle group. A Martial Artist or enthusiast would recognize this instantly as the typical slow and hard Formal Exercise (*Kata*) of the classical and very powerful Okinawan styles of Karatedo like *Goju-ryu* or *Uechi-ryu* schools. Let the reader note that, for our purposes, all these variations of Isometrics will be considered as general Isometric exercises.

Yoga's Warrior Three

Goju-ryu Karate Kata

<u>Plyometrics</u> could be defined as the training for *explosiveness*. Explosiveness could be defined in turn, for sports, as a combination of **power and speed**. This is what athletes of all fields need for performance, and this is what also gives a truly aesthetic body. The principle behind this kind of exercise is that you drill the muscle by contracting it eccentrically and then immediately, concentrically. The theory and physiology behind it is not of great importance for our purpose, but will be hinted at in the relevant chapter. Just remember that you will usually stretch the muscle before shocking it into contracting...

... For anybody doubting the bump in performance he can expect from serious *Plyometrics* training, the generally agreed upon history of its development would be of interest: The Russians used to dominate Track & Field Athletics in the Nineteen Fifties, until the secret of their success was discovered as the training techniques of *Coach Yuri Verkhoshansky*. Only once these techniques became generally used and refined all over the world, did the field level. *Plyometrics* started to be used in all sports with great success.

There are today many variations and denominations for what is basically *Plyometrics*, like "Kinetic Energy Accumulation Training" or "Shock Training", but the basic ideas behind the drills are the same. Some of the exercises presented will even be outside the physiological theory presented, as what is important for us is not the pure Sport Science, but the contribution of the drill to more athletic muscles.

Plyometrics are used in all sports, Basket Ball for example

It is the author's opinion that *Plyometrics* are not used enough in general training for two basic reasons. **Reason One**: *Plyometrics* have sometimes the bad reputation of being dangerous and detrimental to the joints. To this we reply that *Plyometrics* are a tool and it is the way it is used that will make it beneficial or detrimental. Cautious and gradual drilling will ensure no harm is done while huge progress is achieved.

The **other reason** is probably the fact that "*Plyos*" do not look much like 'sexy muscle-building'. Jumping off boxes may seem 'nerdy' to some. Big mistake!

<u>**Flexiometrics**</u>, the third tenet of this program, is an invented word in the spirit of *Plyometrics*. It should mean, in the author's mind, something like **Intensive Stretching**. The exercises presented are not new or based on any novel theory. The naming we gave comes in here to try to underline the fact that a lot of investment in serious Stretching is required in this program, much more than what is usually done by most trainees. Much too often, Stretching is an annoying part of the warm-up and of the cool-down of training sessions, when it is not completely forgotten. And although it is extremely important to stretch before and after training, this should not be considered in itself as Flexibility Training. "*Flexiometrics*" is therefore, for us, the ***dedicated, systematic and separate work on stretching and flexibility*** that will benefit any athlete.

A minimal amount of theory about Flexibility will be presented in the relevant chapter, but it is the *Yoga-type* work that is favored by the author...

INTRODUCTION

...Just like for *Plyometrics*, the author feels that *Flexibility Training* is looked down upon because it takes away precious time from sexier muscle building. Moreover, flexible trainees tend to believe that they do not need it, while stiff trainees do not believe that the time needed for some small eventual improvement is justified. They are *both* wrong! It is true that flexibility improvements require time and methodical training but they will bring, much faster than thought, huge progress to all: athletic performance, muscle tonus and overall health. It is the premise of both this book and of previous '*PlyoFlex*' that **<u>Flexibility Training synergistically enhances muscle growth and performance from Strength Training.</u>**

Many feel that Flexibility is a genetic given and that not much can be done if one is born stiff. It is true that genetics are important, and that one should start exercising his flexibility as early as possible. But one's flexibility can greatly be improved by regular and intensive training. It has been shown by academic research, and time and again proven in practice and in our own hands-on experience; there is no doubt about it. Moreover, and as mentioned, Flexibility Training tremendously boosts effective muscle building and athletic performance.

Flexibility training should start as early as possible, but can be greatly improved at any age

It should be noted that this book does not pretend to be exhaustive. It will present a range of stretching exercises that the author feels are the most important to drill. But there are many more possible drills, probably all beneficial. There would be no point in an encyclopedic presentation of the subject, and the advanced trainee is invited to do his own research and devise his own variations once all those presented have been mastered.

This book's purpose is to present an exercise program and describe possible drills. Going further into the various theories and current controversies of Sport Science is beyond the scope of this book. There are numerous previous Physiology studies and current research going on about muscles in athletic activities, but we shall limit ourselves to briefly present the general understanding commonly accepted at the time of this writing. We shall not go into physiological details which will not contribute much to the practically-inclined reader.

Good Luck to All!

CHAPTER ONE - ISOPLEX IN BRIEF

ISOPLEX stands for *Isometrics/Plyometrics/Flexiometrics*. As explained in the introduction, the method is simply the optimal combination of those three basic tenets of fitness training. *Isoplex* is designed to achieve the best possible results in the shortest possible time. It is suitable for men and women. It is suitable for beginners, for athletes of for all types, and even for bodybuilders. It is designed to build an aesthetic physique which is also conducive to sport performance and to personal health. We shall further describe each of its three components, but *Isoplex* first must be set apart from some other classic ways of training.

While it is certainly not critical of it, *Isoplex* is not a 'Bodybuilding' program in the sense of voluminous bulging muscles. *Isoplex* does not lead to 'bulking up' *Schwarzenegger*-style; it leads to long, supple, toned, efficient and aesthetic muscles. Bodybuilding is a legitimate sport which I respect wholeheartedly, having both a spouse and a son who practiced it at the competitive level. But bodybuilding has a certain goal in mind that is not suitable or desired by all; it strives for a well-defined but very bulky musculature to be judged against a certain standard. An outstanding bodybuilder will unfortunately lack speed, flexibility and explosive power; most others will also lack aerobic qualities because of the inherent relative high weight they carry. And above all, not all would-be trainees do aspire to a 'Hulk-type' body. When training, and especially when starting a training program, one should know what one's goal is. If it is a bodybuilder body that one strives for, then this book is not it; Isoplex training would be an excellent definition-work addition to a bodybuilding routine, but certainly not the core of it. The reader must bear that in mind.

ISOPLEX is in fact the modern and more scientific version of the training ideals of Greco-Roman Antiquity. As illustrated by many well-known antique sculptures, the athletes of old had aesthetic bodies based on core musculature and long, well-defined and necessarily efficient muscles. I have no doubt in my mind that most laymen, male or female, will find the body of the 'Doryphoros by Polykleitos' more aesthetically pleasing than that of, otherwise legitimate champion, Lou Ferrigno. I again want to apologize and assure all bodybuilding fans that I do not seek to denigrate their sport but only to make clear different possible fitness goals...

Lou Ferrigno

... The word 'Athlete' comes from ancient Greek for 'contestant or prize fighter'. The ancient Olympic Games did in fact have fighting contests much prized by the spectators from all over Ancient Greece. All contest categories required overall athletic proficiency and the contestants were trying hard to build adequate bodies. The categories listed in the heyday of those games were:

Doryphoros by Polykleitos

- The *stadion*, about 200 m sprint
- The *diaulos*, about 400 m sprint
- The *dolichos*, about 5000 m race
- The *hoplitodromos*, about 600 m race in full soldiery gear weighing about 25 kgs
- *Pygme*, extreme boxing
- *Pale*, wrestling
- *Pankration*, 'everything goes' boxing and wrestling bout, something like an extreme form of today's MMA (*Mixed Martial arts of UFC* fame)
- Chariot racing
- *Pentathlon*: Five disciplines-contest composed of stadion race, wrestling, discus throwing, javelin throwing and long jumping.

Those Olympic Games were representative of a culture placing the aesthetic human body at top of its ideals. They were also the pretext for much artistic expression like paintings, sculptures, poems and songs. This cultural trait was later picked up by the Roman conquerors who later excelled at building public bath for training and taking care of the body. Sport performance was a Greek and Roman ideal, and so was the aesthetics of the human body as exemplified in many an antique sculpture and their Renaissance inspirations.

The education of a Greek young man was divided into: grammar, music, and *gymnastics*. But gymnastics was by far the most important tenet, taking more time than all other disciplines together. The Greeks hold that the mind could not possibly be healthy, outside of a healthy body. The Ancient Greeks would certainly not have attained mastery of classic sculpture, if the artists had not been utterly familiar with the athletic human body surrounding them at all times. There was no Ancient Greek town of any significance which did not possess its public gymnasium, usually built on the same basic plan; and these places also showed a strong connection with hygiene, medicinal Arts and healthy nutrition.

...Training in these times was highly specific to the performance required for performance sports, be it Fighting or Track events, and very much in line with Isoplex principles. We shall elaborate further in the text.

These training principles are and were universal. They were to be found in ancient Asian Martial Arts and in Body Cultures like Yoga, in Chi Kung and many others. A truly athletic and functional body needed for realistic fighting was achieved by a mixture of Isometric exercises, intensive Flexibility Training and dynamic (*Plyometric*) drills. Martial Artists and Yogis will immediately grasp the connection. This is the way to train the body for effective and natural aesthetics, and that is what *Isoplex* will try to concentrate on through an optimal and synergistic time-saving program.

Physical fitness is not only one of the most important keys to a healthy body, it is the basis of dynamic and creative intellectual activity.
~John F. Kennedy

CHAPTER TWO - BODYBUILDING

For a better understanding of *Isoplex*, we shall examine first, in brief, the principles behind weight exercises for muscle building, as generally practiced today in modern gyms. Those principles, with added aspects of nutrition and supplementation, are at the basis of the sport of *Bodybuilding*. This is not what *Isoplex* is about, but it is important for clear differentiation and for possible complementary training by some more experienced athletes.

In **Bodybuilding**, growth to *muscle hypertrophy* is the goal to achieve: big skeletal muscles that will make the practitioner large, bulky and strong.

Training for big muscles is based on short sets (anaerobic) of high-intensity weight-lifting exercises in a framework of *Progressive Overload*. Progressive Overload means a gradual increase of the weight, the repetitions and/or the sets. It is the basic principle that will lead, after weeks and months of dedicated training, to muscle hypertrophy. Weight training causes micro-tears to the muscles used; this condition is called micro-trauma and it is the repair of muscle fibers that will result in subsequent muscle growth. The high levels of muscle growth and of repair required by bodybuilders mandate a specialized diet; and nutrition with supplementation is a big part of Bodybuilding. It is interesting to note that it is those muscular micro-tears mentioned that cause soreness a day (or sometimes two) after the training session (*Delayed Onset Muscle Soreness - DOMS*). DOMS levels are reduced by regular training.

Accepted Sport Science and training experience discerns three types of weight lifting execution for different objectives:
- *Strength*, typically for powerlifters and sports requiring pure strength.
- *Volume*, typically for bodybuilders.
- *Endurance*, typically for more aerobic athletic activities requiring 'tonus over time'.

It should be noted that what is truly meant here is *emphasis* on one of the executions while still training across all three methods. All athletes need all three qualities in different measures, and progress can only be made by gradually improving all aspects. Training programs usually cycle between methods with further sophisticated "rep/speeds/sets/weight" set-ups...

- **Strength training** is based on sets of few reps of heavy weights, typically 5 reps of the 80% Maximal Weight (maximum weight one can lift in one-repetition). This usually results in what is called '*myofibrillated hypertrophy*' in which the muscle gains in size because of an increase of *contractile protein fibers.*
- **Volume training** is based on more repetitions with lighter weights, typically sets of 10 reps of the 60% of Maximal Weight. This leads mainly to '*sarcoplasmic hypertrophy*' in which the volume of fluid *(sarcoplasmic fluid)* in the muscle cells themselves increases and allows for more glycogen storage. It should be noted that this has, at least theoretically, no bearing on increased muscular strength.
- **Endurance training** is logically based on more reps with even lighter weight, -typically sets of 12 to 20 reps-, which make the results even more tilted towards sarcoplasmic results, and especially towards increased *glycogen-storing capacity.*

The two different types of hypertrophy, -sarcoplasmic and myofibrillar-, do not really happen independently from one another in the real world, and training will result in a bit of both with some different emphasis. Many athletes do regularly switch between the two methods in order to prevent the body from getting comfortable. By keeping challenging the muscles, they will try to "confuse" the body in order to avoid 'plateauing' at a certain level. In all athletic training, the key is to keep progressing with a slowly and gradually increasing difficulty level (*Gradual Overload principle*)

Bodybuilding today has become something between an Art and a Science: many coaches and gyms have developed their training principles and routines to which they stick religiously, and everyday are published new articles on programs and other insights. Here follows a generally accepted set of rules for **Hypertrophy Training,** just to whet the reader's appetite:

- Always warm-up.
- Use mostly free weights.
- Concentrate on compound exercises (using more than one joint).
- Use perfect technique.
- Always go through full range of motion.
- Breathe out during the effort part.
- Lower the weight slowly.
- Train each body part only once a week.
- Perform around an overall of 10 sets per muscle group.
- Rest around between 1 and 2 minutes between sets.
- Do sets that go from not less than 6 to not more than 12 reps.

...
- Weight used should not exceed 80% of Maximal 1 Rep Weight.
- Increase the weight over time (Overload Principle).
- Training sessions should not exceed 90 minutes at the time.
- Cheat your muscles by changing workout programs.
- Start your workout with the biggest muscle groups first, smaller muscles later.
- Start with the heavy Compound Drills first and progress to lighter Isolation Exercises.
- Thoroughly stretch the trained muscles at the end of the workout.
- Cardio is required at least twice a week.

That's *Bodybuilding*...

Isoplex, unlike traditional training and Bodybuilding, is not based on reps and sets; strength training will be based on a limited number of 'long' contractions. But changing programs regularly will always be beneficial. More to follow.

CHAPTER THREE - PLYOMETRICS THEORY

3.1 General

The Merriam-Webster dictionary defines *Plyometrics* as: "Exercise involving repeated rapid stretching and contracting of muscles (as by jumping and rebounding) to increase muscle power". The stretching before contracting ensures a more intense contraction, and therefore more explosive power. The use of "explosive" tries to convey a dimension of time to the qualities gained by such training: The muscles so-trained will so be stronger *while contracting faster at peak power*.
Muscle Strength is the maximum force one can squeeze out of his muscles, like the heaviest weight one can lift. **Muscle Power** is different: it is achieving this full strength **fast**.
A muscle needs to contract in order to cause movement. It has been demonstrated that this *concentric contraction* will be all the more energetic if the muscle has been stretched immediately before in what is called *eccentric contraction*, storing in fact some *elastic energy*. In layman's terms, you get more bang for the buck if you lengthen your muscle just before you contract it into the required move, and this because it adds the energy from your muscle elasticity to the whole equation. This is often referred to as the <u>stretch shortening cycle</u>. A muscle stretched just before it contracts will do so with more energy. As the muscles become used to the extra power, they become more efficient at storing elastic energy. The total amount of power exerted during the exercise is more than with regular exercise, therefore causing more muscle potential power with time. The muscles become able to go from the eccentric contraction to the concentric contraction faster, thus creating "<u>peak power</u>" – fast maximum energy. This is what is referred to, in Sport Science, as <u>"shortening the stretch cycle"</u>.This is one of the reasons why most plyometric exercises should be executed in a "multi-response" way, meaning in series and *with no pause* in between the jumps. Multi-response keeps fast alternating of stretch and contract; and it challenges the muscle accordingly. All exercises should be started single-response to let the body familiarize itself with the specific move (For example, jumping up after jumping off a box, then rest). But, when adequate, one should gradually strive to go multi-response: back and forth fast and with no rest (Jumping back onto the box immediately after landing from the jump-up). It is then important to remember that the key is to keep the 'landing and rebounding' (*muscle amortization phase*) as short as possible. **Behave as if the ground is toxic** or made of burning coal!

… There is much more to the full physiological theory than what has been presented: there is a part played by the *Myotatic Reflex*, which is the automatic contraction of a stretched muscle; and a neurological part played by this same "Stretch" Reflex which lowers the body's tendency to automatically limit maximum power exerted. *Plyometrics* drills will therefore improve gradually the neuro-muscular interactions while allowing for the highest possible energy application in training. Each time a specific and correct plyometric jump is practiced, the nerve endings become better at transmitting the same signal to the muscle. These nervous interfaces (*synapses*) develop over time for a more powerful stimulation of the muscle: you become better at getting a bigger muscle contraction.

The several existing different theories on how and why it works are probably all valid and do complement each other. There is no controversy though that **Plyometrics do work!**

For the reader who is interested in the theories behind *Plyometrics* and wants to dwell into the very interesting physiological details, I would recommend to start with the works of the "father" of modern Plyometrics: *Prof. Yuri Verkhoshansky*. His books are readily available in English and extremely detailed.

3.2   *Caution*

Plyometrics are not for the untrained. Some coaches have given them a bad reputation and are firmly against their practice on the grounds of safety. They argue that the benefits are largely outweighed by the damage they can cause, because they apply to the muscles, joints and connective tissues more energy 'than what they are built for'. The author will argue that it is exactly what sport is all about: furthering gradually the border of human potential, with the emphasis on **gradually**. All physical activities lead to some fiber destruction that will allow the body to re-build stronger fibers to adapt to what is regularly asked from the same body. Ask, -slowly-, more and more of your body and it will adapt. Accordingly, **only** *Plyometrics* will be able to let you access the next stage of muscular *Explosive Power*. Just make sure you proceed carefully.

Here is maybe the place for a little illustrative story. As mentioned, *Plyometrics* were part of Ancient Times' ways to train for efficiency. The well-known *Shaolin* monks, forefathers of all Oriental Fighting Arts, had among many a Plyometric-looking drill of jumping out of a hole in the ground with no hands. The training monk started jumping easily from a very shallow hole but he had to dig out a very thin layer of soil every day, making the exercise more difficult in an extremely gradual way. Chinese patience and caution! At the end, the results were astonishing and the monk could jump out of surprisingly deep holes with ease. That is *gradual* for you…

...*Plyometrics* have, in fact, a proven long-term effect of *injury prevention*; but it should be underscored again that these exercises have to be taken up very gradually and after a minimum level of muscle tone has been achieved. Because all their purpose is to maximize the amount of energy applied to the muscles, tendons and joints, it is easy to understand that they require slow and methodical implementation.

As a rule of thumb, the Plyometrics total beginner will have to develop average muscle strength first by regular training and muscle-building exercises. Only after a few months, should he start carefully doing these drills, after warm-up, and under professional supervision. He should always ensure that he is properly warmed up, and that he stops at the first sign of joint pain.

For a total beginner, a stand-alone plyometric session should always start with a ten minutes warm-up and light stretching. Then five minutes of plyometric exercises. No more. Then five minutes cool-down stretching. The "*Plyometrics*" part of the session can then be increased by a weekly five more minutes, with caution and stopping at the first hint of joint pain. The cool down should become a full ten minutes. Altogether, a training session should never go over one hour, which means about forty net minutes of high energy *Plyos*. One of the advantages of the **Isoplex Method** is that the *Plyo* part is always well seconded into a warming flexibility session, for optimal results and time saving.

Generally speaking:

Training sessions should be two a week at the start, then three a week, but never more.

Plyometrics should not be done day after day, and there always should be one day in between sessions. The Isoplex method takes care of that.

It is recommended to practice on soft flooring, like grass, carpet or indoor sports halls. Never on hard floors like concrete. The wearing of running trainers, reducing impact shock, can be of big help.

Above all, the trainee is advised to use common sense and to "listen" to his body.

3.3   Plyometrics in the Isoplex Program

The athletic benefits of plyometric training are now clear to the reader. They will give the trainee effective powerful muscles able to contract fast and strong. Moreover, the training sessions are obviously high-impact, causing cardio-vascular enhancement and fat-burning. What is not to like?

But as mentioned, *Plyometrics* do require basic strength. This will be achieved by *Isometrics*, which will be presented later. The last tenet of real fitness is then: Flexibility, which enhances athletic performance, both inherently, and also by synergistically boosting strength and power training results. *Flexiometrics*, basically Intense Stretching, will therefore close the training triangle.

One of the advantages of **Isoplex** is that it places the plyometric session in the middle of Flexibility training. It both saves training time and ensures that Plyometrics are executed when well warmed-up. It also ensures that the challenged muscles are later stretched thoroughly for better recovery and overall tonus. Isometric and Plyometric sessions will also be alternated daily to allow for more effective recovery.

3.4   Equipment

Another advantages of *Plyometrics* is that it requires little equipment and that everyday objects can usually be used as replacements. Many exercises will also be executed with no equipment necessary at all.

The most ubiquitous piece of equipment needed is probably the "*Box*". It can be especially built, or it can simply be a sturdy stool, an aerobic step or a stack of them, a low wall in the garden, steps,... The height will depend on your proficiency and can be increased gradually. The author personally likes a stack of aerobic steps: you can use one step at the beginning, and later stack a few to the required height.

Traffic plastic Cones are often used to safely signal height and place. They are cheap and easy to procure.

Hurdles are used, but must not be fixed to avoid dangerous tripping. If you bump into them, they should fall down. *Do not* use a Doorframe Bar or a fixed rope: they are immovable and could make you trip dangerously.

Medicine Balls are necessary for some exercises; they are also easy to procure.

Drills with a *partner* will be presented, but will not be introduced in the basic regular training programs. Training with a partner is ideal, but not always possible. Therefore, the gradual training programs will be doable alone. A special program for two will be presented separately, and proficient athletes will also be able to use the book to design their own partners-training routines.

CHAPTER FOUR - FLEXIOMETRICS THEORY

4.1 General

Flexibility could be defined as the ability to use the full Range of Movement (*ROM*) of a joint or of a combination of joints, and of the relevant muscles attached to those joints. Flexibility, or rather the personal "full range" of an individual is very much determined by genetics but it can be improved markedly by Stretching. But more importantly, it can also *be severely decreased by the absence of stretching*, especially when combined with aggressive muscle growth.
Stretching is the elongation of the muscles, joints and connective tissues in order to improve Flexibility. It should be noted that Flexibility is *not* necessarily a *general* attribute: it is specific to each joint. One can be very flexible at the hips but stiff at the shoulders, or vice versa; or one could be more flexible at the right leg than at the left.

Speed, -being a part of the "explosiveness" equation mentioned before-, is important for most athletic activities. Flexibility inherently improves *Speed Potential*. Moreover, the reader will remember that Plyometrics are based on contracting a *stretched* muscle, and therefore Flexibility will also likely improve potential results from plyometric training. The reader understands now that all three tenets of **Isoplex** are intimately linked.

The other benefits of stretching are common to all sports: better muscle tone, less danger of injury, easy use of the full range of joint movement and reduction of muscle soreness. And the relaxing effect of stretching is clear to anyone who has capped a full Yoga session with a meditation and relaxation posture: care must be taken in order not to fall asleep, and the feeling of well-being is incredible and very different from any other brought by exercise.

The generally accepted theory of *Stretching* will be now briefly presented. It differentiates between several types of stretching, generally four types, that will be introduced at the top of next page:...

4.1.1 _Static Stretching_: You basically hold a position at its full-range of motion, like the 'Splits'. Some authors differentiate further between _Static-Passive_ where gravity helps to maintain the position (Splits); and _Static-Active_ where the muscles are used to maintain the position (Also called _Active Flexibility Stretching_). Yoga is the embodiment of _Static Stretching_, and its results for flexibility improvement speak for themselves. The accepted physiological theory stresses that there is no need to hold a stretch longer than twenty seconds to benefit from it, although twelve seconds is a minimum.

Static Passive Stretching – gravity helped

4.1.2 _Dynamic Stretching_: This is obviously stretching while moving and it uses the full range of a joint movement at regular or high speed, and usually in a specific sport application. You basically stretch the muscle dynamically into an extended range of motion, BUT not exceeding your _static-passive stretching ability_. An example is the straight-leg Front Kick, in which you balance your leg higher and higher, but not more than the front splits you could potentially do on the floor.

Dynamic Stretching: Straight-leg Front Kick

4.1.3 _Ballistic Stretching_: This is the "old" and bad way to stretch. It uses the energy of bouncing motions to further lengthen the muscles and increase the range of motion, trying to gradually force your way a bit further. This has a greater potential to cause injury and does not lengthen the tissues. Moreover, do you remember the injury-preventing _Stretch Reflex_ mentioned in "Plyometrics" above? Bouncing causes this reflex and therefore the automatic _contracting_ of the muscle! Not good!

4.1.4 _Passive Stretching_: This is another word for _partner training_, although the partner can also be replaced by common equipment or stretching machines. In principle, you relax your muscles and let the partner increase slowly and gradually the range of motion. It has the great advantage to allow for stretching beyond the static range of motion, but it requires great care and sensitivity from your partner. Also, the speed of pressure increase must be **slow** and **carefully controlled** to avoid the infamous _Stretch Reflex_ to set in.

Passive stretching: The hip joint in Roundhouse Kick Chamber

...There are more sophisticated stretching strategies, but they are beyond the scope of this book.

We shall not dwell deep into the physiology of stretching, as it has no direct bearing in how to train besides what has already been written. But let us just say this: the muscles are composed of different sorts of fibers, based on different proteins and configurations. Some specific proteins have more bearing to the elasticity of the fiber than others but their names will not help the trainee. The joints and connective tissues also play a key role, but most of it is common sense. Most of the connective tissues that include well-known collagen are *viscoelastic* in nature. It simply means that, when stretched, they do not revert immediately to their former state like an elastic band, but do so very slowly and gradually. This explains partly why flexibility will tend to decrease if you stop training.

While stretching, the artist has to cause the body to reconfigure itself in a more flexible set-up; this will be achieved by going very slowly and gradually a bit further each time, by avoiding the "*Stretch Reflex*" to kick in, and by lowering the sensitivity signals (pain) sent by the neurological interfaces to the muscles and joints. When a muscle is stretched, the nerve interface sends a message to the central nervous system to cause a reflex contraction in order to prevent damage. But, if the stretch is maintained for longer than about 6 seconds, the '*Golgi*' tendon organs send another signal which will cause the muscle to now relax. The only way to progress then, is by stretching SLOWLY, by relaxing. More advanced trainees will also be making use of the *reciprocal inhibition reflex*. This is fancy wording for the body's tendency to relax a muscle when the antagonistic muscle is contracted. In other words and for example, in your full stretch, you will then slowly contract your quadriceps to further relax your hamstrings (*Reciprocal Innervation*).

It should be noted, that a new Sensory Theory is being put forward that proposes that increases in muscle extensibility are at least partially a consequence of an improved (mental) stretch *tolerance* rather than only a physical change in the muscle fibers themselves. This theory is challenged by some, but enough to have mentioned it and to hope that it also plays a role in the well documented progress that regular stretching brings.

4.2 Caution

Stretching must be done very *carefully*. It is obvious, as it is dealing with elasticity. Overstretching anything elastic can cause irreversible damage; it is common sense. On the other hand, stretching has been demonstrated to prevent future injuries when done properly, and it is known to have a long-term protective effect.

Our '*Plyo-Flex*' book did advocate training sessions fully dedicated to stretching, because it was aiming at a specific goal for accomplished athletes; but appropriate stretching should also be practiced in the warm-up and cool-down parts of **any** regular training session; more on that further on. *Isoplex* being more general, it will pair **Stretching** with either *Plyometrics* or *Isometrics* for synergy and optimal time management.

Dedicated stretching should only be done *after warming-up*, as the warmed muscle lends itself to more stretching and to less danger of injury.
Stretching must be done carefully, by "listening" to your body: You have to reach your maximum static range of motion slowly, with relaxed muscles and *without bouncing*. The position should be held comfortably **for about 20 seconds**. If you feel it is not possible, you are already too far; more on the methodology further on.

Never stretch an injured muscle. *Do not* use warming balms (Deep Heat, Ben-Gay, Tiger Balm, and others) as substitutes to a physical warm-up; those are excellent for after-training, or in combination with a real physical warm-up.

It will never be said enough: *NEVER bounce* or use jerky movements when you stretch!

Stretching is no contest: Do not try to "beat" a partner or friend! Stretching is doing your own best in the framework of your genetic potential, and improving yourself slowly and gradually: You can compare to yourself only! *Leave your ego out of the training room.*

4.3 Stretching methodology for Isoplex training

It has already been made clear how important **Stretching** is for all athletes. Just to remind the reader of its advantages: Flexibility, injury protection, speed and better muscle development.

This training program includes the stretching part into composite sessions: either with *Plyometrics* or with *Isometrics*. Basically, **Stretching** will be "sort of" the warm-up and **Intensive Stretching** will be the cool-down. This will allow to save precious training time and to compound the muscle building results. The general principles of stretching stay the same, with a bit more dynamic stretching during warm-up. Any stretch can be done during cool-down as the muscles and joints are then very warm and supple, but it adds qualities of relaxation to avoid a shortening of the muscle, later in the recuperation phase of previous high impact training. All the stretching exercises presented in the book can be done in the cool-down part of any regular training. At this stage, it is needless to remind the reader that a stretching cool-down is a must after plyometric, weight or isometrics sessions.

In the *Isoplex* program, trainees are expected to mainly stretch in the *Static-Passive* way, in the way Yogis do train. A few drills of Passive Stretching with a partner will also be presented, as those, when well done, are beneficial and do tend to promote camaraderie. They are, in fact, similar to the help provided by the teacher or props in Yoga classes.

The constant reference of the author to **Yoga** is not random: Yoga, from most schools, is definitely the best way to promote flexibility. It also promotes core-muscles building, balance, breathing and concentration; and the cross-practice of Yoga is highly recommended to all athletes. Unfortunately, not every trainee has the time or opportunity to add Yoga to his crammed schedule. Therefore, this book will present the most important stretching moves and whenever relevant, will mention the original Yoga posture (*Asana*) Sanskrit name.

The drill methodology is also close to that of Yoga, and is presented at the top of next page...

… The drill methodology is also close to that of Yoga:

After warming up, the trainee will take the position described and do so slowly. He will then stretch very gradually close to his maximum. He will then hold this position for approximately 20 seconds, while trying to relax the stretched muscles. He should, when possible, try to go a bit further by contracting slowly the antagonists (*opposing muscles*), and then relaxing the stretched muscle even more. Once relaxed and while breathing out, the trainee will try to slowly deepen his range of motion a little bit more, but while avoiding the kick-in of the "*Stretch Reflex*". He should try to hold this maximum position for another 10 to 20 seconds. Going out of the stretch should also be done slowly and gradually. A stretch should be executed twice, before progressing to another one.

Relaxing and controlling your breath will be key to your progress, by allowing you better control of the *Stretch Reflex* and of the automatic antagonistic body reaction. Dedicated stretching sessions will help you access a higher level. But it is important to know that the body needs rest from stretching as well. There should be at least one day of rest between the *intensive* sessions, and more than three sessions a week is not recommended for middle-of-the-way trainees. *Isoplex*, being a daily routine, will therefore aim at concentrating the flexibility work alternatively to different areas.

4.4 The Golden Rules of Stretching

And we shall repeat them further later on…

4.4.1   *Always warm up before stretching.*
4.4.2   *Proceed slowly and gradually. No bouncing or jerky moves!*
4.4.3   *Avoid direct air flow while stretching. No Air Conditioning or Fan directed towards you.*
4.4.4   *Do not over-train. Full sessions of Intense Training: never on consecutive days. No more than one day on/one day off. If training daily, alternate areas trained*
4.4.5   *Do not stretch injured muscles or joints. In stretching, "No pain, no gain" is a counter-truth. If a stretch hurts, stop immediately.*
4.4.6   *No need to hold a final position more than twenty seconds*
4.4.7   *Come out of stretch poses slowly. Help with your hands if necessary.*

4.5 Dynamic Stretching

The **Dynamic Stretching** exercises, as mentioned above, are more for the *warm-up* phase of any work-out, and including *Flexiometrics* sessions. We shall only present a few drills as it is not the core matter of this book. The moves must be practiced *gradually and carefully*. The range of motion should never exceed the maximum static stretch range.

A *warm–up session* should be started with an overall warming exercise like hopping, rope skipping or light jogging. The author believes that a subsequent good way to warm up would be abdominal exercises, as they also have tremendous overall benefits. Crunches, leg raises and similar drills will both warm up safely, while strengthening the abdominal belt. Further warming-up can be achieved with regular old-fashioned calisthenics. In the *Plyo-Flex* book, the author naturally proposes instead to execute slow-motion kicking maneuvers, increasing speed and height slowly and gradually; but this is highly specific for kicking Martial Artists and not relevant to **Isoplex**.
Once the body is warmed up, there are a few iconic dynamic stretching exercises that will be presented. They are to be performed, of course, on both sides.

CHAPTER FIVE - ISOMETRICS THEORY

5.1 Definition and History

Isometrics are *static* strength-boosting exercises in which *the joint angle and the length of the muscle do not change during the contraction*. The term "isometric" comes from the Greek "Iso" (equal) and "metria" (length). This is in contrast to *Dynamic Isotonic* training, -traditional weight training-, in which the contraction strength supposedly does not change much, though the muscle length and the joint angle do [In fact, the strength does change slightly as per gravity and muscle fatigue]. The examples will make all this theory clear. In the meantime, the easiest way to understand the principle, is to imagine the drill in which you try to push away the wall with all your power for 10 seconds, although you know you will not succeed.

For the purpose of this book, **Dynamic Self-resistance** will be also considered *Isometrics* although purists could argue: it is the use of *your own muscles against their opposites* in order to develop a very slow and concentrated resistance movement.

As mentioned, Isometric exercises were at the heart of strength training in the Antique Greek and Roman world of perfect-body-idealization fame. Together with flexibility and Plyometrics-like exercises, it was the basis of improvement for competing athletes.

Yoga static power poses are also millennia old, and their isometric core building properties are legendary (not to mention flexibility).

The Indian Buddhist monk *Bodhidharma* brought a series of twelve basic tension exercises called the Yi Jin Jing, to the monks of the *Shaolin Temple* in China. This was the accepted basis of *Kung Fu* and *Chi Kung* that spread all over the ancient world. Oriental Martial Arts were thus based originally on Isometrics (or more precisely on *Dynamic Self-resistance*); and one should remember that they were not sports but reality-based in search of fighting results. *Shaolin* monks were also known to be holding <u>static</u> difficult poses for hours and this kind of training has survived to date in all Fighting Arts. And shall we mention the late *Bruce Lee*? He was an exceptional fighter capable of fantastic physical feats, whose training regimen did include a lot of the *Isometrics* he was also actively promoting...

...But modern *Isometrics* were first brought to the masses' attention in the early days of what was called "Physical Culture". People in my age-bracket will all remember the popular Old School 'Strongmen' capable of extraordinary physical feats: *Eugene Sandow, Charles Atlas* (famous for "Dynamic tension method" ads in comic books), *Bernarr MacFadden* and the great *Alexander Zass*. Those were in fact the pioneers of the wave that would become modern *Bodybuilding*, and they were all *Isometrics* and *Dynamic Resistance* practitioners. It should be noted also that many regular bodybuilders do incorporate isometric exercises in their routines, for example by maintaining the mid- or end-position in order to further "squeeze" the muscle.
A question that asks itself therefore is: If they are so good, why are *Isometrics* and *Dynamic Self-resistance* exercises not more widely used today?

Eugene Sandow

My first answer is that they are used universally but under disguise. *Yoga*, *Pilates* and weight-free exercises do use many an Isometric drill. Even many weight routines of Bodybuilding incorporate very slow reps, or static stops in the middle or at the end of a rep. And as mentioned, Martial Artists of all types do drill Isometric exercises widely, even if not under this name.

My second answer rotates around the success of modern *Bodybuilding* and weight machines. Exercise equipment is everywhere and aggressively marketed. Gyms with sophisticated equipment are located everywhere and do not want you to believe that there is another way than join them and spend hours lifting in an endless routine of sets and reps. Home gyms are all the rage and fitness gadgets take most of the air time of the TV shopping channels. All this, while time-tested training methods requiring no expensive equipment will give you the same, or even better results. Money talks...

My third answer is that *Isometrics* require a secret ingredient for optimal results, and that ingredient is nowadays in short supply. While you execute the Isometric Contraction, you must be totally ***focused and concentrated***! No texting, no selfie, no tweeting or no checking facebook; no listening to music or watching Youtube,... That is probably the most difficult part of the drill

ISOMETRICS THEORY

5.2 *Isometrics differentiations*

In an **Overcoming Isometric**, the joint and the muscle do work against an immovable object (Think of a wall). This is 'true and pure' *Isometrics*: you will exert as much force as possible without being able to move the object and therefore will keep the muscle at exactly the same length during the exercise. Think of pushing back against the wall, for example, or bench-pressing a fixed bar. The advantage of *Overcoming Isometrics* is that they safely allow for the use of 100% of the trainee's power. The resisting object will not move and will never be "too much" for the muscle trained. Progress is possible by increasing the contraction duration, as per the Universal rule of the *Progressive Overload Principle*. The disadvantage of *Overcoming Isometrics* is the subjective perception of effort: it is difficult to measure how much power you put in. The trainee will therefore have to be very concentrated and always strive to give 100% for a given time. But, it is the well-executed *Overcoming Isometrics* that will give you the best and fastest results because of the full use of maximum power on all muscle fibers.

In contrast, in a **Yielding Isometric**, the joint and the muscle are held in a static position while opposed by a resisting weight or force. The amount of muscle contraction will be what is needed to counteract the resistance, in fact oscillating continuously between overcoming the resistance and yielding to it. Think of holding a weighted bar at mid-development of a Bench Press or think of a Low Plank Pose (See Illustrations). *Yielding Isometrics* with weights have the advantage of giving measurable results. For a given holding time, the weight can gradually be increased for progress from session to session. But the trainee will never be able to have a maximum 100% contraction while staying safe.

Taking the specific examples given further on in a logical way, the reader can conclude that doing a *very very slow* and focused Bench Press or a *very very slow* and focused push-up could be the dynamic equivalent of *Yielding Isometrics*. This is in fact called *Dynamic Resistance*, and it carries some of the benefits of a real Yielding Isometric contraction. It is a great training method as well.

Keep a static mid-Bench Press: Yielding Isometrics

It is now clear to the reader that what we call *Isometrics* does encompass many variations, each with advantages and inconveniences. It could be further added that many more classifications are possible: the *Isometric Contraction* can make use of many props as antagonists: the body itself, the ground, structural items like walls or fences, free weights, weight machines, elastic equipment or a simple pulley. We shall present drills from all types in our *Isoplex* program, although the specific programs will tend to be based on minimal equipment.

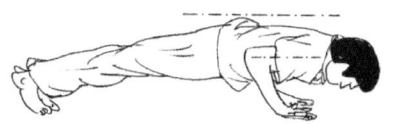 *Keeping the Low Plank Pose: an Isometric Drill*

5.3   How do Isometrics work?

A program of Isometric strength training will build *true muscle power* in the shortest time possible when compared to other training methods. As mentioned, the famous strongmen of old trained with *Isometrics* and they were able to perform feats of strength we have not seen since.
Isometrics works; it is abundantly clear. But how?
If you press the palms of your hands together, you can willingly use humongous force even though there is no actual movement. How? The following would be a layman's simplified explanation: Your brain activates some muscle fibers to accomplish the mutual pressing task required. As your hands do not move, your brain is fooled into "thinking" more power is needed. Therefore, it will put into play even more muscle fibers in an effort to execute your focused will. As your hands neutralize one another and stay in place, all your muscle fibers will finally be activated. The full complete muscle has therefore been trained at its maximum in a very short time. In fact, another simplistic way to make the reader understand is using the well-known Isometrics motto, which goes: '*In Isometrics, the last rep comes first*'.

Most people in the gym will lift a weight in sets in order to develop a certain muscle. For example, 3 sets of 10 reps is common for muscle hypertrophy training. As they start, the body will set in play the necessary amount of fibers to achieve the move. As they intend to do 30 reps all in all, not all muscle fibers will be needed for the first few reps. As they keep going and it becomes more difficult, the body will add fibers to the contracting ones in order to keep going. Ideally for regular training progress, *the last rep of the third set should be nearly a no-success*; that's the way most body builders will work. This means that they are using all the available fibers and that the body gives it all at *the last rep*. This will cause the body to plan for more fibers in the future, but it will happen only if all fibers have been challenged. *This same full use of 100% of the muscle fibers happens immediately if you give everything you have against an immovable object.* In other words: **Isometrics allow you to start with the "last rep".**

...When you start pushing against an immovable object or against yourself, your body orders the contraction of as much muscle fibers as needed to execute the order given by your brain; and that means **all of them**!

To sum up the principles and the advantages of the Isometric Exercise Method, when compared to regular weight training:

5.3.1 Maximum muscle tension is attained for only a brief period in weight training (dynamic exercises), as you obviously are moving. In comparison, isometric exercises allow to hold that maximal tension for longer.

5.3.2 Isometric exercise is also energy efficient: you don't expend much energy by holding a maximum tension for only 10 seconds.

5.4 Equipment

Most Isometric exercises presented in the programs will be without any equipment; this will allow training anywhere and at any time. The drills are simple but effective. Sometimes everyday objects or locations will be necessary for executing the drill: a doorframe, a chair, a stool, a broomstick… These are trivial and are not to be considered equipment *per se*.

The serious practitioners of *Isometrics* **of old** did have sophisticated Isometric Racks which allowed for many types of specialized drills. Such a rack is illustrated, although it is by far unnecessary for the purpose of this Program. The famous Martial artist and Actor *Bruce Lee* was using and promoting such a Rack. It allowed to place iron bars in fixed positions at different heights; the Isometrics exercises being to try to move these immovable iron bars in different manners conducive to muscle growth.

Old Isometric Rack

A cheap alternative to such a complex equipment piece is simply one or more '**Doorframe Hanging Bar**'. This ubiquitous fitness prop is easy to procure and can be set at the right height in any door frame to allow for some Isometric drills. A few examples will be given and the more advanced trainee is invited to experiment. These bars simply allow to reproduce in a static way the equivalent classic weight-lifting exercises, like the squat for example.

Drill in Isometric Rack

Drill with Doorframe Bar

It should be noted that another way to drill *Isometrics* in the gym would be to stack *so much weight* on the machine as to make the weight lifting exercise totally impossible to execute. One can then execute the exercise in an Isometric way, contracting the muscle against an 'immovable weight'. In the case of a weight machine with a locking system, you do not even need to place weight on; it is enough to lock the bar in place (see Photos).

This weight machine has a lock system for the bar, the bar can then be used as an immovable object

Another cheap piece of equipment that would allow many Isometric exercises, is a simple cable with handles and various possible positions. Pulling the cable while blocking it with your body weight, with opposing muscles or with stronger muscles, would allow *Isometrics* nearly anywhere and at any time. We have developed such a piece of equipment and called it the '<u>**Isoplex Prop**</u>'. For the reader convenience, we shall sell the prop on our web site at near-cost. More further on…

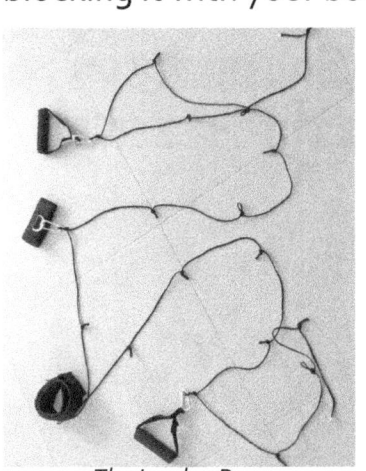
The Isoplex Prop

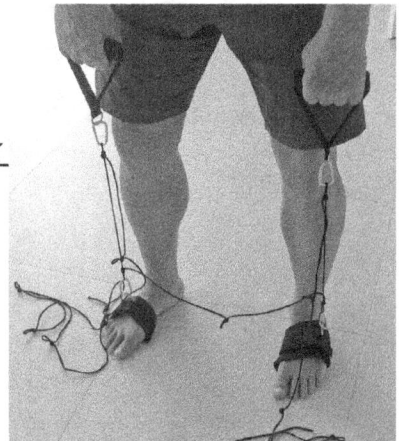
Using the Isoplex Prop

ISOMETRICS THEORY

5.5   The Secret

There is a secret behind the incredible success of *Isometrics*! And this mysterious and big secret will be revealed to you…

It is very simple: **FOCUS**. While executing an Isometric exercise, it is important to be fully invested in a 100% contraction. This is a thing of the mind first and foremost. If you let your mind wander, you will not push the wall as if you really expect to be able to move it. You will use less than a 100% contraction for the duration of the drill and progress will not come.

Only serious and focused trainees will be able to enjoy the fast and incredible results of *Isometrics*. Concentrate and give every contraction everything you have!
And remember that all great champions have underlined this point over and over.
The old masters of *Chi Kung* and *Tai Chi*, the *Yoga* guru of ancient times, all always did underscore this basic principle: concentrate and visualize. People like *Arnold Schwarzenegger* and *Bruce Lee* made a point of concentrating on the muscle trained and on visualizing its contraction. Do not snigger at this; these people obviously knew what they were talking about.
Forget distractions, and do focus. Do concentrate. Then results will come. That is the only '*secret*'!

> **What do I mean by concentration? I mean focusing totally on the business at hand and commanding your body to do exactly what you want it to do.**
> **~Arnold Palmer**

CHAPTER SIX - ISOPLEX: PUTTING IT ALL TOGETHER

It is now time to put it all together. *Isoplex* is a training program aiming at combining in an optimal way *Isometrics, Plyometrics and Flexiometrics* for synergistically effective results (together with adequate nutrition and sleep). The purpose of the program is to achieve as quickly as possible an aesthetic body that is *also* athletically efficient. The program should work for the novice trainee as well as for more advanced sport enthusiasts looking to complement their activities.

The principles behind the design of the program will be explained below. They should be made clear to the reader, so as to allow for individual tweaks in the program, and so as to allow advanced trainees to go further in their *Isoplex* training.

6.1   The Isoplex programs are based on *6 sessions a week*. One full day rest is a must for muscle growth and improvement.

6.2   There should be *a day hiatus* between high impact Plyometric workouts. There should be a day hiatus between high impact Isometric workouts. Specific training cause specific muscle fiber damage that require time for healing.

6.3   *Low impact* Plyometrics, *Low impact* Isometrics and light Stretching should be used for *warming up*. Abdominal exercises are particularly good at the warm-up stage, on top of building important core musculature.

6.4   All training sessions should *end with at least 10 minutes* of intensive *Flexiometrics*. The trainee who has more time than an hour a day is invited to keep stretching.

6.5   *Progress* within a program routine must be executed and *measured*: longer time in Isometric contractions, and more reps in Plyometric drills. In flexibility, it is simply about going gradually further in the stretch, while being careful and mindful of the body.

6.6   You should *switch programs every 3 months*, to "fool" the body into progress and out of its comfort zone.

...As a matter of principle, a weekly session would therefore generally look like this:

Day 1: 10 minutes Warm-up; 40 minutes Isometrics (Upper body emphasis); 10 minutes Flexiometrics (Upper body emphasis)

Day 2: 10 minutes Warm-up; 40 minutes Plyometrics (Lower body emphasis); 10 minutes Flexiometrics (Lower body emphasis)

Day 3: 10 minutes Warm-up; 30 minutes Isometrics (General); 20 minutes Intense Flexiometrics

Day 4: 10 minutes Warm-up; 40 minutes Plyometrics (Upper body emphasis); 10 minutes Flexiometrics (Upper body emphasis)

Day 5: 10 minutes Warm-up; 40 minutes Isometrics (Lower body emphasis); 10 minutes Flexiometrics (Lower Body emphasis)

Day 6: 10 minutes Warm-up; 30 minutes to Plyometrics (General); 20 minutes intense Flexiometrics

There will be some differences in the specific programs presented later in the book to ensure the progression of the trainee. Four programs of increasing difficulty will be detailed, with an additional advanced program for partner training. The First program will use minimum equipment; the following programs will require more props, but always simple and easily available. The Fourth program will be relatively challenging. Once the trainee is proficient in a high impact well-focused execution of the Fourth program, he will easily be able to design his own programs based on the principles presented and the lists of exercises we shall give further on.

It should be noted that one of the special traits of the *Isoplex Method*, is the use of low impact Isometric and Plyometric drills in the warm-up phase. The other key ingredients are the synergistic effect of Intense Stretching and the focus on Isometrics for muscle growth.

If the trainee sticks to those very simple but important principles, progress should come fast and noticeably.

I still believe in synergy, but I call it natural law.
~Barry Diller

CHAPTER 7 - NUTRITION AND SLEEP

There are two other important underpins to the success of *Isoplex*: **Nutrition and Sleep**. The success of *Isoplex* is therefore based on a **Five** Prongs approach: *Isometrics, Plyometrics, Flexiometrics, Good Nutrition and Sufficient Sleep.*

It may seem prosaic to mention nutrition and sleep, but, -as well-known by bodybuilders-, there will be no good muscle growth without those. For the body to repair the muscles and joints micro-tears, it will need *proteins and rest*; it is logical and self-evident. And it is also clear to all that a Six-pack belly is not compatible with a high sugar diet!

A weekly day of no-exercise rest is a must for healthy progress; doing 'too much' is not only detrimental to health, but it could also slow your progress.

Eight hours sleep a night is also a must for general health and athletic development. The good thing about the program is that it should help you get tired enough to sleep more easily; although it is not recommended to train just before going to bed. In general, morning sessions are preferable; if not possible, do train then at the earliest possible during the day. Dealing with sleep is beyond the scope of this book though, and the insomniac reader is invited to consult other works on the subject.

Nutrition is also beyond the scope of this book which is restricting itself to present training programs. An appropriate diet is also very personal as many individual factors come into play. There is no universal diet and a Nutrition Professional should be consulted by the interested reader. We shall only present general guidelines and salient points.

A trainee's diet should be well-balanced and rich in proteins; proteins are needed for muscle repair and growth.

A trainee should always be well-hydrated; in fact, he should start his day with gulping half-a-liter of water just when getting out of bed. A practicing athlete should be also drinking water all day, and especially a lot during exercise.

The modern scourge of high refined carbohydrates must be avoided at all costs: No sugary treats, at all.

One should ingest the amount of calories necessary for his individual development; it is very different from one physiology to another: if you are too skinny (ectomorph) to your taste, increase the size of your portions; if you are too chubby (endomorph), decrease the overall size of all your servings. But all around, your diet must stay balanced.

The reader is invited to research the type of diet best suited for himself, based on his goals and physiology. Vitamins and supplements may also be needed.

In the writer's opinion and experience, the most suitable and balanced diet would be the well-known and much touted *Mediterranean* one. A lot of: Vegetables, Olive Oil, Fish and Nuts; in moderation Cheese, Yoghurt, Chicken, Red Wine (1 glass a day), Eggs (no more than 4 yolks a day), unrefined Cereals and Fruits. Lettuce, raw green vegetables, egg whites and more nuts can be nibbling additions. Protein shakes low in carbs can also help to fight cravings in a constructive way.

And a few more pointers:

- Black coffee in the morning and before exercising is considered good!
- The use of Whey Protein supplements is conducive to muscle building and repair, if high carbs (generally pre-workout) versions are avoided.
- Never skip a meal and try to divide your food intake into smaller meals, but every two hours. It keeps the metabolism churning and provides nutrients optimally in a regular debit. Certainly do not skip breakfast, it is an important meal!
- Avoid processed foods and refined sugar at all costs.
- Drink lots of water all day: it is necessary for muscle-building metabolic processes.
- Take a daily multi-vitamin and minerals supplement (make sure that it contains iodine, copper and zinc).

The rest is left to the reader's common sense and further research.

One digs his grave with his teeth.
~French Proverb

CHAPTER EIGHT - PLYOMETRIC EXERCISES

8.1 Warming-up Drills

8.1.1 High-knee March

Just march forcefully, army-like, while lifting the knees to waist level. You can march in place or walk around the room. 1 to 3 minutes

8.1.2 On-toes Jog

Jog lightly on your toes, in place or around the room. Make sure you stay on your toes. 1 to 3 minutes.

8.1.3 Butt-kicking Jog

Jog lightly in place. Lift the heels higher and higher and aim at kicking yourself in the bottom each time. In place, or around the room. 1 to 3 minutes.

8.1.4 Skipping Jog

Skip around the room, hopping airborne with each step. 1 to 3 minutes.

8.1.5 Lateral Crosses

Jog laterally around the room crossing your legs each time. 1 to 3 minutes. Make sure to stay sideways.

8.1.6 Low Hops

Hop in place or slightly forward *by using your calves*: jump from the feet, not the knees. Keep the knees slightly bent, but use the ankles. Try to jump high. Hop in series with no rest. 1 minute.

8.1.7 Lateral Low Hops

Hop laterally, back and forth, by using the *calves* only. Try to jump as *high* as possible, and back and forth as *fast* as possible. Use the *ankles*, not the knees.

8.1.8 Box Switch Jumps

Hop in place in front of a box or a flight of stairs. Each time you hop you touch the top of the box with alternating feet. Hop fast, in series, *with no rest*. 1 to 2 minutes.

8.1.9 Jumping Jacks

A classic exercise, but plyometric if executed *in series*. Jump in place with simultaneous opening of arms and legs. Execute in series *with no rest* during 1 to 2 minutes. Increase speed with proficiency.

PLYOMETRIC EXERCISES

8.1.10 Alternate Arms Opening

An important arms plyometric exercise: open the arms forcefully, then cross them fast in front of you. Uncross them fast, but brake as soon as uncrossed in order to re-cross while switching upper and lower arms. Then back again with the whole series. The plyometric effect comes from the *speed* of the move, the speed of the braking and the alternating move. Increase speed with proficiency. Drill for 1 to 3 minutes.

8.1.11 Push-up to High Jumps

This is the classic and supreme '**Burpee**', with a dynamic push-up in between. Start slowly and increase speed with coming proficiency. Make sure your back is straight and you jump *as high as possible*. Drill *in series with no rest*, from 5 to 20 reps.

THE ISOPLEX METHOD

8.2 Ground Drills

8.2.1 Flying Butt Kicks

Slightly bend the knees and jump up while trying to kick yourself in the bottom. Concentrate on hitting your buttocks. When proficient, aim at also jumping as high as possible. Then focus on speed: aim at *minimizing 'ground time'*. Jump in series as fast as possible. 5 series of 10 jumps.

8.2.2 Flying Double Knee Kicks

Slightly bend the knees and jump up while trying to knee yourself in the chest. Concentrate on lifting the knees *as high as possible*. When proficient, aim also at *jumping* as high as possible. Then focus on speed: aim at minimizing 'ground time'. Jump in series as fast as possible. 5 series of 10 jumps.

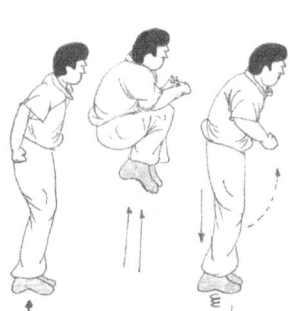

8.2.3 Flying Double Knee Wide Kicks

This drill is identical to the previous one (*Flying Double Knee Kicks*), but is executed with the knees opened as wide as possible. You are trying to have your knees *as high and as wide as possible*. Everything else is identical. 5 series of 10 jumps.

8.2.4 Flying Twists

This is again a variation of the *Flying Double Knee Kicks* (8.2.2): you simultaneously twist 180 degrees while you are airborne. You should become gradually proficient at lifting the knees as high as possible, completing the full 180 degrees, jumping as high as possible and minimizing ground time (no rest between the jumps). 5 series of 10 jumps.

PLYOMETRIC EXERCISES

8.2.5 Lateral Long Jumps

You crouch and touch the ground. From this position, you immediately jump *laterally* as far as possible with one leg. Close the crouching posture at reception while touching the ground again. Jump *immediately* back with the other leg to your starting station. Repeat in series. When you become proficient, aim at minimizing ground time: jump back and forth as far as possible but also as fast as possible. 'Explode' into the jump. 5 series of 10 jumps

8.2.6 Joined Legs Lateral Jumps

You jump back and forth, laterally with feet together, over a line on the floor. The purpose of the drill is to jump *as fast as possible* from one side to the other, neither high nor far. Minimize ground time. The drill can be executed in place, or while gradually progressing forward. 5 series of 20 jumps.

8.2.7 Hop into Jumps

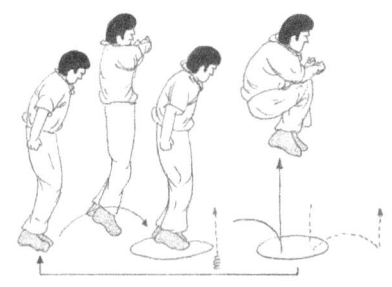

This drill looks simple but is very effective and truly plyometric. Hop forward, using your ankles, not your knees. As soon as you land, you jump up as high as possible while kneeing your chest. As you land, you repeat by hopping forward again. You need to concentrate: hop, jump, hop, jump, ... Focus on jumping as high as possible, lifting the knees as high as possible, and especially focus on minimizing ground time between the hop and the jump. This drill is a combination of the '*Low Hops*' (8.1.6) and the '*Flying Double Knee Kicks*' (8.2.2), and a very important exercise. 5 series of 10 jumps.

PLYOMETRIC EXERCISES

8.2.8 One Leg Lateral Jumps

This is a difficult drill to be executed when warmed-up; and it is a *jump*, not a hop. You stand on one leg and jump *laterally*, as high as possible, in the direction of the standing leg. The purpose is not to jump far, but *to lift the standing knee high* while going laterally. Repeat as you land, minimizing ground time. Execute fast 5 times, then switch legs and direction to come back. 2 to 3 series will suffice.

8.2.9 One Leg Lateral Hops

This typical multi-response isometric drill is the fast version of the one-legged lateral hop: you hop laterally, back and forth, over a line. You can do so in place or while progressing forward gradually. The purpose is to jump fast, back and forth, while minimizing ground time. It is all about *speed*, and not about height or distance. Execute 20 hops, then switch legs. 4 series of 20 hops per leg.

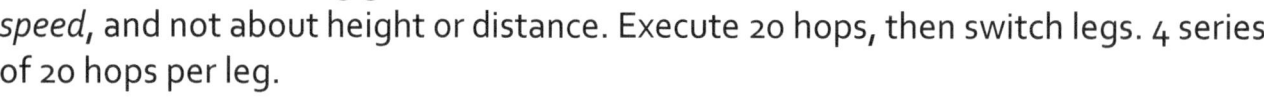

8.2.10 Long Jumps

This is simply the longest possible jump executed *in series* with no momentum. Crouch in place, feet together, and jump *long*. Land with feet together and *immediately* jump again from landing position. Execute 10 jumps in series, with no stop and no step between the jumps. Minimize ground time, but concentrate first on the length of the jump, not on height or speed. Make sure that you do not use momentum: jump off from a fully static position, feet together. 5 series of 10.

8.2.11 Frog Long Jumps

This is again a long jump, *but from hands on floor*, knees bent. From this low squat, you jump like a frog *as far as possible* and reception on your hands first. You land into starting position and repeat. Execute with minimum time between the jumps, but concentrate on the length of the jump and the depth of the squat. 3 series of 10 jumps.

8.2.12 Split Jumps

Jump as *high* as possible from a *deep lunge* and switch legs airborne. Land in opposite lunge position. Repeat immediately. Make your jump as high as possible and your lunging position as low as possible. Once you are proficient, concentrate on minimizing ground time. 4 series of 10 jumps

8.2.13 High Jumps to Reach

In place, bend the knees and jump as high as possible. Land with knees bent and *rebound immediately* into another high jump. Repeat 10 times, while trying to minimize ground time. This drill is best executed below a high target and you will aim at touching it each jump; increase height as proficiency comes. It could be a basketball ring, a dangling rope, etc... 5 series of 10.

8.2.14 Skipping

This may seem like a little girl going happily skipping to school, but it is a true isometric exercise. You jump off both feet and lift one knee. Once you land, you repeat while lifting the other knee, and then again and again. To make it a serious drill, concentrate on *jumping as high* as possible and *lifting the knee as high* as possible. This drill requires some room as you will progress forward with each hop. It is also a good warm-up exercise. 3 series of 20 jumps.

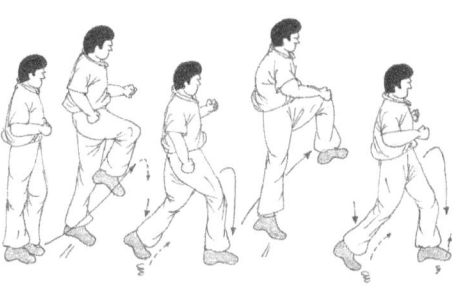

PLYOMETRIC EXERCISES

8.2.15 Clapping Push-ups

This is the isometric version of the classic push-up. From a straight-back *High Plank Position*, you bend the arms in a classic Push-up. Only feet and hands touch the floor. From the *Low Plank Position* so achieved, you explode up by pushing on your hands and then clap while 'airborne'. You fall back on your hands and brake your fall by bending the arms, therefore landing back in Low Plank. Explode up *immediately* again, and keep repeating. In order to achieve maximum plyometric effect, you have to aim at minimizing ground time between the 'hops' and to aim at lifting the straight trunk as high as possible. 3 series of 10.

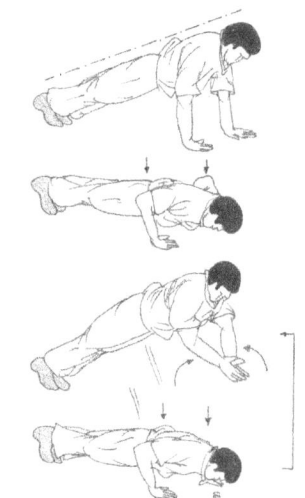

8.2.16 One-armed Push-ups to Down Dog

This is a challenging shoulder exercise. Lie on your belly with one arm behind your back; the other hand is below your shoulder. Push your chest-up, *Cobra*-like. Then lift your whole body into a straight *one-armed High Plank Pose*. Then push your bottom back into a *one-armed Down Dog Pose*. Go back down by inversing the process: *Down Dog* to *High Plank* to *Cobra*. Repeat with the same arm 5 to 10 times, then switch arms. Unlike the previous exercises, you do not try to minimize ground time or to go fast: you clearly mark each step and hold the pose for a second or two. Once proficient, execute 3 series of 10 for each arm.

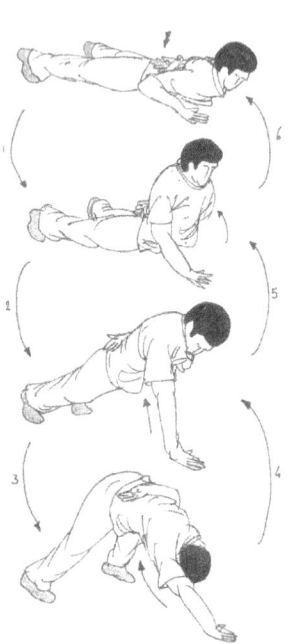

8.2.17 Jumping Jacks Push-ups

This Push-up variation starts in a *High Plank* pose with feet together. As you start the push-up by bending your arms, you hop outwards with your feet to land with open legs (just as for a standing '*Jumping Jack*'). This places more body weight on the arms during the descent. The hop and arm flexion are simultaneous. Once you are down with open legs, you straighten the arms up while jumping back with feet together. Repeat 10 times, and make sure your back stays straight during the whole exercise. 3 series of 10.

8.3 Box Drills

As previously mentioned, a "**Box**" can be anything: a real Plyometric Box of course but also an Aerobic Step, a stack of 'Steps', the lower step of a staircase, a sturdy stool or chair,…The "Box Drills" just require something you can step or jump on, or from.

These drills are the first "new and spectacular" plyometrics discovered by Western coaches in the Sixties, and they are the bread-and-butter of plyometric training. The height of the box is dependant on the type of exercise or the proficiency of the trainee. It is usually beneficial to gradually increase the height of the box. That is why a stack of aerobic steps is a good solution: they are stable and stackable to the desired height. But anything goes: It is the drill that counts!

8.3.1 On-box Jump

Simple, iconic, fully plyometric: hop on the box and rebound to jump back down. Repeat *immediately* and try to minimize ground time. Up, down, up, down… You do not need to try to jump high or far. Just on the box and off as *fast* as possible. 3 series of 20

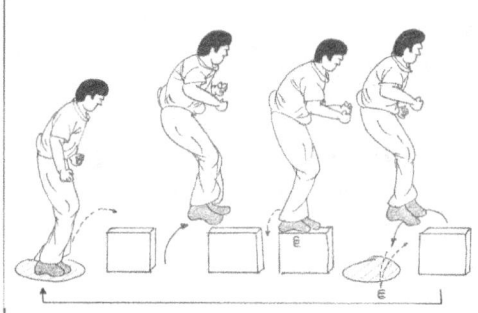

8.3.2 On-box High Jumps

You will, again, jump onto the box. But, this time, the box is much higher. The purpose of the drill is to jump high from a static 'feet-together-position. The best prop for this exercise is a stack of aerobic steps. The height of the stack should be such that you can (just) complete a series of 10 jumps [5 jumps for beginners].

You jump onto the box, stand up, and jump back down. You will not rest between the jumps, but there is no need to strive for minimum ground time. The purpose of the drill is not speed, but height. Once the drill becomes easy, you add another step on the stack. 3 series of 10 jumps.

8.3.3 On-box Twist Jumps

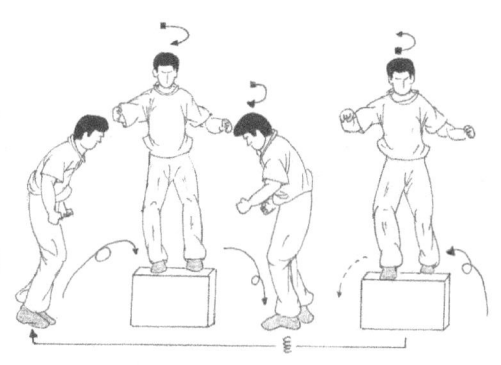

This is a simple On-box Jump (*8.3.1*) in which you *twist 90 degrees* while being airborne. You therefore land on the box laterally to your starting pose. You then immediately jump down while keeping the 90 degrees airborne twist and therefore land facing the opposite side of the starting position. You then jump back on the box while twisting airborne in the other direction. And then down, and then up,... You must strive to do a perfect *90 degrees twist*, and then *minimize ground time*. 3 series of 20 jumps (10 times on the box).

8.3.4 On-box One-leg Jumps

This is again a simple but more challenging variation of the On-box Jump (*8.3.1*): you just execute it *on one leg*. You execute 10 jumps on the same leg while minimizing ground time. Concentrate on *rebounding fast* from the ground for 10 times, then switch legs. 3 series of 10 jumps per leg.

8.3.5 On-box One-leg Twisted Jumps

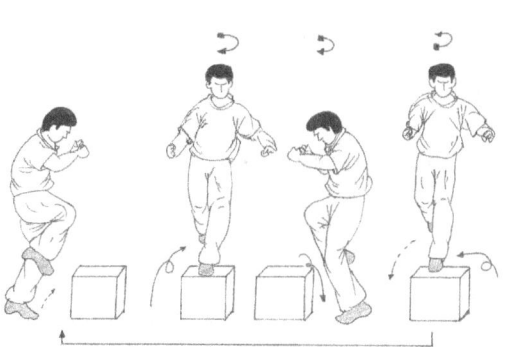

This is a compounded variation of the On-box Jump: at the same time *twisting* and *one-legged*. It is simply but more challengingly the On-box Twist Jump (*8.3.3*) executed on one-leg (*8.3.4*). Once you have mastered the drill, concentrate on fast rebounding within the series. 3 series of 10 jumps per leg.

8.3.6 Box-on and Up

You jump onto the box, *on which you will rebound immediately for a <u>height</u> jump*. The double jump is very 'plyometric'. You have to minimize the time spent on the box itself *by rebounding as fast as possible*. Jump from the box itself *as high as possible*. You land on the floor behind the box, pivot and repeat in the other direction. You do not need to rush when on the ground: pivot at normal speed before jumping again, but do not rest. *Concentrate on the height of the second jump*; a target, like a basketball ring, can help. 3 series of 10 'double' jumps (5 in each direction).

PLYOMETRIC EXERCISES

8.3.7 Box-off and High

This is a typical "off-box" plyometric exercise, also called depth jump. You jump from the box and land with bent knees in order *to rebound* for a high jump from the floor. The strong plyometric effect comes from the braking landing on flexed legs followed by the full-powered *height* jump. Concentrate on minimizing ground time and jumping (from the ground) as high as possible. After the high jump, climb back on the block for an encore: do not rest, but there is no need to minimize ground time then. 5 series of 10 jumps.

8.3.8 Box-off and Long

This is another classic *depth jump*. Just like with the previous drill, you will jump off the box for a rebounding jump. But this time you will aim at jumping *as far* as possible. The principles stay the same: minimize ground time and try to jump *as long as possible*. After you land, go back to the box for a repeat, with no rest but no haste either. 3 series of 10 jumps.

8.3.9 Box Cross-over Jumps

This is an important speed drill of a simple Lateral Jump. With one foot on the box besides you, you jump over the box to land with the other foot on the box. Your landing foot then rebounds on the ground to repeat the jump in the opposite direction. And then repeat… The height of the jump is of no importance, but you must aim at jumping to and fro *as fast as possible*, minimizing ground time as much as possible. 3 series of 20 jumps, 10 in each direction.

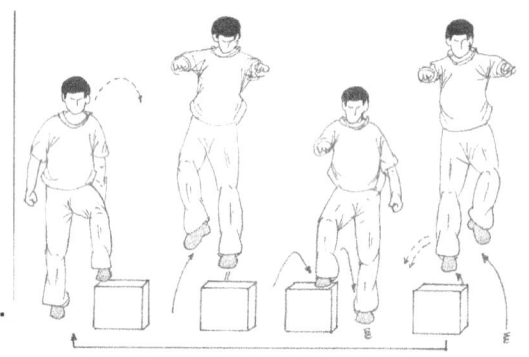

8.3.10 Lateral On-box/ Off-box Jumps

This is again a Lateral Jump drill to be executed in series *while minimizing ground time*. Jump laterally with both feet on to the box on your side. Immediately jump off to the other side. Rebound on the ground to jump back up, and then down on the other (original starting) side. Jump with both feet together

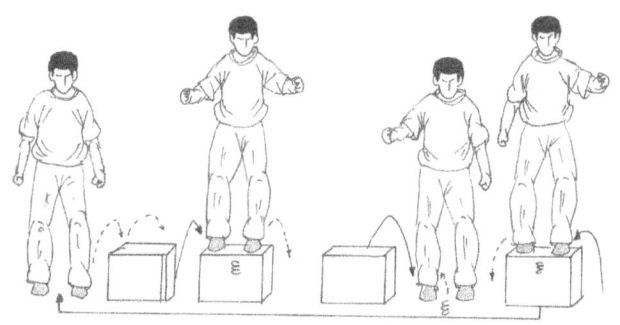

and concentrate on *rebounding* speed for maximum plyometric effect: jump back up immediately as your feet touch the ground from the jump-off. 3 series of 10 jumps (5 to each side).

8.3.11 Double-box Jumps

This is simply the basic 'On-box' drill (*See section 8.3.1*), but executed *in series*. We called it the '**Double Box Jump**' because you would need at minimum Two boxes. You can use a stair or a stool as the second box, but it is best if all boxes are identical. If you have enough equipment, you can do the drill with

up to Five boxes placed one after the other; if not, do the Double Jump and pivot to execute it in the opposite direction, and repeat. You must *rebound* both on the box and on the ground and execute the drill as *fast* as possible: on/off/on/off/... 3 series of a total of 20 jumps.

8.3.12 On-box Squat Jumps

This is again a variation of the *basic On-box Jump* (8.3.1): this time you execute it **in squat position**. You squat in the starting position and land on the box in squat position. You then *rebound* back down to a squat position and repeat with no pause. You should squat as illustrated, unless you

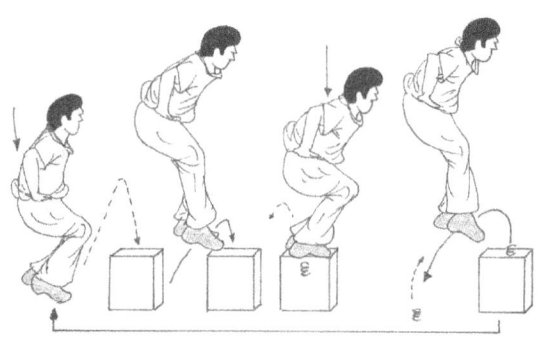

have knee problems or lack flexibility. If you are flexible or are an advanced athlete, you can squat deeper. *The plyometric effect comes from the rebounding*: you brake the landing (both on the box and on the ground) by squatting and rebound up from this low position. Therefore, there is no rest between the jumps within the series. 3 series of 10.

PLYOMETRIC EXERCISES

8.3.13 Off-box Squat Hops to High Jumps

The plyometric angle of this drill is identical to that of the previous exercise. But you now *start on the box*, in squat position. Squat and jump off the box to land in squat position. *Rebound* immediately from this low position to jump *as high as possible*. Land from the high jump into another *low squat*. You can then straighten up and climb leisurely onto the box for a repeat. The rebounding is the key: *minimize ground time* between the two jumps. 3 series of 10.

8.3.14 Off-box to 360 Jumps

This is an advanced variation of the classic 'Off-box and High' (8.3.7). You jump *off* the box, land in a *squat* and then jump *high* while executing a full circle *spin while airborne*. Land in a squat and then climb back on the box for a repeat. Concentrate on the squat landings and the full airborne spin (*which requires jumping high*). 5 series of 5 jumps.

8.3.15 One-leg Off-box Jumps

This is an advanced version of the basic 'Box-off and High' (8.3.7). It is simple to understand, but advanced because difficult and hard on the joints. It is not to be drilled by beginners. You simply execute the 'Box-off and High' five times in a row <u>on one leg</u> (*the same leg!*). Then switch legs for another five Double Jumps, and repeat. Once you have the gist of the exercise, concentrate on jumping *as high as possible* and on *minimizing ground time* between the drop-off and the high jump. 3 series of 10 jumps, five each leg in series.

THE ISOPLEX METHOD

8.3.16 Clapping Depth Push-ups

This is the advanced version of the *Clapping Push-up* (8.2.15), not to be drilled by beginners. You simply execute the plyometric *Clapping Push-up* <u>with your feet on the 'box'</u>, which will put more weight on your arms. Make sure that you keep the spine straight and that you *minimize ground time* within the series. Start with series of five claps to familiarize yourself with the drill. 5 series of 10 claps.

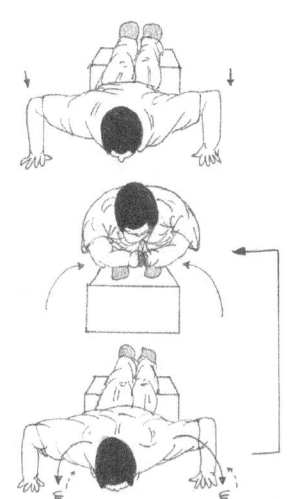

8.3.17 Drop Push-ups

This is also an advanced drill based on the same plyometric principles as the previous exercise. It is not to be executed by beginners and must be approached gradually. From a *High Plank Pose* with your hands wide and on 'boxes', you hop off into a narrower *Low Plank Pose*, from which you *rebound* immediately. The rebound is in fact a dynamic push-up that takes you back into the starting position (*High Plank Pose on the boxes*). You repeat *immediately*. The boxes would best be Aerobic Steps, which will allow for an easier gradual progression. You should start with one Step on each side and a series of 4 push-ups. You should then gradually attempt to get to a series of 10 push-ups from two stacks of two Steps. 3 series of 10 push-ups.

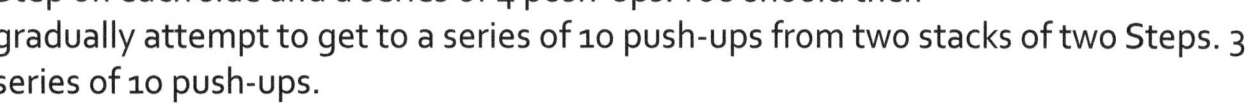

8.3.18 Push-up and Rotation

This is another advanced push-up. From a *Low Plank Pose*, you push up *while simultaneously pivoting into Side Plank*. You hold the *Side Plank* for two seconds, then pivot back into the starting position (*Low Plank*). You immediately repeat on the same side. Make sure your spine is straight in both the *Low Plank* and the *Side Plank* poses. Concentrate on the <u>simultaneous</u> push-up and pivot; this will place more weight on the 'staying' arm while it straightens and while the body changes alignment. Start with series of five push-ups on each side: 5 push-ups on one side, then five push-ups in series on the other side. *Gradually* increase to series of 10 per side. 4 series of 10 push-ups on each side.

PLYOMETRIC EXERCISES

8.3.19 Triceps Dips

This is a classic Triceps exercise that you will execute *slowly on the way down*, as low as possible, and then *fast on the way back up*. Start as illustrated with the feet on the floor and execute series of 10 dips. If it is difficult for you, you can bend the legs to bring them closer to the chair. When you become proficient, you should aim for series of 20. Once you can do series of 20, you should go back to 10 but execute the drill with your feet on a chair, at same height as the hands. Gradually climb back to series of 20 in this more difficult set-up. 5 series of 20.

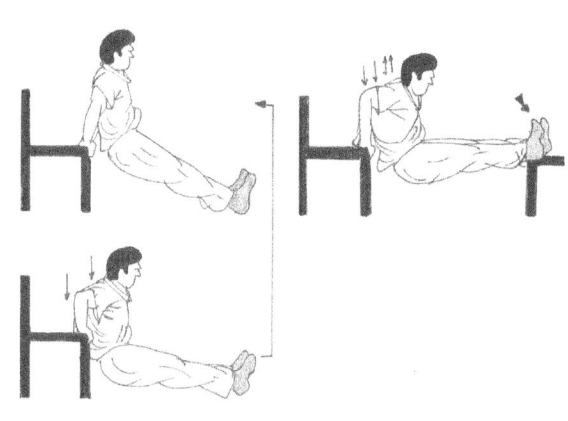

8.4 Cone Drills (and rope variation)

Cones are a very useful prop for plyometric exercises: they are cheap, stackable and easily stored. They are the equipment of choice for jumping over in series. The important thing to remember though is to jump without trying to avoid the cone in unorthodox ways (like opening the feet): jump over it as if it was a full hurdle!

8.4.1 Front Cone Jumps in Series

The example uses 3 cones; but if you have the room and the equipment, you could use as much as 10 cones in series. As many cones as possible will make the drill more efficient and less cumbersome. You jump over the cones in series with knees and feet together, and you concentrate in minimizing ground time. Rebound as fast as possible. At the end of the cone line, pivot and repeat back in the other direction until you have jumped 10 times. Make sure you do not "cheat" by opening the feet and knees to "clear" the cone height. 5 series of 10 jumps.

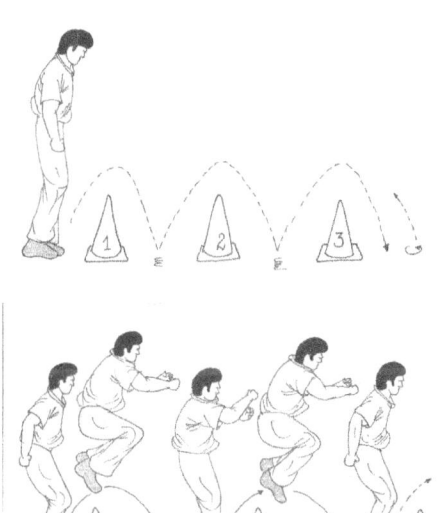

8.4.2 Lateral Cone Jumps in Series

This is a similar drill as the preceding one, but executed laterally. You jump in series laterally over 3 cones and concentrate on *minimizing ground time*. After three jumps, you rebound <u>immediately</u> in the opposite direction for another three lateral jumps. And again, and again. 3 sets of 18 jumps, 9 in each direction.

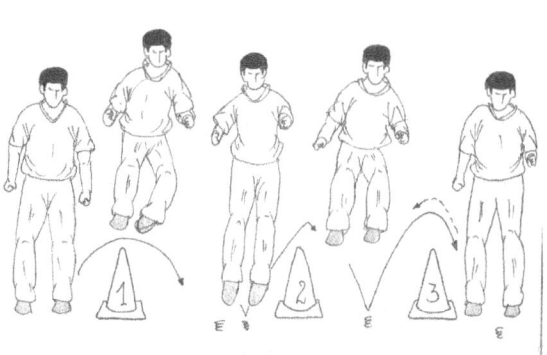

PLYOMETRIC EXERCISES 63

8.4.3 Diagonal Cone Jumps in Series

This is simply a combination of the two first drills presented in the section: you jump in series *diagonally*, which is both forward and sideways. The cones are, obviously not aligned but alternate to form two lines and to allow for the diagonal jumps. The best options is to jump in series over 10 cones and then back. If you do not have 10 cones, then you should have a line of at least 3 placed adequately. 3 sets of a total of 18 to 20 jumps, according to the number of available cones.

8.4.4 One-leg Lateral Cone Jumps in Series

This is the advanced version of drill *8.4.2*, executed on one leg. Three cones will suffice and you jump laterally on one foot between them while concentrating on *minimizing ground time*. After the third jump, you rebound <u>immediately</u> for three more jumps in the opposite direction, still *on the same leg*. Once you have completed 6 jumps on the same leg (back and forth), you switch legs and repeat. Notice that the muscles involved in the jump are different for each jumping direction of a given one-leg position. 2 series of 6 jumps for each standing leg.

8.4.5 Incremental Height Jumps

This important exercise can be drilled with cones of increasing height. But if such cones are not available, it is best executed with a *rope* tied as to give a *gradual slope of increasing height*. In order to avoid accidents, one of the ends should be tied loosely, so as to 'give' if the rope is touched.

The best set-up is a rope tied to the floor and hold at suitable by a partner. The drill is an advanced version of *Diagonal Jumps in Series* (8.4.3), <u>but executed with increasing height</u>. The more gradual the slope, the better, as you'll be able to execute a long series of jumps of slowly increasing height. Once you have *mastered* the height part of the drill, you should concentrate on *speed* and *minimizing ground time*. Aim at achieving 3 series of 10 jumps. If your rope is short (at least 3 jumps though!), go back immediately to start position for a non-stop 10 jumps series.

8.5 Various Drills (Hurdles, Dumbbells and Bar)

Hurdles allow for high jumps. they can be replaced by everyday objects that can mark a certain height, for example, a rope stretched between 2 objects. But it is imperative that the Hurdle or any other prop *be set to fall if hit by the trainee*. Be careful: It would be extremely dangerous to fall during the drill from hitting a high immovable object. Common sense is *de rigueur*!

An **Exercise Bar** could be purchased at the sport store, but it could also be a simple broomstick, a regular barbell bar or even a weighted barbell bar.

Dumbells can be easily procured, but they can be replaced by bottles of household liquids (with handles!). For even more weight, these bottles can subsequently filled with sand.

Hurdle

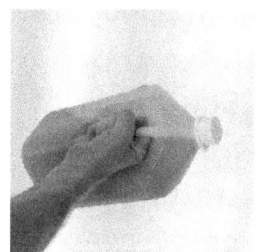
A household bottle can be used as a dumbell

8.5.1 Hurdle Forward Jumps (in Series)

You simply jump over hurdles in series *while minimizing ground time*. There should be a line of at least 3 hurdles at optimal intervals for the drill to be effective. Series of about 10 jumps are ideal; if you have only three hurdles, pivot immediately at the end of the line and repeat. Once you clear the hurdle height easily, concentrate on *speed*. 3 series of 9 to 10 jumps.

8.5.2 Hops to Hurdle Jumps

For this drill, one hurdle will suffice; after the jump-over, you either pivot and repeat in the opposite direction, or you go back to your starting place. The exercise is simple: *you execute a hop <u>and then</u> jump over the hurdle*. You then repeat. You must concentrate on the plyometric *rebound between the hop and the jump:* bend the knees as you land and rebound as fast as possible to clear the hurdle. Then position yourself for a repeat. 5 series of 10.

PLYOMETRIC EXERCISES

8.5.3 Long Jump to Hurdle Jumps

This drill also requires only one hurdle. It is best done with a mark on the floor for good distance. You execute a *Long Jump*, followed immediately by a *Hurdle Jump*. The plyometric effect comes from the *rebound between the two jumps*, and it is important to minimize ground time. After the double jump, go back to starting position and repeat. 3 series of 10 jumps.

8.5.4 Squat to Hurdle Jumps

Squat in front of a single hurdle, and jump directly *from the squat over the hurdle*. Go back to the starting position for a repeat. Squat for *as low as you can*, according to your own flexibility, and touch the floor with both hands before you **explode** up. 3 series of 10 jumps.

8.5.5 Off-box to Hurdle Jumps

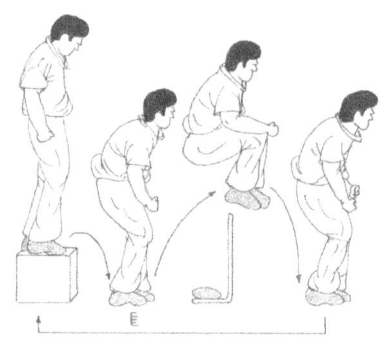

Jump off a plyometric box and *rebound for an immediate jump over the hurdle*. Go back to starting position on the box and repeat. The plyometric effect comes from landing off the box with bent knees and then *minimizing ground time* before the hurdle jump. 3 series of 10 jumps.

8.5.6 Bar Twist

Start this simple exercise with a simple stick. When proficient, you can proceed with a heavier bar or with a weighted bar. It is not recommended to go over 20 lbs. (10 kgs.) though. Open your feet hip width and twist the trunk fully from one side to the other. The feet do not move. The plyometric effect comes from starting to twist in the opposite direction just before you reach the maximum on one side. Increase speed gradually with proficiency and experience, in order to maximize this effect. 2 series of 50 to 100 twists (according to progress).

8.5.7 Dumbbell Twist

The drill is similar to the previous one, but you hold a dumbbell at arms-reach and at shoulder height instead of a bar on your shoulders. Twist with arm straight at all times and without moving the feet. The plyometric principle is the same as in the previous drill: *start switching directions just before you reach the maximum twist.* Start with a low weight (3 to 10 lbs.) and increase speed gradually. Once you become proficient and can execute the direction switch fast enough, you can very gradually increase the weight of the dumbbell. It is not recommended to go over 30 lbs. (15 kgs.) in any case, even if you are strong and proficient. 3 series of 30 twists.

8.5.8 Dumbbell Arm Swings

In a semi-squat, you swing your arms holding dumbbells in opposite directions: one in front up to face level, while the other is going back as high as the shoulder joint allows. The arms are slightly bent. As soon as the hands reach their apex, you switch directions. And repeat. The plyometric effect comes, again, *from starting the opposite move just before you reach the end of the swing*: you therefore have to brake a very fast move and switch directions powerfully. It is recommended to start with a low weight (3 to 10 lbs.) and concentrate on speed. Once you become proficient, you can very gradually increase the weight of the dumbbells, but it is not recommended to get over 30 lbs. (15 kgs.) in any case. 3 series of 20 swings.

Start where you are. Use what you have. Do what you can.
~Arthur Ashe

8.6 Stairs Drills

Stairs allow for a combination of both height and distance when jumping.
Stairs are a great prop for Plyometrics, but they must be used with the utmost caution. Only use the lowest part of the staircase, make sure they are not slippery and that you wear suitable antislip footwear.
Stairs can replace Plyometric boxes for numerous drills.
Please be very careful!

8.6.1 Front Stairs Jumps

Front Stairs Jumps are in fact simple *On-box Jumps,* but the stairs add a dimension of distance to the simple height parameter: the higher step you try to reach, the further away it is also. The aim of the drill is to jump with both feet on to the highest (furthest) step possible. You then either climb down to repeat, or you eventually keep jumping up if you are on a long flight of stairs (like a stadium). Once you become proficient, you should gradually try to carefully reach the next step. 3 series of 10.

8.6.2 Lateral Stairs Jumps

Just like for the previous drill, you aim at reaching the highest, and therefore furthest step. But you will not keep the feet together, and you will bound *laterally*. You start by squatting and touching the floor with your fingers before exploding in the jump. You can then either keep jumping up if the stairs are suitable, or you can go back down to the starting point for a repeat. Of course, this drill must be executed *on both sides*, jumping with each leg on the stairs side in turn. Once proficient, try carefully to reach the next step. 3 series of 10 bounds, 5 on each side.

8.6.3 Off-box to Stairs Jump

This is simply the Front Stairs Jump (*8.6.1*) executed *after an Off-box drop*. You will try to jump onto the highest possible step while minimizing ground time. The plyometric effect comes from the *rebound* between the jumps. 2 series of 10.

8.6.4 Lateral Climb with Knee-up

This is a very important exercise. Stand sideways to the staircase and place your foot on a step, as high as possible for you. From this starting position, *explode up* and lift yourself on to the step while lifting the other knee as *high* as possible. Think of it as a climb with a powerful knee strike. Lower the kneeing leg and take back the starting position. Repeat for another 10 times before switching sides. The beginner is invited to start drilling at a lower step than his maximum; the drill is not as easy as it looks. <u>The exercise also requires a good warm-up</u>. 3 series of 20 climbs (10 on each side).

Sports do not build character. They reveal it.
~Heywood Broun

8.7 Medicine Ball Drills

A **Medicine Ball** is a weighted ball for exercizing, sometimes with handles, that is very common and easy to procure. They exist in a range of weights, usually from 2 to 20 lbs and have been in use for over 100 years for fitness and rehabilitation. It is even believed that the arch-ancestor of medicine Hippocrates used a similar contraption for his patients. You should use the ball of the weight most suited to you and to the specific drill. Always start at low weight and increase very gradually.
Used judiciously, the Medicine Ball is a fantastic Plyometric tool.

8.7.1 Squat Jumps with Ball

Hold the Medicine Ball on the back of your neck, squat and *jump as high as possible*. Land in squat and *rebound up immediately*. Make sure that you keep the ball in contact with the neck and that your squat is square (thighs parallel to the ground). If you cannot squat that deep, do as much as possible for you. In any case, do not squat deeper than square. The plyometric effect is achieved by *minimizing rebounding ground time* and making sure that the squat is deep. When proficient, you can increase Medicine Ball weight. 3 series of 10 jumps.

8.7.2 Eight around the Legs Ab Drill

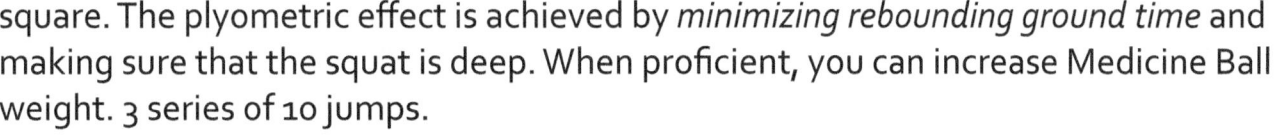

Sitting on the floor, pass the ball over and under your legs in a 'Figure Eight' pattern, lifting your legs alternatively. After

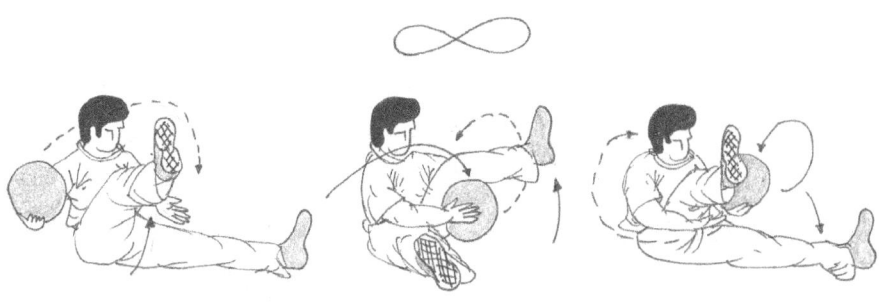

10 'Figures Eight', switch the direction of the movement. Once you are proficient, concentrate on speed. You can later use a heavier Ball. 2 series of 20 'Figures Eight' (10 in each direction).

PLYOMETRIC EXERCISES

8.7.3 Sitting Trunk Rotation with Ball

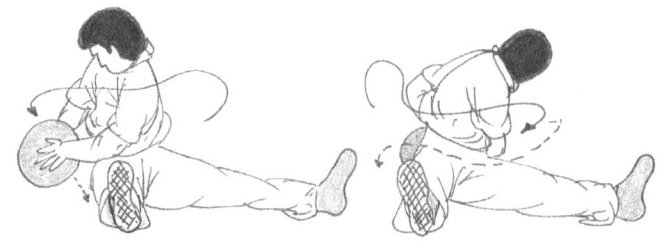

Sitting on the floor with legs stretched wide open, you twist the trunk to lay the Ball behind your back. *Immediately* twist in the opposite direction to pick the Ball back up and change twisting direction to set the ball back behind your back. The Ball is basically flowing in a constant circle around you. The plyometric effect comes from the *sudden change in the twisting direction* of your trunk. Therefore, you must concentrate on <u>speed</u>. After you have set the Ball ten times behind you, you change the direction of the flow. Once you are proficient, you can increase the weight of the ball, but you must keep concentrating on the speed of the twists. 5 series of 20 circle flows (10 in each direction).

8.7.4 Squat to Underhand Wall Throw

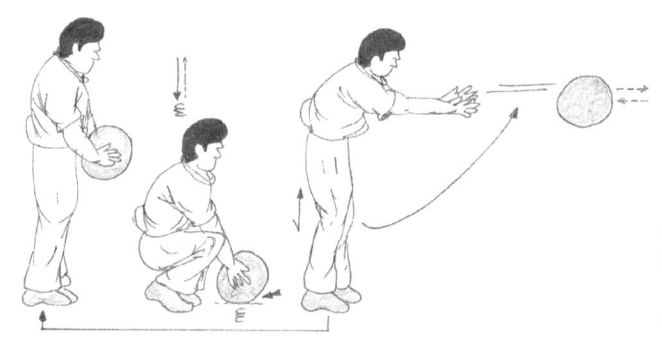

(This is also a <u>partner</u> drill). From a standing position holding the Ball with two hands, you squat and touch the floor with the Ball. You immediately *explode* back up while throwing the Ball against a wall. The throw is underhanded: straight from the floor by lifting your arms. The Ball rebounds on the wall you are facing and comes back to you for a repeat from the standing position. Position yourself in such a way that you can easily catch or collect the ball coming back. This drill can also be executed with a partner who will catch the Ball and throw it back to you. You should concentrate on *rebounding up from the squat as soon as the Ball touches the floor*. Once you are proficient, you should also try to throw the Ball as powerfully as possible. You can then increase the Ball weight gradually with time. 3 sets of 10 throws.

8.7.5 Overhead Wall Throw

(This is also a <u>partner</u> drill). From a standing position, holding the Ball with both hands, you lift it overhead. As soon as you reach your apex, you immediately explode forward with a stepping throw. You lower the arms while letting go of the ball in a classic overhead throw forward. The Ball rebounds on the wall in front of you, and you collect it when it comes back for a repeat. You should alternate the side of the stepping, either at each rep (right/left/right..) or at half-the-set (5 right/ 5 left). The plyometric effect comes from the *change of direction as you reach your apex*: you should start throwing as fast as possible once you are overhead. Once you are proficient, you should then try to throw as powerfully as possible, and eventually start to increase the weight of the Ball. Please note that the wall can be replaced by a training partner who will catch the Ball and throw it back to you. 3 series of 10 throws with alternating steps.

8.7.6 Lateral Wall Throw

(This is also a <u>partner</u> drill). Standing sideways to the wall, you hold the Ball in front of you. Twist away from the wall, and then explode into a counter-twist during which you release the Ball forcefully towards the wall. Pick up the Ball as it comes back to you and repeat from the normal sideways position. The plyometric effect comes from *the fast transition from twist to counter-twist*, to be executed forcefully and as explosively as possible. Once you become proficient, concentrate on the speed of the overall move and of the transition. You can gradually use heavier Medicine Balls and throw them as powerfully as possible. This exercise can be drilled with a partner who will catch the Ball and throw it back to you. 3 series of 10 throws (5 each side).

8.7.7 Medicine Ball Push-ups

This is a simple Push-up exercise, but with your hands on a Medicine Ball as illustrated. This set-up emphasizes the work of the Triceps muscle and *the balance adjustment required do put in play the smaller core muscles*. It is a great overall drill, but it is best executed as follows for optimal results: (1) Go down very *slowly* and <u>explode up</u> *fast*, and (2) make sure your spine is straight and unchanged during the whole drill. 3 series of 10 to 15, according to your level.

8.7.8 One-hand Medicine Ball 'Twist and Switch' Push-ups

This is an advanced exercise, once regular Ball Push-ups become easy. You start with both hands on the Ball and go down. While you push up, you lift one of your arms and open your chest by twisting on that side.

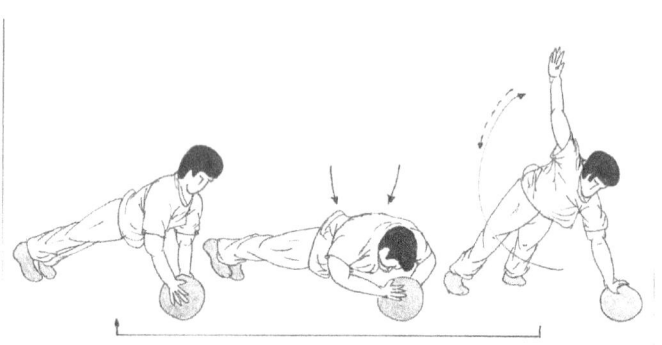

Your hand goes back to the Ball and you go down again. You push up again while lifting the other arm. You keep going and you alternate the direction of the twists. As you push up and lift the arm simultaneously, *the push-up is partially a One-arm Push-up.* Best results are achieved if you drill at slow and constant speed, but *concentrate on no stops during the flow of the exercise.* 3 sets of 8 to 12 repetitions.

8.7.9 Twisting Lunges

This is a drill that exercises: *abs, obliques, shoulders, gluteals, quads and more*. Standing with the Ball hold at arm's length, you lunge *deep and low*, while twisting sideways. Go back to standing and repeat on the other side.

Make sure you keep the arms as straight as possible and at shoulder height. Make sure you *lunge far and deep*; ideally the rear knee should nearly touch the ground while the front thigh should be parallel to the ground. Make sure you *twist as far as possible*, while keeping your back straight; and that you *minimize the time you spend standing up:* the move must not necessarily be executed fast, but the *transition time between the twists must be minimized*. 5 series of 10 alternating lunges (Five to each side)

THE ISOPLEX METHOD

8.7.10 Asymmetric Ball Push-ups

In *High Plank Pose*, you have one hand on a Medicine Ball, and the other on the floor. Execute an <u>Asymmetric Push-up</u>. When back up, roll the ball towards the other hand to take the opposite position. Execute another *Asymmetric Push-up* with the other hand on the Ball. Push the Ball back to the original hand and repeat. Make sure your back is straight. Strive to minimize transition time: there is no need to rush but speed should be constant *with no interruptions or slow-downs.* 3 series of 10 to 16 Push-ups.

8.8 Partner Drills

Working with a partner is great if he is as motivated as you are. It makes the training more fun, more competitively challenging and it allows for specific drills some of which we shall present here. The examples presented will be either with no equipment at all, with a Medicine Ball, or with an **Elastic Band**.
The Fitness Elastic Band used should be sturdy and resistant: go for the estabished brands. This is because a band tearing in the middle of a drill can cause serious bodily damage. Caution is warranted!

8.8.1 Forward Pushed Lunges

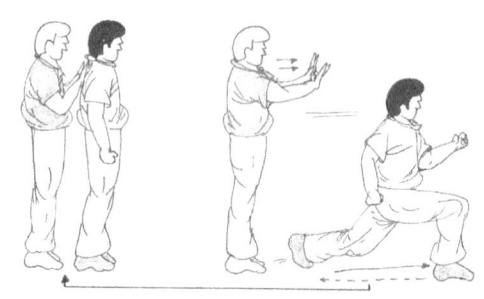

Your partner stands behind you and he *pushes* you forward. You brake the strong forward impetus by lunging *deep and low*. You then step back to the original position. As your partner pushes you again, you lunge with the other leg. *The push is powerful but not explosive* (violent). You must neither anticipate nor resist the push. You must strive to lunge as deep and as low as possible, and *then rebound back up and rearwards as fast as possible*. You must be well warmed-up to do this advanced drill and execute it at constant speed with no downtime. 3 series of 20 lunges (10 each side)

8.8.2 Lateral Pushed Lunges

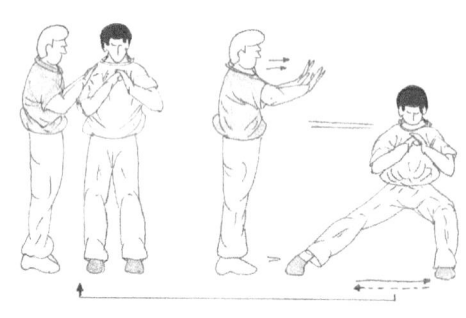

This is the *lateral* version of the previous drill. You stand sideways to your partner and he *pushes* you laterally at shoulder level. You *brake* the momentum with *a deep low lateral lunge.* You immediately rebound back to the original position for a repeat.
After 10 lunges, you switch sides to train the other leg. The push is *powerful but not explosive* (violent). You must neither anticipate nor resist the push. You must strive to lunge *as deep and as low as possible, and then rebound back up as fast as possible*. You must be well warmed-up to do this advanced drill and execute it at constant speed with no downtime. 2 series of 20 lunges (10 each side)

8.8.3 Abdominal Leg Throws

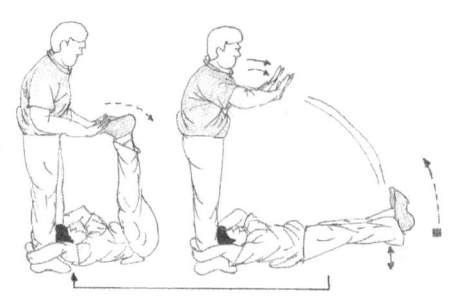

This is a classic and very important exercise. As you lie supine on the floor, you catch the ankles of your partner standing over your head. You lift your straight legs to vertical and your partner *pushes* them back down forcefully. You will fight the fall of your legs *in order to stop the momentum a few inches from the floor and immediately lift them back* to vertical. It is a classic '**stop-and-rebound**' Plyo, but your legs *never* touch the floor. The Plyometric effect comes from this abrupt and forceful change of direction, from powerfully down to powerfully up. Once you become proficient, your partner should throw your legs down as powerfully as possible. You should strive to drill as fast as possible and minimize the time at near-horizontal. 3 series of 20 leg lifts.

8.8.4 Elastic Band Sprints

You simply sprint forward while your partner is *pulling you back* with a sturdy elastic band. The actions must be proportional and constant: **your partner** pulls just enough to let you progress forward *slowly*, and he pulls steadily and with no sudden changes. **You** sprint forward for 10 seconds, then rest for 30. If you can do the drill outside or in a large room, your opponent can let you progress faster; if you exercise in a smaller room, your partner will have to restrain your progress more. If you drill outside, you can add to the drill by executing a real *unrestrained 10 seconds sprint* after the restrained one. You can do the drill without a partner, if you can hook the elastic band to the wall <u>in a secure and safe way</u>. *{It is important to take note of the fact that this drill can be dangerous and all precautions must be taken by the reader: wall anchors must be of the highest quality and checked before exercise; elastic bands are prone to tear when old and cause both sudden loss of balance as well as very serious whipping wounds. CAUTION is required!}* 3 sprints of 10 seconds.

8.8.5 Elastic Band Lateral Steps

This is the *lateral* version of the previous exercise, although you will not sprint but simply execute fast. While your opponent restrains you, you will *cross-step sideways as fast as possible*. The opponent must apply just enough force to let you cross-step away, but with difficulty. If you can drill outside, he can let you cover more distance during the drill while still making it difficult. You must strive to do as large steps as possible, as fast as possible, and make sure you alternate legs at each step. In spite of this alternation, *it is imperative to execute the drill in both directions* (to both sides!). Once you have executed 10 cross-steps to your right, you should switch and executed 10 restrained steps to your left. Again, in the absence of partner, the elastic band can be hooked safely to a wall. *{The precautions explained in the previous exercise apply here as well, and the reader is invited to refer to them and do all necessary safety checks}* 4 series of 10 cross-steps, two in each direction.

8.8.6 Medicine Ball Twists

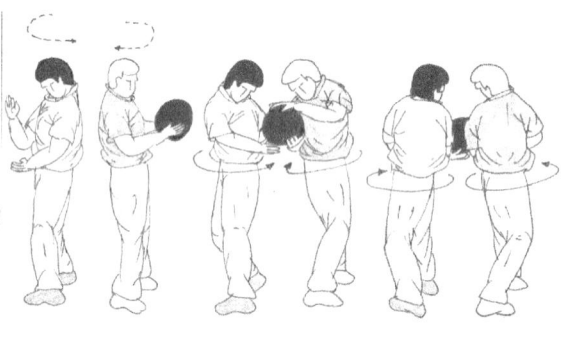

Back to back with your partner, you twist *without moving your feet* in order to pass a ball to one another. In this drill, you and your partner twist *in opposite directions*: when you twist left, he twists right. The Ball therefore makes a circle around the two partners. *The plyometric effect comes from the abrupt change of direction*, and therefore you must execute the drill as *fast* as possible with no hesitations. Once you become proficient, you can increase the weight of the Ball. Make sure you do not move your feet at all. It is advised to switch the direction on the Ball circle from series to series. 4 series of 20 full circles of the Ball.

8.8.7 Medicine Ball Extended Twists

This second Medicine Ball Twist drill will cause the Ball to travel in a '**Figure Eight**' pattern. The two partners will twist simultaneously in the *same* direction: both to their right or both to their left. This requires a deeper twist and makes it a more advanced and difficult exercise. Again, you must strive to twist as *fast* as possible and make sure that your feet do not move at all. 3 series of 20 full '*Figure Eight*' patterns.

8.8.8 Various Medicine Ball Throws

Those drills were described above as 'Wall Throws'. They can all be executed with a partner instead of a wall. You throw the Ball to your partner and he will throw it back to you. This is pretty straightforward and refers to drills 8.7.4, 8.7.5 and 8.7.6.

8.8.9 Shoulders Ball Throw

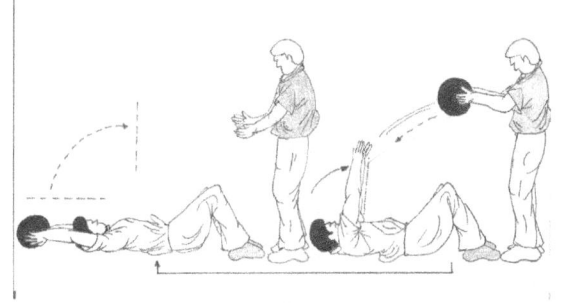

Lying on your back, you hold the Medicine Ball with stretched arms over your head. Your partner stands at your feet. You throw him the Ball forcefully by lifting your outstretched arms (only). Your back stays on the floor and your arms do not bend: *the only muscles working are the pectorals, the upper back muscles and the shoulders*. Your partner catches the Ball and throws it back to you for a repeat. As you catch the Ball, you *immediately* stretch the arms overhead to "rebound" into the throw. Make sure that you minimize the 'overhead' time and that you keep your arms straight. Once you are proficient, have your partner stand gradually further to force you to throw longer. You can also gradually increase the weight of the Ball. 3 series of 15 uninterrupted throws.

8.8.10 Sit-up Ball Throw

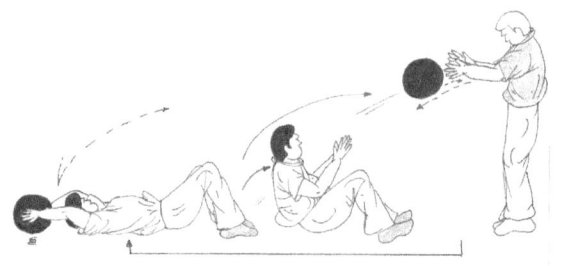

This drill starts like the previous one, but you *sit up* while throwing the Ball to your partner. You still throw the Ball overhead and do not use the arms for the throw, *but it is the abdominals which give the momentum*. As your partner throws you the Ball back, you lie down with stretched arms for a 'rebound' into a new throw. The plyometric effect comes from *minimizing the 'lying down' time between the throws*. Once proficient, you progress by using heavier Balls and/or throwing further. 4 series of 10 throws.

8.8.11 Lateral Ball Throw on knees

You sit on your knees with your partner standing to your side at adequate distance. You hold the Ball in front of you. Twist away with the Ball to gather momentum and *explode in a counter-twist* towards your standing partner. Let go of the Ball for him to catch. He'll throw it back to you for a repeat. The plyometric effect comes from *the abrupt change in twisting direction*: ensure that the transition is as short as possible. Then, explode into a 'twist and throw' as powerful as possible. After 10 reps, turn around to drill your other side. When proficient, you can have your partner standing further away and you can use (gradually) heavier Balls. 2 series of 20 throws (10 to each side).

8.8.12 Overhead Backward Ball Throw

This time your partner will be standing *behind* you. You stand normally, holding the Ball in both hands. Bend forward to gather momentum; the *Ball nearly touches the floor*. Explode immediately back up while throwing the Ball overhead towards your partner. Your partner will catch the Ball and throw it back to you for a repeat. The plyometric effect comes, again, *from the abrupt change of direction*: make sure you bend forward and immediately 'rebound' up while minimizing the transition time. This drill cannot be executed everywhere; it is best done outside or in a Sport Hall, as low ceilings can be a serious hinder. Once you are proficient, you can progress with gradually heavier Balls. 3 series of 10 throws.

8.8.13 Lying-down Ball Catch

You lie on your back while your partner stands over your head, preferably on a stool or on a plyometric box. Your partner holds a Ball above your chest and you extend your hands towards the Ball. Your partner lets go when you are ready, and you catch the Ball. *You bend your arms to soften the drop and immediately throw back the Ball* to your partner. The plyometric effect comes from the arms bending and exploding back up in a classic 'rebound'. This drill is not easy and requires a reliable partner. Your partner must make sure the Ball is not over your face and he must not *throw* the Ball (unless you are an advanced athlete). He must also be proficient in catching the Ball thrown back at him. The trainee must exercise caution by himself and take care of not getting hit in the face by a falling Medicine Ball. Once the trainee is proficient, he must concentrate on *minimizing the transition time* and on throwing the Ball back *as high as possible*. To progress, the Ball can be thrown from higher and can be of heavier weight; but increases must always be very *gradual*. 3 series of 10 throws.

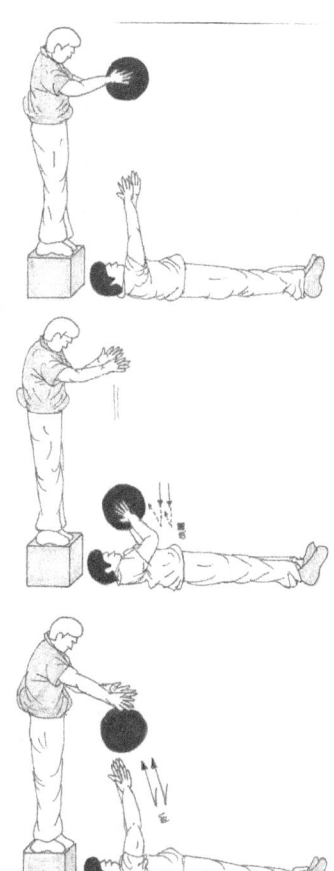

8.8.14 Powerful Basketball Pass

This is a simple Basketball basic *Chest Pass*, but executed with a heavier Medicine Ball and *as powerfully as possible*. The drill allows both partners to train simultaneously by throwing the Ball back and fro. The classic Chest Pass requires throwing at chest level while twisting the wrist to the inside during arm extension (See illustrations). The plyometric effect comes from throwing the Ball *as fast as possible after reception*: you catch and immediately throw back. It is important to minimize transition time while still executing in good form. The distance between the partners must allow for the most powerful throw possible at chest level. Once proficient, distance can be increased and/or Ball weight can be increased. 3 series of 15 throws per partner (30 back and fro).

8.8.15 Handstand hopping Push-ups

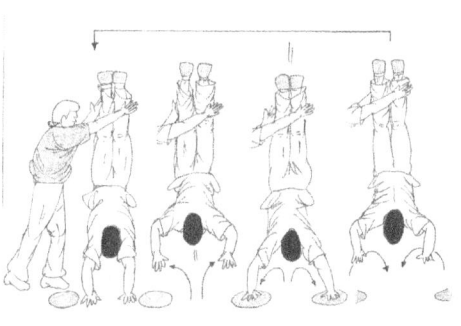

Definitely an advanced exercise! You are helped in a handstand by either the wall, your partner or preferably both. Being stabilized by your partner, you execute the arm equivalent of Jumping Jacks. Propel yourself up and land in a wide handstand; then immediately *rebound* up to land in a normal (narrower) handstand. This drill is best executed on a mat or with towels for a softer landing. It is also good to mark on the floor the place of the 'wide landing'. The partner's job is to help you keep your balance, nothing much more. You must concentrate on *minimizing the ground time in 'wide' position* for optimal plyometric benefits. 3 series; you should gradually work your way up to 10 reps (A rep includes both jumps to 'wide' and to 'narrow').

8.8.16 Incremental Height Jumps

This is the excellent drill presented in 8.4.5, but the high extremity of the rope will be held by a partner instead of being hooked to the wall or any other solid object. This has several advantages on top of the camaraderie of working with a friend. It allows dynamic fine tuning of the height gradient. It is also safer, as your partner can let go of the rope in the event you touch it and are about to fall. Refer to section 8.4.5.

We are what we repeatedly do. Excellence, therefore, is not an act but a habit.
~Aristotle

CHAPTER NINE - FLEXIOMETRIC EXERCISES

This intensive Stretching part of Isoplex is best drilled with bare feet and loose clothing.

9.1 Warm-up Stretches

These exercises have to be drilled dynamically, but very gradually. The purpose is to warm up the muscles, tendons and ligaments in order to allow safe stretching afterwards. The safe way to train is to bring the body's temperature up slowly and to loosen up the muscles before we really start to stretch. Once the muscles have worked and are warm, they are ready to let us stretch further than we normally could, without risking an injury. Stretching methodology has been described in detail in Chapter Four.

9.1.1 Straight-leg Front-Back Pendulum Kick

Standing straight, you throw your straightened leg up forward and then, pendulum-like, up behind you. You keep the pendulum movement going, forward and backward, and gradually increase height and speed. It is important to both stand straight (*no leaning*) and keep the swinging leg straight (*no bending*). Keep going gradually higher, but without forcing. Obviously, the straight leg will go much higher in front than in the back. Beginners are invited to use the wall or a piece of furniture to keep their balance while doing the exercise. Proficient trainees can stand on their own and use the hand as a target for the lift forward (illustrated). Both beginners and advanced athletes must make sure to be well warmed-up before the drill, and must increase height and speed only *gradually and carefully*. By drilling fast and high, after warm up, the drill has some plyometric effects (*at the abrupt change of direction*). 3 series of 30 kicks (15 full kicks each leg).

9.1.2 Inside Crescent Kick

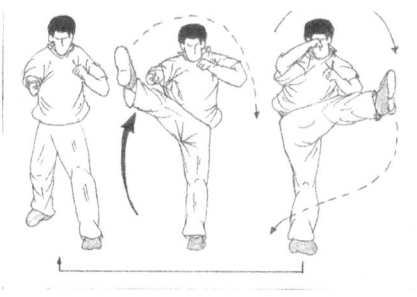

This is a classic Kick which is found in most Martial Arts, whether hard or soft. As a warming-up drill it must be executed slowly at first, with a gradual increase in speed, in height and in width of the trajectory. Once the trainee is proficient, the exercise is best drilled as a full-fledged Kick, with intent. In something akin to a guard stance, you lift your straightened rear leg *forward and outside* to describe an arc in front of you. The leg then goes back to initial position for an immediate repeat. Make sure your back is straight and your leg stays straight during the whole movement. If working with a partner, you can use his extended hand as an obstacle to clear height-wise. 1 series of 10 kicks per leg.

FLEXIOMETRIC EXERCISES

9.1.3 Outside Crescent Kick

This is the mirror maneuver of the previous drill: from the same starting position, the straight leg goes forward *and inside* to cover the trajectory in the opposite direction. This is, again, a classic Kick which is found in most Martial Arts, whether hard or soft. As a warming-up drill it must be executed *slowly at first*, with a *gradual* increase in speed height and width of the trajectory. Once the trainee is proficient, the exercise is best drilled as a full-fledged Kick, with intent. In something akin to a guard stance, you lift your straightened rear leg *forward and inside* to describe an arc in front of you. The leg then goes back to initial position for an immediate repeat. Make sure your back is *straight* and your leg stays *straight* during the whole movement. If working with a partner, you can use his extended hand as an obstacle to clear height-wise. 1 series of 10 kicks per leg.

9.1.4 Cobbler Dynamic Stretch

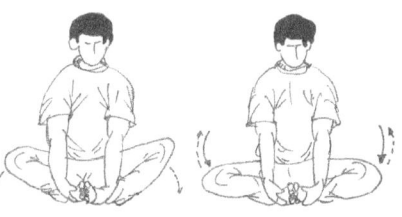

This is Yoga's *Cobbler's Pose* (or *Bound Angle Pose* – **Baddha Konasana**) but executed in a *dynamic* way to warm up the hip joints. Sitting with the plants of your feet together, and as close as possible to your crotch, you lift and lower your knees. Start slowly and at minimal amplitude and increase both speed and momentum *very gradually*. 1 series of 50 'bumps'.

9.1.5 Sitting One-legged Stretch

This is Yoga's **Janu Sirsasana**. You are sitting on the floor with one leg extended and the other bent with the plant of the foot on the inner thigh as high as possible. Bend forward and catch your ankle or foot for a *gentle and progressing stretch*. Make sur to lengthen your spine and stretch slowly. Try to keep the bent knee on the ground and the extended leg as straight as possible. Hold the slowly deepening stretch for 30 seconds each leg. *If you are stiff*, you can use a belt to pull yourself down while keeping the extended leg straight (As illustrated -1). *If you are flexible*, you can do the advanced version with the ankle of the bent leg on top of the thigh. In that case, you should also try to keep the bent knee as close to the floor as possible (Illustrated - 2).

1
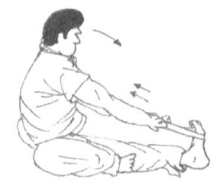

2

86   THE ISOPLEX METHOD

9.1.6 Bent-leg Pull

Sitting on the floor, you will catch one foot and pull it towards your face while bending the knee outwards. Go *gradually and slowly*. Use one hand on the foot and the other on the knee. Make sure you sit *straight* and hold the slowly deepening stretch for 30 seconds each leg.

If you are flexible, the drill is best executed as you lie on the floor on your back. See second Illustration.

9.1.7 Standing Front Bends

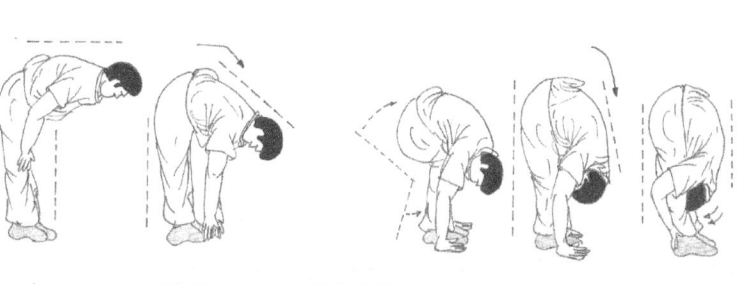

This is simply bending forward as deeply as possible when standing. Make sure you stretch your spine and keep it *as straight as possible*. Use your core muscles as much as possible to bend and aim at *fully straightening the knees*. The Illustrations show the natural progression of the drill according to your progress or to your natural flexibility.
Bend forward as much as possible with straight legs and a straight back. (2) Touch the floor with the fingers with straight back and legs. (3) Place your palms on the floor and then straighten your legs gradually until you can hold the position. (4) Hold your heels and pull to bend even deeper while trying to place the forehead on the knees. (5) Place your palms on the floor behind you and bend deeper.
60 seconds of slowly deepening bend.

9.1.8 Standing Side Bends

Extend your joined hands over your head and stretch your spine as much as possible. Keep straight and start bending to one side *without bending forward* or backwards. *Keep the spine stretched* and deepen the posture gradually by relaxing. Keep the deepest bend for 30 seconds; then repeat on the other side. 2 times 30 seconds on each side.

FLEXIOMETRIC EXERCISES

9.2 Lower Leg Stretches

9.2.1 Sitting on the knees Poses

Yoga's **Vajrasana Pose** is simply sitting on your heels. Make sure your *back is straight* and feel the stretch in your knees and ankles. The Illustrations show

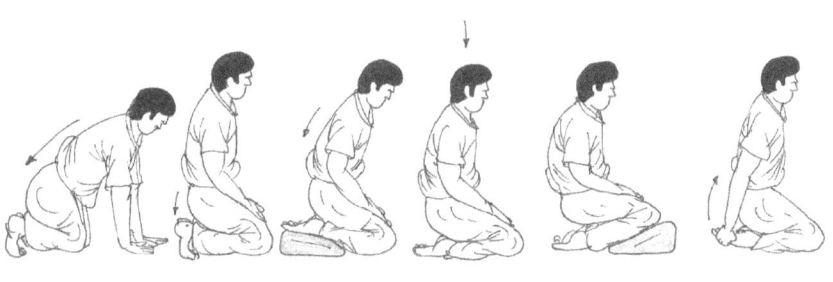

the progression for the stiff trainee to gradually improve the posture. Once you can sit easily on your heels, you should then use an inclined cushion or should pull your feet up to deepen the stretch, as illustrated. Once it becomes easy, you should switch to the next stretch. Keep 2 minutes in your deepest pose.

9.2.2 Hero's Pose

Yoga's **Virasana Pose,** or Hero's Pose is simply sitting on your knees *with your bottom between your heels;* ideally, you should be sitting with your buttocks on the floor. This allows for a further stretch from the previous pose (*do not try this stretch if you are not proficient in the previous one*). Relax and try to lower your buttocks further. Keep the stretch for 2 minutes.

9.2.3 Downward Dog Poses

Yoga's **Adho Mukha Svanasana** is an iconic pose, much used to relax and stretch between difficult stretches and exercises. With your feet flat on the floor, and your arms extended, you take

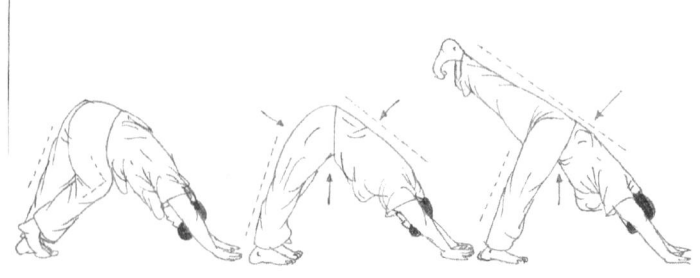

the basic position and try to sharpen the pyramid 'form' you are in. Your *buttocks and hips should stretch up*, as you *push down with your thighs and (straight) back*. A further distance between hands and feet will stretch the lower leg more intensely. A 'shorter' dog, will stretch the hamstrings more. A beginner should start by alternating a raised heel, slowly switching from foot to foot. An advanced student should raise one straightened leg to get a more intense stretch on the other one; then switch legs. Keep the deepest stretch for 2 minutes

9.2.4 Flexed Foot Front Leg Stretch

Rear foot flat on the floor; front foot on the heel; straight legs. Bend forward with *stretched spine* and aim at placing your *forehead on your front knee*. *Lift your front toes* as high as possible and deepen the stretch. Make sure your front leg is absolutely *straight*. Keep the deepest stretch for 60 seconds before you switch legs.

9.2.5 Sitting Two-legged Stretch

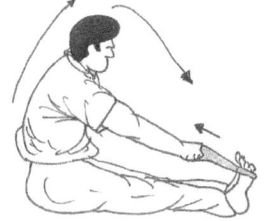 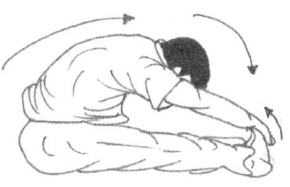

Yoga's iconic **Paschimottanasana** stretches the spine, the hamstrings and the ankles. Sitting on the floor, you simply bend over your straight extended legs. *Lengthen your spine* and pull on your toes to try to get your *forehead on your knees*. If you are stiff, use a band or a towel to help you at the beginning, as illustrated. Make sure you pull on your toes and not lower, in order to also stretch the feet and ankles. Relax, pull yourself down and forward. Keep the deepest pose for 30 seconds. Repeat 3 times.

9.2.6 Crossed-legs Standing Forward Bends

Very simple but very effective: you cross your feet in standing position, and then bend forward. Keep your *spine stretched* and aim at placing the *palm of the hands on the floor*. Relax to get as deep as possible, then keep the stretch for 30 seconds. Switch legs and repeat, twice each leg.

9.2.7 Lying One-legged Stretch

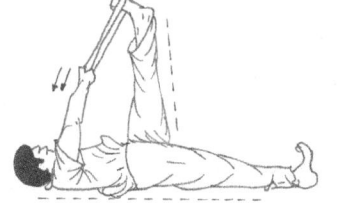 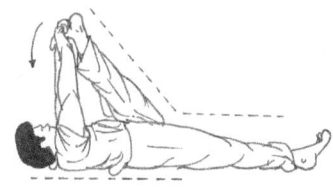

Lying on the floor, you pull a straight leg towards your trunk. Start with the help of a belt, a band or a towel at first, if needed. Make sure you keep your *back and both your legs straight*. Do not lift the head and pull gradually to deepen the stretch. Make sure you *pull at your toes level*, not the ankle, in order to make sure that the feet and ankles are stretched as well. Keep the deepest pose for 1 minute, then switch legs.

9.2.8 Dance positions

These are pretty straightforward but more challenging than they look. Take the dancing positions illustrated in their order of progress; hold a chair, a dance bar or any other possible support. *Flex the knees while keeping the feet in place.* Go down slowly and deepen the stance *gradually*. Make sure you *open the hips* and <u>do not</u> use over-rotation of the knees themselves. Keep the deepest possible stance for twice 1 minute.

9.3 Hamstring Stretches

9.3.1 Sitting Bends

Those are the sitting bends already encountered for stretching the lower leg: sitting stretches on one or on both extended legs. This time though, the poses are executed with emphasis on the *hamstrings*

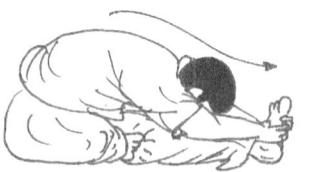

and not the ankles: you do not pull on your toes to stretch the feet, *but you pull on your heels*. Your feet are not flexed but relaxed and all the stretching concentration goes *to the back of the leg and the lower back*. The stretches are still the classic Yoga's poses **Janu Sirsasana** and **Paschimottanasana**, but concentrating on the

hamstrings. As illustrated, you can enroll a reliable partner to help you deepen the stances gradually and carefully. Keep the deepest stance for 2 minutes; of course switch legs for a repeat in the case of the one-legged stretch.

THE ISOPLEX METHOD

9.3.2 Open-legged Sitting Bends

Yoga's **Upavistha Konasana** pose is an important classic. Sitting on the floor, you open your *straightened* legs as much as you can. Bend down with *stretched spine* towards the floor and place your hands *as far as possible* forward. Aim at slowly going further while placing the chin on the floor. Keep the deepest position for 90 seconds.

9.3.3 Lying Leg Pulls

Yoga's **Supta Padangustasana** looks easy but requires concentration. Lying on your back, you pull one *straightened* leg towards your face while the other leg *stays straight on the floor.* Make sure your back and head stay straight on the floor as well. Pull the leg *slowly and gradually* towards your face. Beginners should start with the leg on the floor slightly bent (Illustrated) and then,

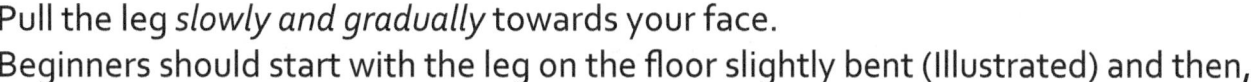

when getting better, should proceed to use a belt or band to pull the leg in the right classic position (Illustrated). Proficient trainees can use the help of a reliable partner for a careful deeper stretch (Illustrated). Keep the deepest possible stretch for 1 minute before switching legs.

9.3.4 Standing Elevated One Legged Bends

This is a classic stretch for runners and cyclists, but it requires an elevated support. Place your *straight* leg on this support at about waist height. Keep your *standing leg straight* and bend with a stretched spine towards your elevated knee. Keep stretching the spine while trying to get a little deeper. Keep the deepest position for 30 seconds, then switch legs. When proficient, aim at lifting the leg on a higher support. *It is best to keep the standing leg about vertical*: going for a splits-like position is not the same stretch. 2 times 30 seconds per leg.

FLEXIOMETRIC EXERCISES

9.3.5 Front Leg Bends

This is Yoga's **Parsvottanasana**, a much deeper stretch than it looks. You stand with one leg in front, and *both legs totally straight*. Bend gradually over your straight front leg, *aiming at the knee with your forehead*. Keep your spine elongated and your legs straight. Keep the deepest stretch for 30 seconds, then switch legs. 2 times 30 seconds per leg.

9.3.6 Classic Front Bends

Iconic Yoga's **Uttanasana** is a simple standing front bend. But it is one of those unavoidable basic exercises that must always be done, at all levels of proficiency. The Illustrations show the gradual progression towards the posture, according to your flexibility. Strive to get there *gradually*, with no forcing. Always keep your *back straight and stretched*, at all levels. (1) Beginners can then start practicing with hands on the floor, but knee bent; they should strive to straighten their legs gradually, until they can touch the floor with straight legs. (2) Touch the floor with fingers first, then gradually keep training until you can place your palms flat on the floor (3). From then on, start to hold your ankles and pull your forehead to your knees (4). Legs and spine must be pulled straight. Hold deepest position for 1 minute. Rest and repeat for another minute.

9.3.7 Open Legs Front Bends

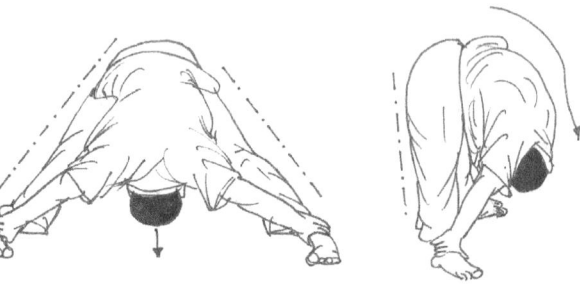

Prasarita Padottanasana is basically the previous front bend executed *in a wide open stance*. The legs must be opened about twice the waist width and the trainee must strive *to lower the top of his head to the floor*. The spine and legs must be *straight* and stretched; and pulling on the anshould help reach the deepest possible bend. Keep the bend for 1 minute. Rest and repeat.

9.3.8 Front Splits

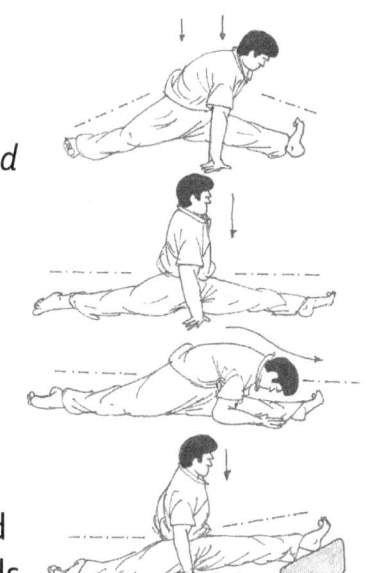

Yoga's **Hanumanasana** is simply the *Front Splits.* This is a very deep hamstring stretch, but it needs to approached *carefully and gradually*. At the start, use your hands to support your weight while going down; make sure your *front leg and your back are straight*. Once you can hold the pose all the way down, make sure both legs and the spine are straight and stretched. When proficient you can gradually bend forward and strive to place the face near the front knee. And if you are very flexible, you can place the front heel on a cushion to achieve a more than a 180 angle. But careful is the word. Proceed slowly, patiently and very gradually. Hold your deepest possible stretch for 30 seconds before switching legs.

9.3.9 Heron's Poses

Sit on the floor with one leg bent and lift the other leg towards your face. Hold your ankle and heel and make sure the leg is totally *straight*. Try to keep your *back as straight as possible*. Hold for 30 seconds and switch legs. Once you are proficient, you can proceed to the Yoga version (**Krounchasana**), in which you sit with bottom close to your heel (See Illustration). This adds a knee stretch for the flexible trainees. The pose is difficult, though, and unnecessary as a hamstring stretch; do not go there if it is too difficult or if you have knee problems. Whichever pose you are holding, do so at its maximum for 30 seconds each leg.

It always seems impossible until its done.
~Nelson Mandela

FLEXIOMETRIC EXERCISES

9.4 Adductors Stretches

9.4.1 Cobbler Poses

Baddha Konasana, or *Bound Angle Pose*, is commonly referred to as Cobbler's Pose. You sit and hold your feet with their soles fully touching. Try to have your heels as close as possible to your groin and to keep your *spine erect and stretched*.

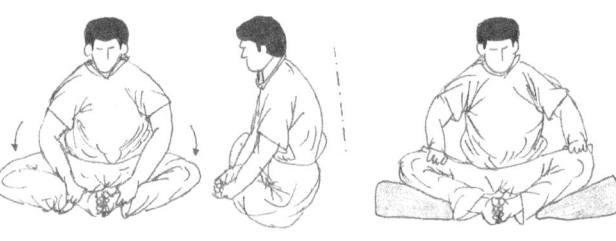

Then use your elbows to push the knees down and gradually stretch your adductors. Keep the deepest possible stretch for 1 minute. Beginners should proceed cautiously and start with cushions under their knees, as illustrated.

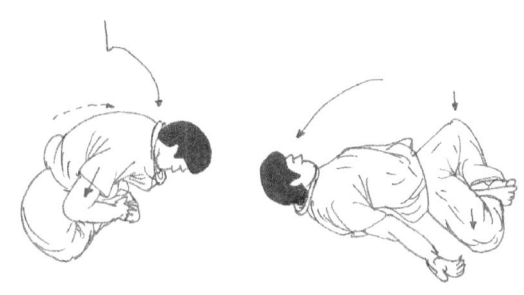

Once you are proficient, you can deepen the stretch by bending forward and by trying to place your forehead to the floor while pushing the knees down. After the stretch, classic or advanced, let your back lie on the floor while keeping the legs in a light stretch (as Illustrated); hold the pose (**Supta Baddha Konasana**) for 1 minute as well.

The Cobbler's Pose is a stretch that is definitely suited to partner training: a deeper (passive-assisted) stretch is generally attained safely if a careful partner presses your knees down very gradually, instead of letting you do it yourself. The partner-helped stretch is then maintained in the lying down phase.

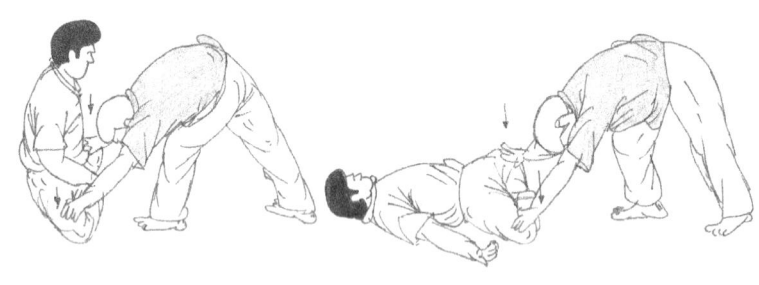

9.4.2 Lying Wide Stretch

Lie on the floor; lift your *straightened* legs and catch your ankles. Open your legs *as wide as possible* and pull your feet towards the floor. Keep the legs totally straight. Make sure that your back and head stay on the floor and that you do not lift your bottom. *The hips stay down as you aim at stretching the adductors*. Pull on your ankles: try to simultaneously open your legs as wide as possible *and reach the floor with your toes*. Keep the deepest possible stretch for 30 seconds.

9.4.3 Sitting Wide One-leg Side Stretch

Yoga's **Parivratta Upavistha Konasana** is a very important stretch that is not that easy to execute well. It must be approached carefully, very gradually and tenaciously. Sitting with legs opened as wide as possible, you lean sideways, aiming with your head towards one knee. Place the shoulder *inside* the thigh, while the other arm goes over your head. Both hands then go to grab the foot to pull you further down, with one elbow over your head and the other on the ground. Keep the *spine stretched*; keep the legs *straight*, make sure you lean *sideways*; pull down and forward and try to look up to the ceiling. Once you become proficient, you can progress by trying to open the legs even wider. Keep your deepest stretch for 30 seconds, before you switch legs.

9.4.4 Sitting Wide One-leg Front Stretch

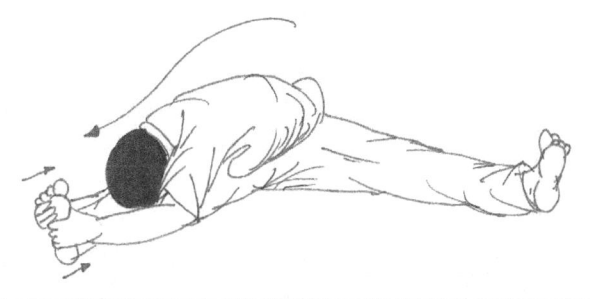

Parsva Upavistha Konasana must not be confused with the previous posture. In fact, they are best drilled one after the other because they emphasize different muscles. With legs opened as wide as possible, you will now twist your trunk to be *parallel* to the leg to be stretched. You then lower gradually your chest towards your thigh. You are not stretching sideways *but straight*! Extend the spine and pull both down and forward over you straight leg. Keep the deepest stretch for 30 seconds before you switch sides.

If you're going through hell, keep going.
~Winston Churchill

FLEXIOMETRIC EXERCISES

9.4.5 Sitting Wide Middle Stretch

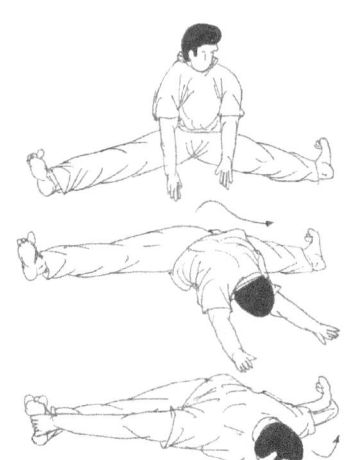

After the two previous exercises, it is natural to finally get to the 'Seated Angle Pose', Yoga's **Upavistha Konasana**. Sitting, again with the legs opened *as wide as possible*, you will now go down forward between your legs. You aim to place your whole chest and belly on the floor. When proficient, you then lift your head and place your chin on the floor. Keep the legs *straight* and as wide open as possible, and keep the *spine stretched* as you pull forward. Your hands can either catch your feet to help pulling you forward, or can stretch forward on the floor in front of you. Once you have reached your deepest stretch, relax and keep it for 1 minute. <u>Go back up slowly and use your hands to help close your legs again</u>.
This is a very important pose, and it definitely helps to drill it with a careful partner.

You partner helps to deepen the stretch, either by pushing your lower back forward and down, or by pulling your hands forward while pushing your legs open with his feet (Illustrated).

9.4.6 Lying One-legged Stretch

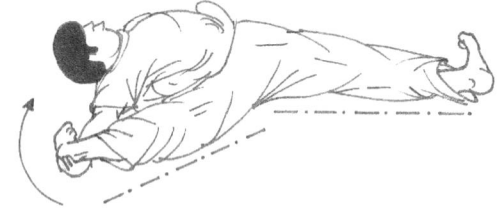

Lying on the floor on your back, you glide one straight leg to the side *while staying in contact with the floor*. Catch your heel or grab your ankle and pull the leg towards your head slowly and gradually. Your back, your head and both of your straight legs *stay in full contact with the floor*. If you need it, use a towel or a belt to pull the foot up, as the leg must be straight. Hold your deepest pose for 30 seconds and switch legs.

9.4.7 Frog

Squat down and place your elbows between your knees. Push the knees out with the elbows to stretch the adductors. *Keep your back straight* and sit as low as possible. Keep the deepest stretch for 1 minute.

9.4.8 Side Splits

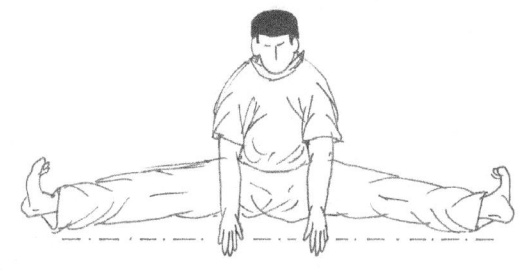

Sit on the floor with your *straightened* legs opened as much as possible. Lean on your hands to lift your bottom and inch forward slowly; the heels stay in place. When you sit back down you have opened the stretch a little more. Keep inching gradually towards your maximum and hopefully aim for the full Side Splits. Keep your maximum stretch for 1 minute. Relax when finished and *use your hands to help the legs close back slowly*.

9.4.9 One-legged Chair Bend

Stand next to a Plyo-box or a chair and place one feet on it. Keep the other leg *totally straight* and bend forward. Aim at touching the floor with your fingers and *place your forehead to your straight knee*. This should pull the adductors of your bent leg. If you are flexible, the foot must be placed higher and you should keep lifting it more and more as you become proficient. Keep your deepest stretch for 1 minute, before switching legs.

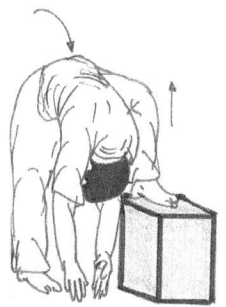

FLEXIOMETRIC EXERCISES

9.5 Quadriceps Stretches

9.5.1 Standing Quad Stretches

Standing on one leg, you catch the ankle of the other leg (with same side hand) and *pull your heel towards your bottom*. Pull gradually to stretch the quadriceps to his maximum. Beginners should start while using a wall in front of them for balance, or should do the exercise while lying on their bellies. Once you become proficient doing the basic standing pose, you can increase the difficulty by using the opposite hand to pull the ankle. You can then also increase the pressure by using a table or a wall while pushing back with your whole body weight. Keep the deepest stretch for 1 minute before switching legs.

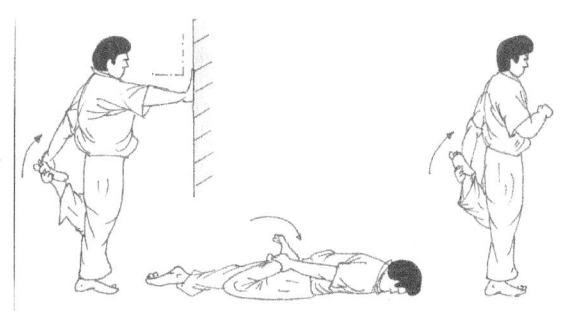

9.5.2 Kneeling Quad Stretch

Kneel with one leg forward. Catch the ankle of the back leg and pull it up while keeping the knee on the floor. At the same time, lean forward on the lunging leg. Try to pull *the heel to the bottom* and lunge forward *as deep as possible*. Keep the spine elongated. Keep the deepest possible stretch, to be felt at the front of the thigh, for 30 seconds before switching sides.

9.5.3 Reclining Hero's Pose

Yoga's **Supta Virasana** is an important but difficult pose. It is to be approached carefully and gradually because it challenges the knee. *Sitting on the floor with your bottom between your heels, you should gradually lean back and place the whole back on the floor.* You then relax and enjoy the stretch for 1 full minute. *In order to achieve the stretch gradually, you should start with one leg bent and the other stretched in front, all the while you support yourself back on your elbows.* When you become more flexible, you can bend both legs while supporting yourself on your elbows. Keep going down gradually until you can get to the floor and do not need the support of the elbows any more. Keep your deepest possible stretch for 1 full minute. (If one leg is straight, repeat the drill while switching sides).

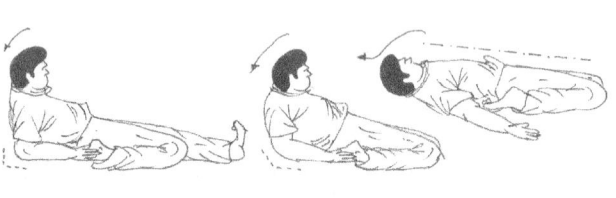

9.5.4 Lying Quad Stretches

Place your front thigh and hip on the edge of a table or a bench; the height of the prop is not important. Your other foot is on the floor. *Catch your ankle and pull the heel towards your bottom while lifting the trunk.* If you lack flexibility, use a belt or a towel to reach your ankle. Keep your deepest stretch for one minute, before you switch legs.

9.6 Glutei and Hip Stretches

9.6.1 Deep Lunge

Anjaneyasana is a very important stretch that anyone can do to his own limits and reap the benefits. The rear knee is on the floor and the front leg is bent *perpendicular to the floor* (90 degrees). Push your hips forward. You must keep your *spine straight* and place your front foot *as far as possible forward*. Feel the stretch in your rear hip and deepen slowly and carefully. Keep your deepest lunge for 1 full minute before repeating on the other side.

9.6.2 Front Splits

The Front Splits are called **Hanumanasana** in Yoga. The final pose is not for everyone, but the trainee must strive to achieve it gradually. The beginner should concentrate on the *Deep Lunge* first (Previous exercise); he should then try the Front Splits *with the rear leg bent and while supporting his body weight on his hands.* Keep the spine straight and erect. Flexible trainees who can do the classic Splits can progress by *bending the trunk towards the front thigh, and by elevating the front foot on a pillow or a soft block*. Keep your deepest Pose for 30 seconds, release the Pose slowly and carefully, and switch legs.

9.6.3 Lying Knee Twists

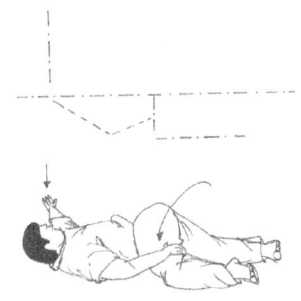

This drill, unlike the previous one, can be, and *should be* executed regularly by everyone. Lying on your back, you bend your knee at 90 degrees and pull it to the floor on the opposite side. *You make sure that everything else stays in contact with the floor: the head, both shoulders, the full back, the (other) straight leg.* The arm and hand of the stretching side should also stay in contact with the floor at a 90 degrees angle to the body. You can help the stretch by using the other hand to push the knee even further down. Make sure the shoulders stay in contact with the floor and keep the deepest stretch for 1 full minute before you switch sides.

9.6.4 Lying Leg Twists

This important stretch is similar to the previous one, but it is executed *with the whole straightened leg* instead of the knee only. On your back with the arms stretched at 90 degrees, you lift your straightened leg also perpendicularly. While *keeping the back, the other leg and the shoulders fully in contact with the floor*, you lower the leg sideways and aim to place the foot as close as possible to the opposite palm hand. Keep the stretch for 1 full minute before switching legs.

9.6.5 Waist Twists

This simple but very important stretch has a long Yoga name: **Eka Pada Parivrtta Upavisthasana**. Sitting on the floor with one leg straight and the other bent and crossed over, *you twist towards the side of the bent leg and try to look behind you.* Use your elbow to maintain the twist at first, and then later to push the knee and deepen the twisting pose. Make sure the spine stays *straight and elongated, that the foot of the bent leg is flat on the floor and that the straight leg stays straight and in contact with the floor*. Keep your deepest twist for 1 minute before switching sides.

9.6.6 Bent Leg Pulls

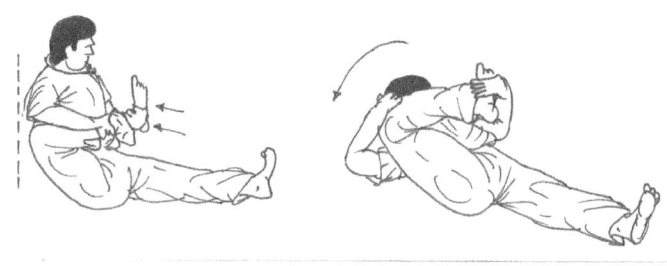

Sitting on the floor with one leg straight, you bend the other one and *pull its ankle towards your face.* The most flexible should aim at placing the foot behind the neck. Proceed slowly and carefully, and make sure you *keep your back straight.* Once you are proficient, you should do the drill while lying on your back to allow for more concentration and a deeper stretch. Keep your deepest pose for 1 minute before switching legs.

9.6.7 Runner's Stretches

Yoga's **Salamba Kapotasana**, the *Supported Pigeon Pose*, is often called in the West the 'Runner's Stretch' because of its importance for running and cycling enthusiasts. You sit on one bent leg and on your hips, with the other leg extended straight behind you. Your *back is straight* and vertical, and you support yourself on your hands. If you are flexible you can gradually 'open' the angle of the bent leg and you should aim for the 90 degrees angle. Release your weight on your hips to deepen the stretch. *When proficient and comfortable, you should bend forward on your bent knee*, but keep pulling the spine for a straight back. Keep the pose for 2 minutes before switching legs.

9.6.8 Cross Side Bends

This drill is simple and easy, but very beneficial. While standing, you simply *cross your legs* and then bend sideways *to place your palms on the floor.* You bend slowly to the side of the crossing leg and try to place the hands perpendicular to your foot. Keep *the legs as straight as possible*. Beginners will warm up by doing the drill with legs uncrossed first and then will try to reach the floor with their fingers first. Keep your deepest stretch for 30 seconds before switching legs (and therefore corresponding bending sides).

FLEXIOMETRIC EXERCISES

9.7 Abdominals

9.7.1 Cobra Stretches

Yoga's **Bhujangasana** (*Cobra Pose*) must be drilled *carefully* to avoid harming the lower back. Lying on your belly, you use your hands at shoulder level to lift your trunk as high as possible. *Your pelvis and legs stay fully on the floor.* Stretch **gradually** by pushing on your hands and looking up as far as possible. Stretch your spine and abdominals by making sure that everything below the belt stays on the floor. You can have a partner help you by pulling you carefully at the arms (extended over your head). Keep your deepest pose for 1 minute.

9.7.2 Camel Stretches

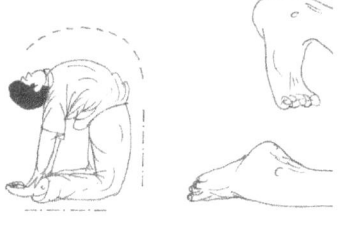

Yoga's *Camel Pose*, **Ustrasana**, usually needs easing into; it is best if you can have a partner support you during your first efforts. On your knees, you bend carefully backwards to go and *place your hands on your heels.* Try to look back and *push your abdominals and pelvis forward.* Beginners will have their heels up by resting on their dorsiflexed feet and raised toes. Advanced trainees will rest on the top of the feet (ankles in plantarflexion) to have the heels as low as possible. Keep the stretch for 30 seconds.

9.7.3 Bow Pose

Dhanurasana, or the Bow Pose, is a great overall Stretch. In this case, you concentrate on stretching the Abdominals. Lying on your belly, you catch your ankles with your hands. You then pull on your ankles while stretching the legs up in order *to arch your back as far as possible.* Concentrate on your abs and keep your knees together. Keep the deepest stretch for 30 seconds, rest 30 seconds and repeat.

9.7.4 Bridge Poses

In prone position with hands near the shoulders and heels near the buttocks, you lift your back as high as possible. Push on your hands to lift the shoulders and use the top of your head as support. *Arch the back as much as possible to stretch the Abdominals*. This is the *Bridge Pose* (**Sirsa Setu Bandhasanasana**), from which you can proceed if you are strong and flexible. Keep pushing on your hands to *lift the head off the floor* and arch the back even more. To progress, you can then inch your hands closer to your feet. This is now, in fact, the challenging *Upward Bow Pose* (**Urdhva Dhanurasana**). All these 'Bridge Poses' have to be executed with great *care* and only *gradually*. Keep your best pose for 30 seconds, rest 30 seconds and repeat.

9.7.5 Hanging Abdominal Stretch

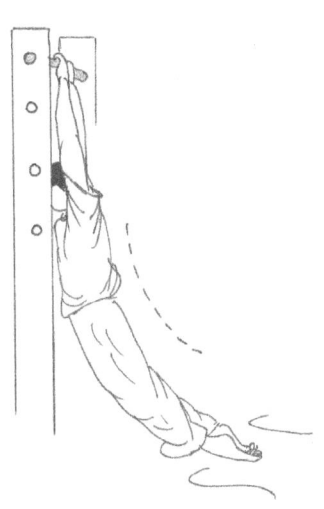

This is a simple hanging exercise for which you need a chin bar in a doorframe, or a sport ladder, or anything you could suspend from that is lower than your chin to start with. Hang from the bar with relaxed shoulders and let some of your weight onto the top of your extended feet. *Arch your back as much as possible* and feel the ab stretch. Keep the pose for 1 minute.

Tight hamstrings are fierce. And I'm guilty of not allocating the time that I should to stretch. I'll put the time in for the runs, but then I go, 'I have to go here. I've got to go there.' Usually, stretching is what gets cut out of the program, <u>but it's so critical.</u>
~Bill Rancic

9.8 Lower Back and Laterals

9.8.1 Standing Bends

These are the simple *Classic Front Bends* (encountered as 9.3.6, in Hamstring Stretches). You will drill the same poses as before, but this time, the emphasis and focus will be **on the lower back** rather than on the Hamstrings. The principles stay the same for this Yoga's **Uttanasana**, but the trainee will concentrate on stretching his back. The Illustrations show, again, the gradual progression towards the posture, according to your flexibility. Strive to get there *gradually*, with no forcing. Always keep your *back straight and stretched*, at all levels. Beginners can then start practicing with hands on the floor, but knee bent; then they should strive to straighten their legs gradually, until they can touch the floor with straight legs. Touch the floor with fingers first, then gradually keep training until you can place your palms flat on the floor. From then on, start to hold your ankles and pull your forehead to your knees. Legs and spine must be pulled straight. Hold deepest position for 1 minute. Rest and repeat for another minute.

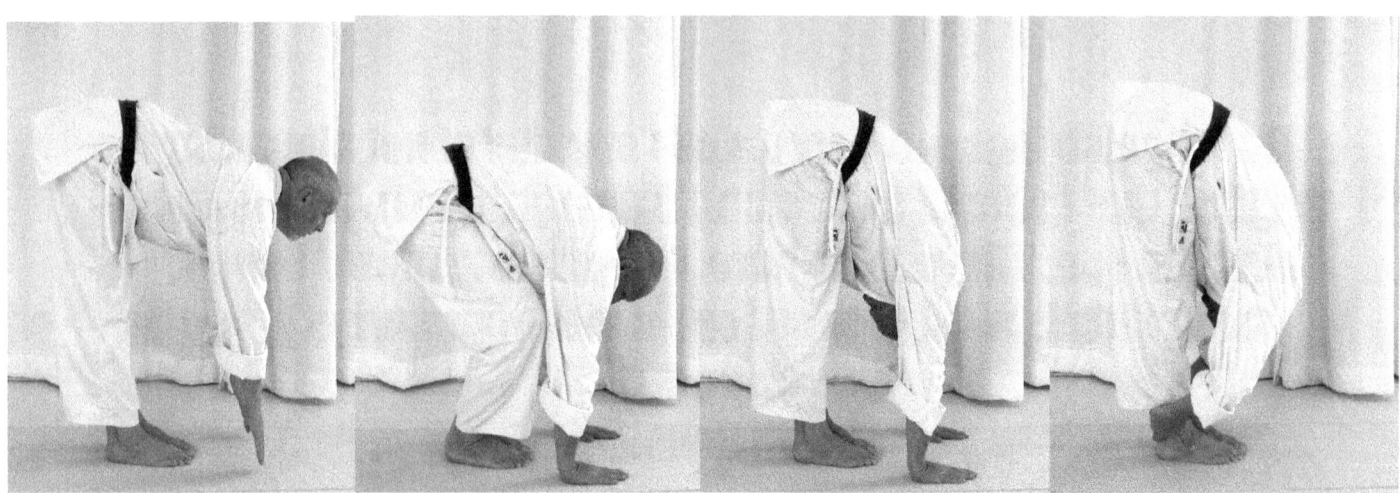

9.8.2 Plough Poses

Yoga'a **Halasana**, known as the Plough Pose, is the ultimate Spine Stretch. It is an important exercise, but it must be approached *carefully and gradually*, especially as far as the neck is concerned. It 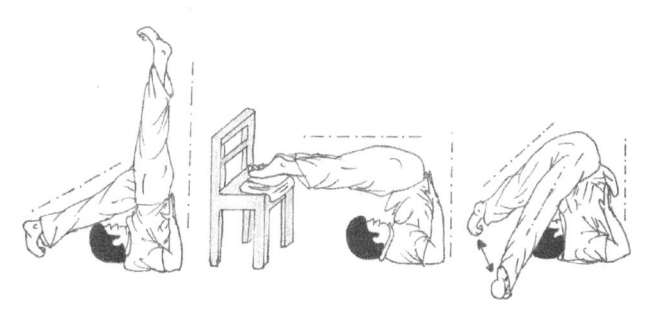 is also a pose difficult to execute if you have belly fat, and therefore progress should go hand in hand with slimming down. The Pose itself is well known: your stretched legs are over your head and both your shouldres and your toes touch the floor. We have shown the preparatory poses for the beginner, in order of gradual difficulty. Take your time. We have then shown more advanced versions for the advanced trainee. Go gradually and *always keep your neck straight*: do not turn your head while in the pose! The beginner will lower one straight leg to the floor while keeping the other one straight and perpendicular to the floor; the back is supported by the elbows. The trainee can then gradually proceed towards the full pose, but using a chair as 'higher ground'. Then, the trainee can approach the full *Plough Pose*, but with legs open which make it easier. Once the trainee can easily hold the Plough Pose, he can proceed to the more sophisticated versions. **Supta Paschimottasana** will have him lower the back to the floor while keeping the legs and back straight and the toes to the floor. **Karnapidasana** will have him bend the knees near the ears from Plough Pose. <u>Always mobilize the neck in slow motion after these poses</u>. Keep your deepest pose for 1 minute, and *come out of it slowly*.

9.8.3 Sitting Side Bends

Yoga's **Parivrtta Upavistha Konasana** consists in sitting on the floor with straight legs wide open. You then lean sideways and reach overhead for your toes. Place the  other elbow on the floor inside your knee and stretch while trying to look up at the ceiling. *Keep your spine stretched, open your legs as wide as possible and pull gently;* you can aim at catching your own wrist with the hand touching the floor. Beginners should start with their hands locked behind the head, leaning sideways and aiming at placing the elbow behind the knee. Progress slowly and carefully. Keep your deepest stretch for 30 seconds, then release the pose slowly and switch sides.

FLEXIOMETRIC EXERCISES

9.8.4 Seated Twists

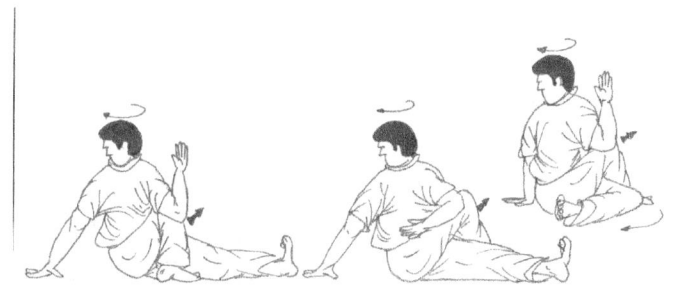

Eka Pada Parivrtta Upavisthasana can be drilled with emphasis *on the lower back and the laterals.* With one leg extended, you place the foot of the other on the floor outside the extended knee. Twist to look behind you and use the elbow to push the knee back in the opposite direction to the twist. Use the other hand to lean slightly on the floor *and keep your spine straight.* The neck stays in line with the trunk; there is no need to twist the neck. Beginners will start with the foot inside the extended leg and use their elbow to deepen the twist; they should aim at having the hand pointing at the ceiling as illustrated. Advanced trainees can compound the pose by then bending the extended leg and bringing the heel towards their buttocks (**Matsiendrasana**). Keep your deepest stretch for 30 seconds and switch sides.

9.8.5 Triangle Pose

Yoga's iconic **Utthita Trikonasana** is an important exercise to be drilled regularly as it stretches nearly the whole body. In a wide stance, you have you front foot pointing forward and the rear foot at about 45 degrees. Lean sideways, *with a straight spine*, towards your front leg and aim at placing your hand flat on the floor outside your front ankle. Beginners will first place the hand on the shin (Illustrated), and then gradually attempt to place the hand inside the ankle, before reaching the classic pose. Make sure your legs and spine are straight; try to have *both arms straight in a single line* perpendicular to the ground; look at your upper hand. Once you have reached your deepest stretch, relax and hold the pose for 1 minute before switching sides.

9.8.6 Inverted Triangle Pose

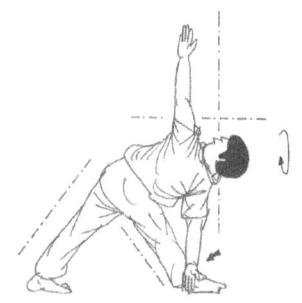

Parivrtta Trikonasana is a more difficult stretch than the previous Triangle Pose; proceed *slowly and gradually*. This time you will twist the trunk 180 degrees before leaning towards the front leg. Place your hand flat on the floor inside the front ankle, though beginners should start by placing the hand on the shin. Advanced trainees will place the hand outside the front ankle (Illustrated). Just like for the previous pose, you should aim at having *legs, spine and arms straight*. Use you core muscles for the twist and look at your upper hand. Relax in your deepest pose and keep it for 1 minute before switching.

9.8.7 Chair Twist

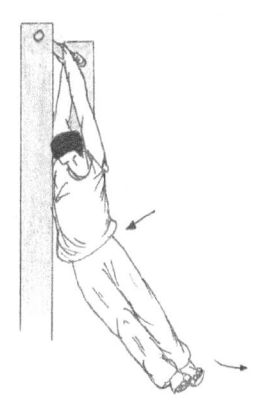

Sit on a chair with a straight back. Hold the back of the chair and twist slowly but *as far as possible*. Keep your feet flat on the ground and your legs and bottom straight and facing the front. Look behind you with a stretched spine and keep the pose for 1 minute before switching sides.

9.8.8 Hanging Lateral Stretch

Hang from a suitable bar (about head height). Place your feet sideways *as far as possible* and keep your arms straight and over your ears. Feel the stretch in your sides. Keep your deepest stretch for 1 minute before switching sides.

FLEXIOMETRIC EXERCISES

9.9 Upper Body Stretches

9.9.1 Pectoral Doorframe Stretch

Use a doorframe or a corner wall to place your arm bent at 90 degrees for a stretch at shoulder height. Push forward with a *straight trunk* to feel the pectoral stretch. Make sure the spine is straight and the arm is at a 90 degree angle. Keep the deepest position for 1 full minute before switching sides.

9.9.2 Pectoral Table Stretch

Place both hands on a sturdy table, arms straight and body bent at 90 degrees. Legs are straight as well. Push the body down to stretch shoulders and pecs. Make sure *spine is erect and limbs are all stretched straight.* Keep the deepest position for 1 minute. Release and repeat after 30 seconds.

9.9.3 Upper Back Stretch

This drill is identical to the previous one, but the hands are placed *higher*. The higher the hands, the more is the **upper back** stretched. Make sure the *back and the legs are straight* and feel the pull in your back shoulders. Hold the deepest stretch for one minute.

9.9.4 Elbow Back Pull

Standing straight with both arms behind your back, catch one elbow with the other hand (from the inside). Relax your shoulders and pull your elbow *slowly and gradually* to the other side. Keep your *back straight and do not twist* in any way. Keep your deepest stretch for 30 seconds before switching sides.

9.9.5 Wall Shoulder Stretch

Use a wall or preferably a wall with an outside corner. Place your hand at shoulder level on the wall and then all the arm, including the shoulder. Make sure *hand arm and shoulder are in full contact* with the wall. Keep the trunk straight. Start twisting the body to look behind you to stretch the shoulder *gradually*. Keep the deepest position for 30 seconds before switching sides.

9.9.6 Eagle Pose Grips

This is the shoulders and arms stretch that is part of yoga's Eagle Pose (**Garudasana**) {Yoga's *Eagle Pose* also includes a difficult lower body set up}. Standing or sitting down with a straight back, you simply aim at placing your palms together, but ... after crossing your elbows. You do this first with the right elbow crossing over the left one, and then repeat with the left elbow crossing over the right one. It is a pretty difficult stretch, and you should aim at keeping your *forearms perpendicular* to the floor, your *upper arms parallel* to the floor and your back straight. Keep your deepest stretch for 30 seconds before switching sides.

9.9.7 Back Namaste

A great and simple drill: place your hands palms together, as if in prayer, but ... behind your back. This upper body stretch is part of several Yoga poses that also challenge the lower body. In our case, you can either stand or sit, but with a *straight back*. Push your palms against one another and try to *gradually* raise your hands higher in your back. Keep the deepest stretch for 1 minute.

9.9.8 Cow's Face Grips

This is also part of a more complex Yoga Pose called *Cow's Face* (**Gomukhasana**), but we shall only drill its upper body stretch. Sitting or standing with a *straight back* you join your hands together behind your back, with one arm up and the other down. Let your fingers grip one another, and then pull gently and progressively up. Beginners will try first to push the elevated elbow down as illustrated. They can then proceed by doing the stretch with the help of a belt or a towel; gradually the grips should come closer to one another. Keep the deepest stretch for 30 seconds before switching sides.

FLEXIOMETRIC EXERCISES

9.9.9 Downward Dog Poses

This is again this king of Yoga's postures, already encountered. This time you take this versatile pose *with your hands a little closer to your feet* and you concentrate on the **shoulder stretch**. Of course, make sure your legs and back are straight. Keep the best possible pose for 1 minute.

9.9.10 Side Praying Grips

This is an easy but very beneficial stretch that can be done anywhere and at any time. Interlock your fingers behind your back, palms together. Use your right hand to pull the left one to your right hip (from behind of course). *Try to gradually pull the hands to the front as much as possible* and feel the stretch in your left shoulder and arm. Keep your deepest stretch for 1 minute before switching sides.

9.9.11 Sitting Knees-to-Elbows Vise

A difficult but important Shoulder Stretch. Sitting on the floor with open bent legs, you place the back of your hands on your hips and pull your elbows in. Lock the position with your knees on the outside of the elbows, relax your shoulders and *start pressing the elbows in with the knees*. Do this drill slowly and progress gradually. Keep your deepest stretch for 30 seconds. Relax 30 seconds and then repeat.

9.9.12 Neck stretches Posterior, Anterior and Lateral

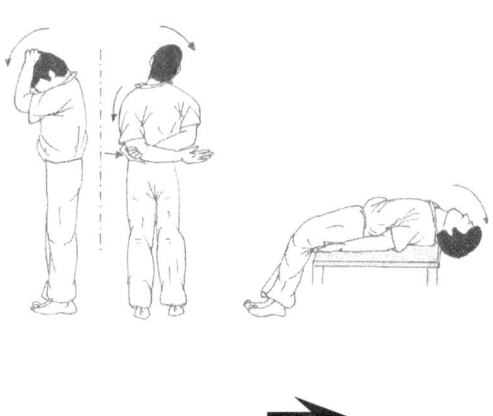

Neck stretches are very important but often neglected exercises. They should be executed often, but **always very carefully, slowly and gradually**. *All three types of neck stretch are best drilled together, one after the other*; that is why they are presented here in the same section. Here come the Posterior, Lateral and Anterior Neck Stretches: …

(9.9.12 - Continued)

... The best **Posterior Neck Stretch** is simply pulling the head forward with the hands and aiming with the chin towards the chest; make sure the back is straight and the shoulders relaxed.

The best **Lateral Neck Stretch** is leaning sideways with the head while pulling on the opposite elbow behind your back; make sure the back is straight and the elbow pulls down a relaxed shoulder. Switch sides after 1 minute.

The best **Anterior Neck Stretch** is letting the head hang down when lying on your back on a bench, table or bed; you are in contact with the bench up to your shoulder line. Relax the shoulders and let the neck stretch naturally. Be very gentle and keep your deepest stretch for 1 minute.

9.9.13 *Chair Dip Shoulder Stretches*

Use a chair or a bench just like for *Triceps Dips*. Hands on the chair behind you and leg stretched in front of you, let your bottom go down by bending the arms. Feel the gradual Shoulder Stretch and keep the deepest position for 30 seconds.

9.9.14 *Twisting One-arm Shoulder Stretch*

Place the back of your hand on your lower back and stand near a wall. *Twist the head and trunk towards the arm bent in your back* and use the wall to deepen the stretch. You can also do the drill sitting on a high back chair. Keep the deepest pose for 30 seconds before switching sides.

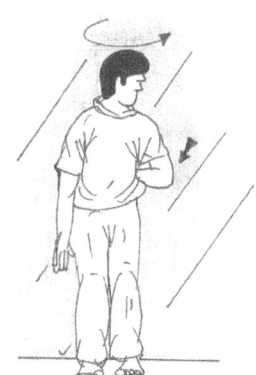

9.9.15 *All-fours Wrist Stretches*

Wrist Stretches should not be forgotten and *they are best drilled altogether, in series* as described. The wrist is an important joint in the exercise chain, but it is often neglected for the bigger joints. **(1)** In regular 'Cat Pose' (All-fours position), *push forward for the simplest wrist stretch*; feel the wrist and forearm and keep the deepest position for 1 minute. **(2)** Keep the 'Cat Pose', but lean on your hands *with the fingers pointing to your knees*; push on your palms and lean rearwards to feel the stretch for 1 additional minute. **(3)** Then lean *on the back of your hands in the same Pose* and lean rearwards slowly and carefully; keep the stretch for 1 more minute.

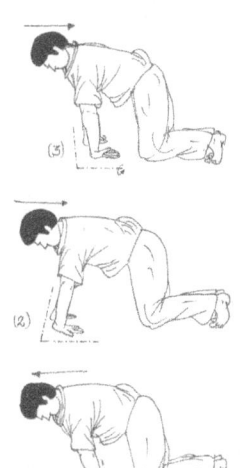

FLEXIOMETRIC EXERCISES

9.10 Partner Stretches

9.10.1 Dynamic Crescent Kicks

This is a <u>Dynamic</u> Stretching Drill, where the muscles are stretched in movement, as explained earlier. It must be executed *slowly and low at first*; then the speed and height can be increased *gradually*. The move is a classic Martial Arts Kick (*Mikazuki Geri* in Japanese Karate) and it can be drilled with that kind of focus in mind. Your partner helps by holding his hand straight to the front, at the adequate height: this will be a hurdle for you to clear. Pass over his hand with the *leg straight* and the foot going along a crescent trajectory, from outside-inwards (illustrated) and then from the inside-outwards (*Gyacku Mikazuki Geri*). Execute 10 inside and 10 outside kicks slowly and at regular height, and then switch legs. Then do 20 of each type and for each leg, while increasing speed and height to your maximum.

9.10.2 Sitting Bends

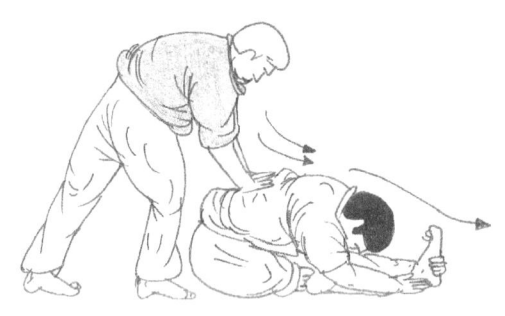

This is the simple *Sitting Forward Bend* (Section 9.3.1) in which a partner helps by *pushing your lower back down and forward*. You can do it with both legs extended forward, or alternating with each time one leg bent and the sole of the foot on the stretched thigh. The help must be light and *very gradually increasing* to take you a bit further than your maximum. Relax and keep the pose for 1 minute.

9.10.3 Pulling sitting bends

In this sitting bends version, your partner helps *by pulling you down and forward*. Sitting with straight legs together, the soles of your feet are in contact with your partner's. Your partner uses a strap, a belt or towel you are holding *to pull you forward gently and gradually.* Keep your legs straight, relax and keep the stretch for 1 minute. In this kind of partner exercise, it is then usually time to switch roles and your partner becomes the trainee.

9.10.4 Pulling Sitting open-legs Bends

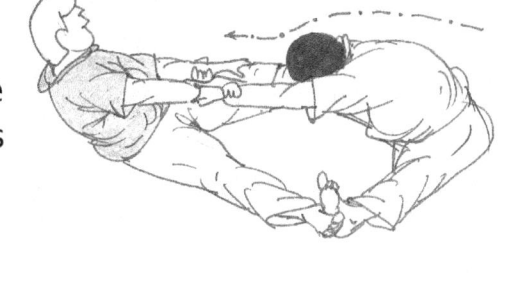

This is the wide open legs version of the previous exercise: both partners have their legs open as wide as possible and their feet touching (or feet to ankles according to respective heights and flexibilities). There is usually no need for a belt, as the partners are close enough to grasp each other's wrists. The helper pulls *gently* while opening the trainee's legs as much as possible. The trainee relaxes and keeps the forward bend for 1 minute.

9.10.5 Assisted Lying Leg Pulls

This is the classic one leg Pull in which a partner helps the stretch by leaning on your straightened leg. He also presses just above your other knee to keep that leg straight and on the floor. This must be done *very carefully, very slowly and with 'feeling'*. Relax during the stretch, but do not hesitate to signal your partner when he is going too far. After 1 minute, switch legs.

9.10.6 Lying Assisted Quad Stretch

You lie on your belly, preferably on a mat. Your partner bends your leg to stretch your quads by pushing your heel slowly towards your buttock. He keeps the hips and thigh in place with his other arm. This, again, has to be done *gradually and very carefully*. Switch legs after 1 minute.

Never, never, never give up.
~Winston Churchill

9.10.7 Assisted Standing Splits

This is a typical Martial Arts stretching exercise. Place your foot on your partner's shoulder and hold him for balance. If you are not flexible enough, your partner can crouch. Keep *both legs straight* and let your partner go slowly rearwards to place you in standing Front Splits. *Gradually is the word*. Keep the deepest stretch for 1 minute and have your partner come back

forward to ease the stretch. You then twist your hips to place your head on your standing knee. Your partner can then deepen the stretch by going back again. Keep the stretch for another 1 minute and come out of it <u>slowly</u>. Repeat the compounded stretch on the other side.

9.10.8 Standing Hip Stretch

Stand in front of a wall for support and lift your bent leg behind you. Your partner will lift your knee up while keeping your hip in place with the other hand. He will push and lift gently and gradually. Keep the upper body in the same position as the stretch progresses; keep the deepest position for 1 minute before switching sides.

9.10.9 Assisted Cobblers

Your partner simply helps you maximize your stretch in the *Cobbler's Pose* already encountered above. He will press your knees down as you make sure to keep *the soles of your feet together and your back straight*. Once you have been helped slowly into your deepest stretch, keep it for 1 minute. If you are proficient, you should repeat the assisted stretch with your back on the floor for an additional 1 minute. Get out of the stretch *slowly*.

9.10.10 Sitting Wide Middle Stretches

There are 2 ways in which a partner can help you deepen your open-legged sitting stretch. (1) He can simply *push your lower back forward and down* while you bend to help you gradually reach forward. (2) The second version, to be executed in turn, has the advantage to also help widen the legs opening during the forward stretch: the partners *sit with their feet touching and holding wrists* and the helper lies down slowly on his back while pulling the trainee forward and while pushing his legs simultaneously wider. Both exercises should be executed *very slowly and carefully*. It is best to do both one after the other, 1 minute each.

9.10.11 Assisted Side Splits

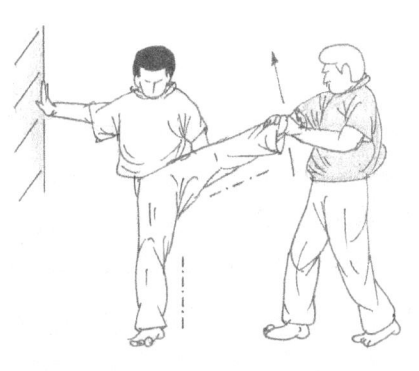

Start by standing near a wall for support and having your partner lift your (straight) leg laterally. Keep your *back and your standing leg straight*. Once you become more flexible, your partner can place your foot on his shoulder and you can hold your own leg instead of the wall. Your partner can gradually stand higher to stretch you more; you should

keep both standing leg and back straight. Once this variation becomes easier, your partner can gradually go back further from you to place you in standing Side Splits. *Be very careful and proceed very slowly.* Hold the stretch for 1 minute before switching legs.

9.10.12 Side Chamber Assisted Stretch

The name of this stretch actually comes from Martial Arts training, but it is a very important stretch overall suitable for all athletes. Use a wall for support and have your partner lift your foot laterally and push you knee towards your face. *Your standing leg must stay straight*. Have him deepen the stretch very gradually and carefully. Keep the stretch for 1 minute before switching legs.

9.10.13 Assisted Cobra Stretches

Your partner will simply help you to deepen your *Cobra Stretch* by carefully pulling you up. Start with the regular Cobra and the partner will *gently* pull your upper arms while you keep your legs *straight on the floor*. When you become flexible, you can start working the **Inverted Cobra Pose** <u>*very carefully*</u> by having your partner lifting slowly your straight legs as you keep your upper body on the floor. Be extremely careful with these potentially *dangerous* poses. Keep the stretch for 1 minute and have your partner take you out of the stretch *very slowly*.

9.10.14 Upper Back Assisted Stretch

You sit on your heels in front of a wall and place both forearms <u>as high as possible</u> *fully* on the wall. Your partner behind you will *gently* push your upper back towards the wall. Feel the back stretch and keep the rest of the body immobile. Keep for 1 minute.

9.10.15 Assisted Shoulder Stretch

Sit on the floor with your hands on the floor behind you, fingers pointing away. Your partner will take your wrists and very carefully move them both *towards him and one towards the other*. Your partner will have to be very careful and proceed slowly. The wrists are not expected to touch in the middle (unless you are extraordinarily flexible). Keep the stretch for 1 minute and have your partner take you out of it gradually.

9.10.16 Assisted Back Namaste

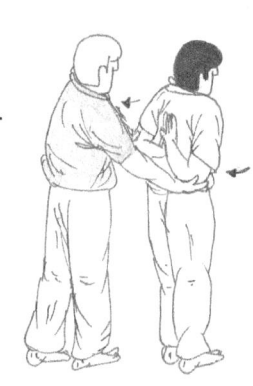

Execute the classic Back Namaste while standing or sitting. Place your hands in prayer behind your back, fingers pointing up, as high as you can. Your partner will then gently pull your elbows back towards him, while keeping a light pressure to stick the hands together. Proceed very carefully and keep the stretch for 1 minute.

CHAPTER TEN - ISOMETRIC DRILLS

And we get now to the part where we build strength and aesthetic muscles. Isometrics means that the angle of the joint and the length of the muscle do not change during the exercise. The reader is invited to refer to the Chapter about Isometrics Theory. We shall present here completely Static Poses, Yoga-style, to be kept for a minute or more, and traditional Isometric drills where maximum effort is to be held for 10 seconds. We shall present exercises needing no props at all, and some using everyday objects. We shall present a simple Isoplex Prop that can help train anywhere. And we shall present some drills that are bordeline orthodox Isometrics, but that work…

The results of proper Isometrics training are simply fantastic. The reader is just invited to remember one important point: in Isometrics, the key to success are _**focus and concentration**_.

10.1 Static Poses for Upper Body and Core

10.1.1 Upward Bow Pose

(Urdhva Dhanurasana)
This is not an easy pose and should not be attempted by beginners. It works both on most of the body muscles and on spine flexibility. Lie on your back, place your palms flat on the floor near your ears, bend your knees and place your feet as close as possible to your bottom. From this position push on hands and feet *to lift your bottom as high as possible*. Hold your highest pose; start with 30 seconds and work your way up to 2 minutes. Get out of the pose slowly. If you have difficulty with the pose, drill the *Upward Table Pose* first or have a partner help you to get into the pose by lifting your hips.

10.1.2 Plank Pose

(Kumbhakasana)
This is a classic and unavoidable pose. Excellent for the abs, the core muscles, the shoulders and more. Just make sure that your hands are *straight below your shoulders* and that *your back is straight*. Start by holding the pose for 30 seconds and work your way up to 3 minutes.

10.1.3 Upward Table Pose

(Sahaja Purvottanasana)
This is a preparatory pose to the coming *Upward Plank Pose*, but a great isometric drill by itself for the back muscles, the shoulders and the thighs. From sitting on the floor, *lift your buttocks by standing on feet and hands, face up*. Make sure your back is straight, your hands are straight below your shoulders and your legs are perpendicular to the floor (90 degrees). Keep the perfect pose for up to 2 minutes, starting at 30 seconds.

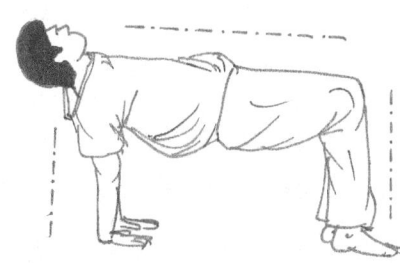

ISOMETRIC DRILLS

10.1.4 Upward Plank Pose

(Purvottanasana)
From the previous pose, simply extend your legs and try to lower the toes to the floor. Make sure the *legs and trunk are straight*, and that the *arms are straight below the shoulders.* You can let your head hang down and look behind yourself. Hold the perfect pose for up to 2 minutes

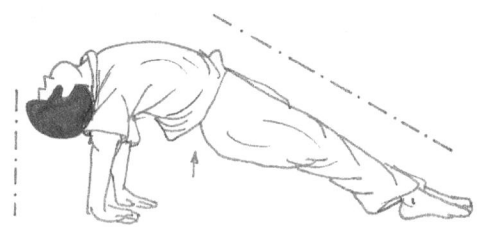

10.1.5 Half Boat Pose

(Ardha Navasana)
This classic abs exercise is also a toner of most other muscles: back, shoulders, legs and more. From sitting on the floor, lift your knees with the *lower legs parallel to the floor*. Lean back about 45 degrees with a *straight back* and lift your straight arms parallel to the floor on both sides of the knees. Keep the pose for up to 2 minutes, starting at 30 seconds.

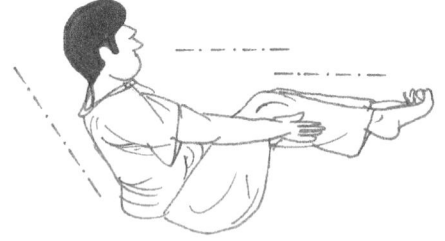

10.1.6 Easy Staff Pose

(Ardha Chaturanga Dandasana)
From a *Plank Pose*, bend your legs a little and lower your knees until they *nearly* touch the floor. Bend your arms until the upper arms are nearly parallel to the floor. Arch your back and keep the pose for at least 30 seconds. Work your way up to 2 minutes. If you cannot hold 30 seconds, you can start drilling with the knees on floor until you can hold this way for 2 minutes; you'll then go back to the original drill.

10.1.7 Side Plank on Elbow

This is not truly *Yoga* but a variation of the (following) Yoga *Side Plank Pose*. It is a great overall exercise that works especially the abs and sides, but also the shoulders and many more. From lying on your side, straight legs together you lift up on your feet and elbow. Use your side muscles to keep a perfectly straight body. Make sure your shoulder is just above your elbow. Keep the pose for up to 2 minutes, with a minimum of 30 seconds; then switch sides.

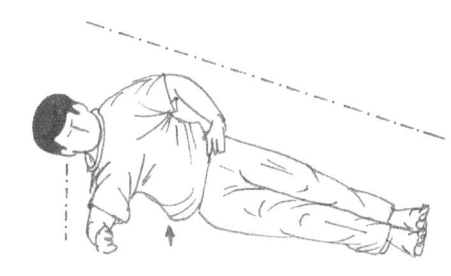

10.1.8 Side Plank Pose

(Vasisthasana)
And here it comes. The corresponding Yoga Pose is identical to the previous one, but you stand on your straightened arm-hand instead of your elbow. Lift your other arm straight in line with the lower one and look up at your hand. Keep the pose for up to 2 minutes before switching sides.

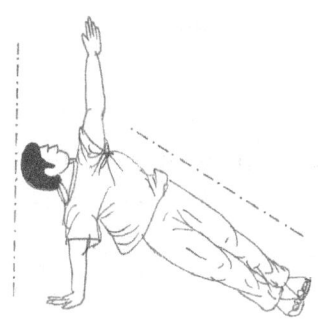

10.1.9 Side Plank Pose with Leg Up

This is the more difficult version of the *Side Plank Pose*: once in the classic Side Plank, you simply lift the *straightened* upper leg and keep the pose. Try to keep the lifted leg parallel to the floor and all other constraints of the regular Side Plank. Start by holding for 30 seconds and work your way up to 2 minutes before switching sides. Do not drill this pose before you can hold the *classic Side Plank* for 2 minutes.

10.1.10 Low Boat Pose

(Navasana)
This is the more difficult version of the previously described *Half Boat Pose*. In this case, you *straighten the legs* and you place your hands with fingers interlocked behind your neck. Make sure your *back is also straight* and keep the pose up to 2 minutes.

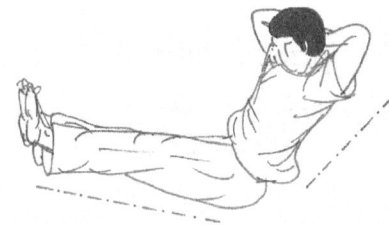

10.1.11 Staff Pose with Leg Up

(Trianga Dandasana)
This is the 'hard' version of the *Four-limbed Staff Pose*, described just after this Pose, and also called *Low Plank Pose*. From classic High Plank Pose with a perfectly *straight back*, bend your arms at 90 degrees. Then lift one *straight leg* to bring it parallel to the floor. Keep the pose for up to 2 minutes before switching legs. If you cannot hold the pose for 30 seconds, you should drill the regular version presented below until you can easily hold for 2 minutes.

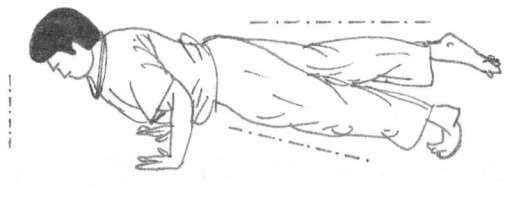

10.1.12 Four-limbed Staff Pose

(Chaturanga Dandasana)

If the previous pose is too hard for you, drill the *Low Plank* without lifting the leg until you become stronger. Work your way up from 30 seconds. Once you can hold easily for 2 minutes, start to lift one leg and do the (previous) more difficult pose.

10.1.13 High Boat Pose

(Paripurna Navasana)

This is the even harder version of the *Boat Pose* for a tough drill of the abs and other core muscles. The idea is to make a *perfect 90 degrees angle* between the straight legs and the body, preferably both at a 45 degrees from the floor. To top those geometric requirements, the arms should be extended straight and parallel to the floor. Keep the perfect pose for 2 minutes, starting at 30 seconds for beginners.

10.1.14 Bridge Pose with Leg Up

(Ekopada Dhanurasana+)

This is a very challenging Pose, putting in play most body muscles, but especially the glutes and the lower back. From the *Upward Bow Pose* (or 'Bridge Pose') described at the beginning of the Chapter, you 'simply' lift one leg straight and perpendicular to the ground. Push your *hips up as much as possible* and extend your arms. Keep the pose for up to 1 minute, starting at 20 seconds. Go down, rest for 30 seconds and start over from the ground to switch legs.

10.1.15 Upward Plank with Leg Up

(Purvottanasana+)

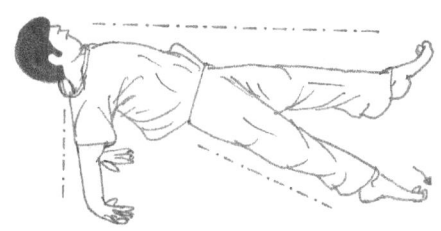

This variation of the Upward Plank is excellent for overall muscling, but especially the core. It is not to be drilled before you can hold a regular Upward Plank for over a minute. From the regular Upward Plank Pose, you lift one straight leg until it is parallel to the ground. Keep the back, the other leg and the arms perfectly straight and keep the pose for up to 2 minutes, starting at 30 seconds. Switch legs.

10.1.16 Staff Pose on Elbows

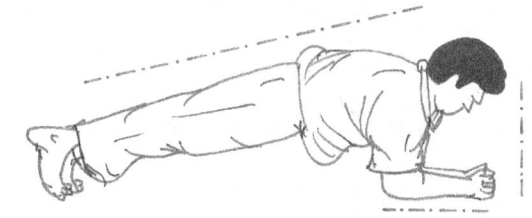

This version of the *Plank (or Staff) Pose* is easier on the abs but harder on the shoulders. It is good to drill both version. You stand, *straight as a staff*, on your toes and elbows. Arms are straight and perpendicular to the floor; the fingers can be interlaced or free. Make sure your *back is totally straight*. Keep the Pose for up to 2 minutes.

10.1.17 Prone Trunk Lift

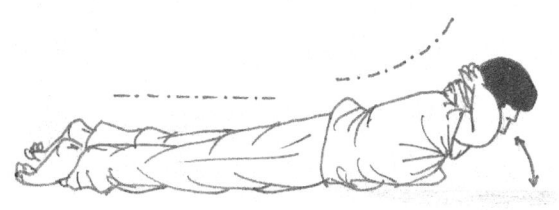

Lying on your belly, legs together and hands on your head, you lift your trunk as high as possible. *Make sure your head stays in line with your body to avoid hurting your neck.* This drill requires a more **active** isometric approach: use your hands to create more back tension by 'resisting' the lift slightly. Keep the maximum tension for 30 seconds only. Rest for 20 seconds and repeat 3 times.

10.1.18 Prone Skewed Trunk Lift

Repeat the previous exercise, *but twist when up*. Keep the twisted position at full tension ('**resist**') for 30 seconds only. Rest for 20 seconds and repeat on the other side.

ISOMETRIC DRILLS

10.2 Static Poses for Lower Body and Core

10.2.1 Chair Pose

(Utkatasana)
This classic *Yoga* pose is a great overall muscle builder, but with emphasis on the legs. Crouch with a *straight back*, arms straightened above your head. Your lower leg should be about perpendicular to the ground and your thighs should be between parallel to 45 degrees. Lean slightly on your heels and *make sure that your knees do not go further forward than your toes*. Your arms are close to your ears, and you should strive for your straight back to be as close as possible to perpendicular to the ground (which will be very difficult). Once you become proficient, you should strive to have your thighs as close as possible to parallelism to the floor. Keep your best pose for 2 minutes, starting at 30 seconds.

10.2.2 Warrior Pose

(Virabhadrasana 1)
Another iconic *Yoga* posture, that is extremely beneficial in spite of looking simple. Stand in deep lunge, front leg bent at 90 degrees and rear leg straight with the foot pointing outwards at 45 degrees. *The trunk is totally aligned with the hips, laterally*. The arms are straight and *parallel* to the floor, one pointing forward, the other rearwards. The *back is straight* and the whole body is fully aligned, with the exception of the front leg at 90/90. Keep the pose for 1 to 2 minutes before switching sides.

10.2.3 Warrior Pose 3

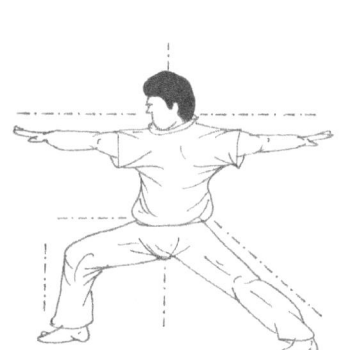

(Virabhadrasana 3)
Standing on one *straight* (but not locked) leg, you bend forward with a *straight back* while lifting the other leg behind you. In the final pose, the back and rear leg are aligned and *parallel* to the floor and the arms are extended in front of you in alignment. Keep the classic Pose, with legs, arms and back straight for 2 minutes before switching sides (beginners start at 30 seconds).

10.2.4 Buddhist Stupa Pose

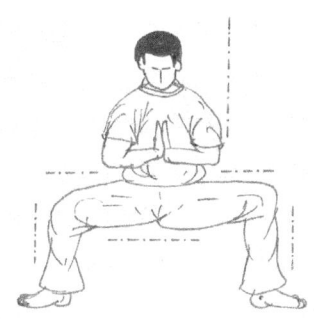

Open your legs at least twice your hips' width and turn your feet *outwards as much as you can*. Bend then the legs to have the thighs parallel to the floor and the lower legs perpendicular. *Keep the back straight*. The hands are traditionally held in *Namaste* position at the solar plexus, but it is optional. Keep this deep pose for 2 minutes without moving; beginners can start at 30 seconds.

10.2.5 Locust Pose with One Leg Up

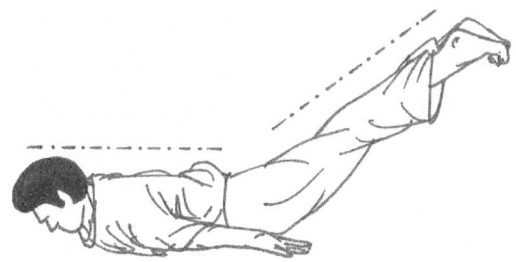

(Ekopada Salambhasana)
Lie on the floor on your belly with your arms along your body, palms on the floor. Lift **one** straightened leg *as high as possible*. Your body and your other leg stay on the floor, both straight. Keep the pose for up to 2 minutes, starting at 30 seconds. Switch legs after 30 seconds rest.

10.2.6 Locust Pose

(Salambhasana)
This is the challenging pose that is prepared by the drilling of the previous exercise. From the same starting position, you will now lift **both** straight legs together *as high as possible*. This is a fantastic exercise for the legs, the gluteal muscles and the lower back. Keep the pose for up to 2 minutes.

10.2.7 Low Lunge

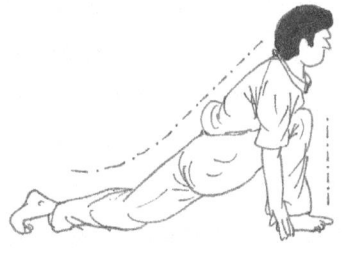

(Ashva Sanchalanasana)
In a lunge position, pull your rear leg back as much as possible (on your toes) and flex your front leg *while keeping the lower leg at 90 degrees*. From your deepest lunge, place your fingers on the floor, without leaning on them. Lift the trunk as high and *as straight as possible*. Keep the position up to 2 minutes before switching legs.

ISOMETRIC DRILLS

10.2.8 Rotated Warrior Pose (or Half Moon Pose)

(Virabhadrasana)

The *Half Moon Pose* is a great isometric core muscle builder. Lift your leg sideways while bending on the opposite side. Place your hand on the floor, straight below your shoulder. Both your standing leg and your lifted leg are straight. Lift your other arm up in line with the one you are leaning on. Look down or up at one of your hands, according to your balance proficiency. Keep the Pose for up to 2 minutes before switching sides.

10.2.9 Forward Stretch Pose (Bend) with Leg Up

(Urdhva Ekopadasana)

Bend forward to place your forehead on (or near) one knee. Lift the other leg behind you as high as possible. Both legs are straight. You can keep your hands on the floor; or, if you have good balance, you can catch the standing ankle with one or two hands (as illustrated). The purpose is to *lift the leg as high as possible* and keep the Pose for up to 2 minutes. Switch legs after 30 seconds rest.

**A goal is a dream with a deadline.
~Napoleon Hill**

10.3 Upper Body No-props Full Isometrics

10.3.1 No props at all

10.3.1.1 Abs-in

Stand with your hands on your head. *Suck in your abdominals as much as you can* and keep the tension while breathing out slowly for 10 seconds. Relax the tension slightly, while keeping your abs sucked in, and breathe in for 5 seconds. Tense to your maximum and start breathing out again in 10 seconds. Repeat 10 times, without releasing the suck-in of your abdominals. Concentrate on the tension and *think of sticking your belly in all the way to your spine*.

10.3.1.2 Bent-over Abs-in

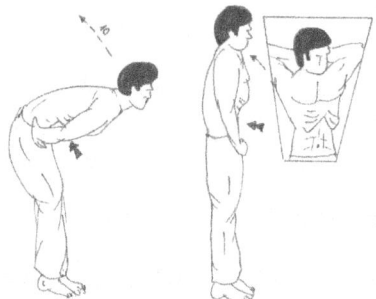

Bend over at the waist *with a straight back* until parallel to the ground. Exhale to your maximum and then *suck in your abs as far in as possible*. Keeping your abs in at maximum tension, slowly stand back up to the count of 10 seconds. Do not inhale. After 10 seconds, inhale and relax your muscles for a few seconds. Repeat 10 times. Concentrate on maximum isometric tension; it is as much a thing of the mind as a thing of the body.

10.3.1.3 Neck Back

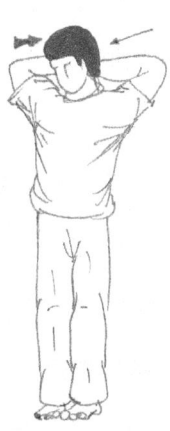

Standing with your hands behind your head, **push** your head back *against the resistance of your hands*. Exhale slowly and use maximum tension according to all the rules of the classic Isometrics. Your head does not move but pushes back at its maximum. After 10 seconds, relax.

ISOMETRIC DRILLS

10.3.1.4 Neck Front

Standing with both hands on your forehead, **push** your head forward *against the resistance of your hands*. Exhale slowly, concentrate and maximize isometric tension. Your head does not move but pushes forward with maximum effort. Relax after 10 seconds.

10.3.1.5 Neck Side

Standing with one palm on the side of your straight head, **push** your head sideways *against the resistance of your arm*. The head does not move but you exert maximum tension. Exhale slowly for 10 seconds while resisting. Relax.

10.3.1.6 Upper Back Squeeze

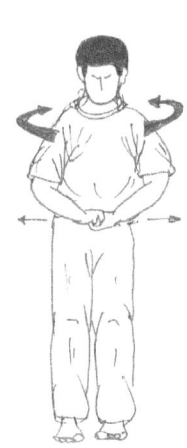

Standing with a straight back, you interlock your fingers in front of you at about navel height. Pull your shoulders back and start to *squeeze your shoulder blades close together*. Keep your maximum position and start to tense your back muscles to keep it that way *while you are pulling on your hands.* Keep the elbows inside and keep maximum tension while exhaling for 10 seconds.

10.3.1.7 Standing Back Pull with Leg

Stand with one leg in front. Interlock your fingers behind your thigh, just above the back of the knee. *Use your back muscles to pull your leg up*. Of course, your leg **pulls down** to keep the body motionless as you exert maximum tension. Exhale for 10 seconds while maximizing isometric tension. Relax for a few seconds and switch legs.

10.3.1.8 Lower Back 'Superman' Pose

You lie on the floor on your belly and extend your arms to the front. Keeping your straightened legs and your feet in contact with the floor, you *lift your trunk as high as possible*. The arms stay straight in front of you. Once in your highest position, contract your lower back muscles as much as possible, concentrate on the drill and exhale for 10 seconds. Relax for a few seconds and repeat once.

10.3.1.9 One-hand Shoulder Press

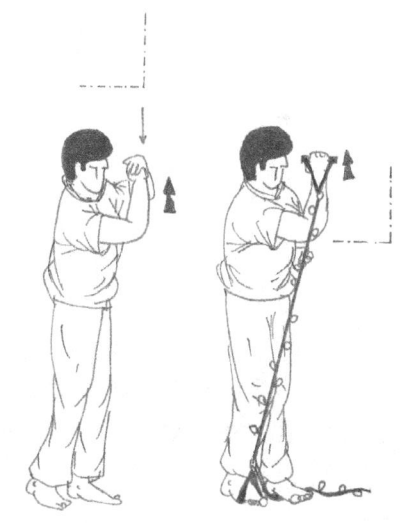

Place one arm bent at shoulder level in front of you. The upper arm is parallel to the floor and the lower arm is at 90 degrees. Make a fist that you will cover with your other hand. **Push up** with your fist *while resisting with your other hand*. Exert maximum tension without any movement and start exhaling for 10 seconds. Push up as hard as possible. Relax for a few seconds and switch arms. *{The illustration shows the use of the 'Isoplex Prop' to execute the same drill: you use your foot and body weight to resist the upward push in the same arm position}*

10.3.1.10 One-hand Shoulder Front Raise

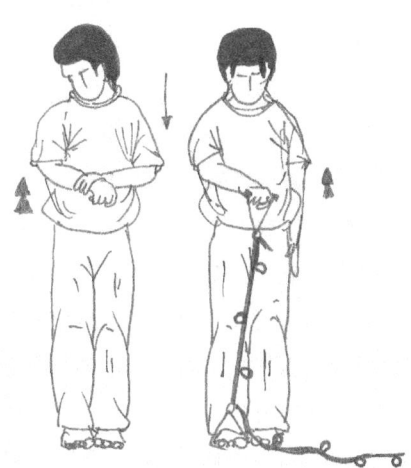

Place one arm in front of you, forearm parallel to the floor. Clasp your wrist from above with the other hand; both arms are in front of you in the middle of your body, more or less at solar plexus height. Try to **lift your arm** while *pushing back down with the other hand*. Concentrate and use your shoulder muscles to lift. At maximum tension, start exhaling for 10 seconds. Relax and switch arms. *{The Illustration shows the use of the 'Isoplex Prop' to execute the same drill: you use your foot and body weight to resist the upward pull in the same arm position}*

10.3.1.11 One-hand Shoulder Side Raise

This is a similar drill to the previous one, but executed on the side for more side-deltoid work. Place one arm on the side with the forearm parallel to the floor. Place your other hand on top, to *resist* the coming **upward push**. The hands do not move but exert maximum isometric tension. At maximum tension, start exhaling for 10 second with no weakening. Relax and repeat on the other side. *{The Illustration shows the use of the 'Isoplex Pro' to execute the same drill: you use your foot and body weight to resist the upward pull in the same arm position}*

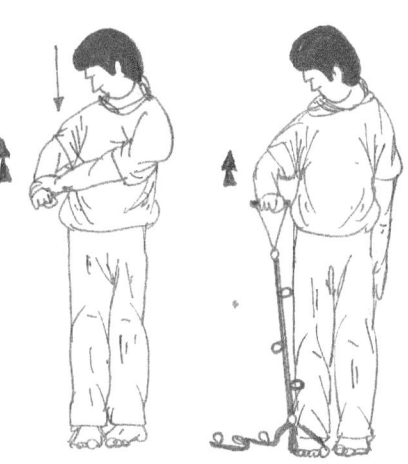

10.3.1.12 One-hand Shoulder Rear Pull

In order to work the rear delts, you execute the inverse of Drill 10.3.1.10. Take the same position with your arms in front of you, catching the wrist of the trained arm from above. But this time, you will *pull the arm down* while resisting the pull with the other hand, **pulling upwards.** *Use your back shoulder to pull the arm down* and concentrate on the tension. Keep your maximum tension while exhaling for 10 seconds. Relax and switch sides.

10.3.1.13 Biceps Curl

With your forearm parallel to the floor, palm up and and fist clenched, place your other hand <u>on</u> the wrist to *resist* the biceps curl. The hands do not move as you give your maximum to **lift the wrist towards your shoulder.** Keep the maximum tension achieved for 10 seconds, while exhaling. Relax and switch sides. *{The Illustration shows the use of the 'Isoplex Pro' to execute the same drill: you use your foot and body weight to resist the upward curl in the same arm position}*

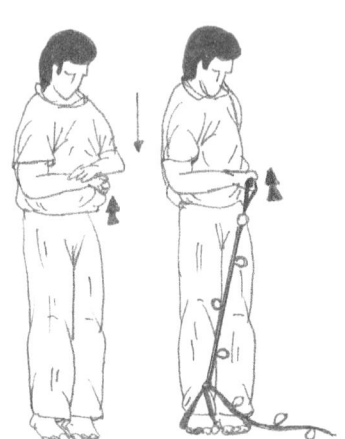

10.3.1.14 Triceps Press

With your forearm parallel to the floor, fist clenched and thumb up, place your other hand <u>under</u> the fist. **Push your fist down** to extend your arm, and *resist* the move to achieve isometric tension. Concentrate. Keep the maximum tension achieved for 10 seconds while exhaling. Relax. Switch arms.

10.3.1.15 Biceps-Triceps Drill

Place both fists in front of you at plexus height and close to the body. Place one fist above the other. **The lower fist pushes up in an attempted Biceps Curl.** *The higher fist pushes down in an attempted Triceps Press.* The arms do not move and you concentrate to achieve maximum tension. Keep the maximum tension for 10 seconds while exhaling. Relax for a few seconds and repeat in the inverse position: the previous lower fist goes up and vice versa.

10.3.1.16 Classic Pectoral Press

Place your hands together at pectoral height in front of you, close to your body. Use your pecs **to push your hands against one another**. Concentrate to achieve maximum tension, and keep it for 10 exhaling seconds.

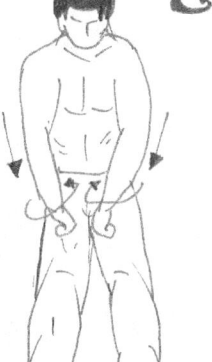

 10.3.1.17 Inside Pectoral Squeeze

In this pectoral exercise, you do not use one arm against the other, but you use your body's limits as the immovable resistance. This is a great drill for the inside pecs, though it requires concentration. Place your arms in front of you and twist both wrists towards the inside in order to have both backs of your fists facing one another at a few inches distance. Concentrate and **pull your arms down while twisting the wrist further as much as possible**. You will feel that the tension builds up in your pecs and a little in your shoulders. Achieve maximum tension and keep it for 10 seconds while exhaling.

ISOMETRIC DRILLS

10.3.1.18 Classic Dorsal Pull

This classic Back and Chest Drill is the opposite of the *Pectoral Press* (See *10.3.1.16*). Clasp your fingers together in a strong grip at pectoral height and **pull with both hands**. The arms do not move as you build maximum tension. Keep your maximum tension for 10 seconds while exhaling.

10.3.1.19 Floor Pectoral 'Plane' Press

Lie on the floor on your belly with your arms extended perpendicular to your body, palms down. Use your pectorals **to push against the immovable floor**. No part of your body moves as you concentrate on the isometric tension. Keep your maximum tension for 10 seconds while exhaling, *as if you expect to push the floor down*.

10.3.1.20 Forearm curls

Sit and place your forearm on your upper leg with the wrist sticking over your knee. The palm of your fisted hand faces the ceiling and you place your other hand on top. Use your forearm muscles to **try to curl the wrist up**, while *resisting down with the other hand*. There is no movement but you exert maximum tension for 10 seconds while exhaling. Relax and switch wrists. The Illustration shows how to do the drill with the help of the '*Isoplex Prop*'.

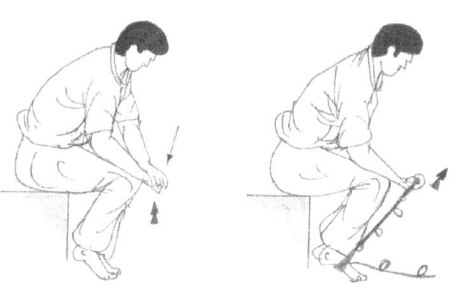

10.3.1.21 Forearm Reverse Curls

This is the same drill like the preceding one, but the drilling wrist faces *down*. Try to **lift your inverted wrist up** while *resisting with the other hand*. Switch wrists after 10 seconds of concentrated maximum tension. Again, the drill can be executed with the '*Isoplex Prop*', as illustrated.

THE ISOPLEX METHOD

10.3.2 Door Frame Drills

10.3.2.1 Oblique Press

Stand in a door frame or near a wall. Take the further arm over your head, to go and place your palm on the wall or onto the side of the door frame. To do so, your body will be bending slightly towards the wall or door frame. Use your side muscles (*Obliques*) to **push the body** more towards the wall/frame, and *resist with your hand*. Doing this properly requires concentration. Keep your maximum Oblique Muscles tension for 10 seconds while exhaling. Relax and switch sides.

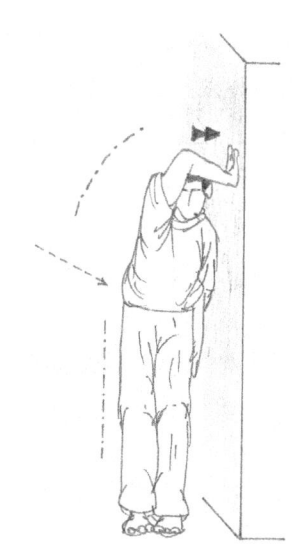

10.3.2.2 Shoulder Press

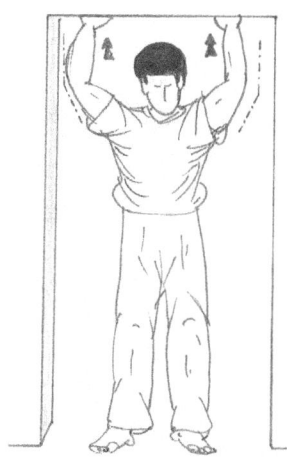

Stand in the door frame with straight legs, and place your hands above your head. Your arms must be partially bent. **Push the top of the frame up,** as if you want to lift it; *use your arms and shoulders only*. At maximum isometric tension, exhale on the count of 10 before relaxing. If you are too short to reach the upper frame as required, climb on a low stool. {***There is a version of the drill with the 'Isoplex Prop'***}

10.3.2.3 Twin Shoulder Raises

Stand in the door frame with arms extended down. Place the backs of your hands on the sides of the frame; the arms stay straight. Try to **lift your straight arms up** (to bring them at shoulder height) *against the immovable resistance*. Keep the maximum tension for 10 seconds while exhaling.

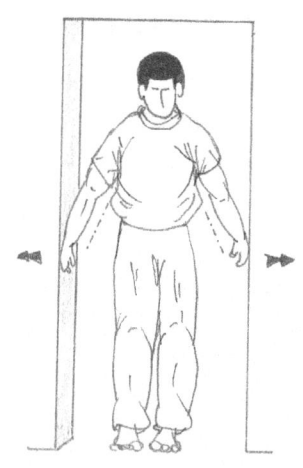

ISOMETRIC DRILLS

10.3.2.4 Leg and Shoulder Press

This is an overall drill for the whole body; it is excellent but requires concentration. You place your hands on the top of the frame and you will push up. But this time, you will not only use the arms, *but the legs as well*, as if you are using your whole body to lift something heavy. In order to do the Drill, you need to be able to stand in a position in which both your arms and your legs are slightly bent. If you are too small to do that in the specific door frame, you will need to place a step or a box below your feet. **Push up with arms and legs as much as possible**, and keep the maximum tension for 10 seconds while exhaling.

10.3.2.5 Front Neck Press

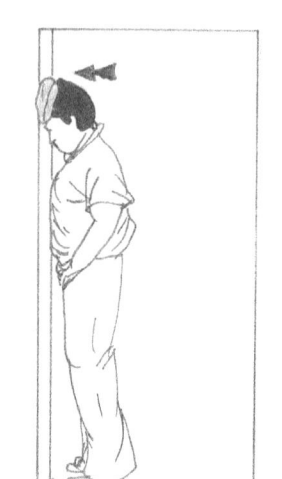

Neck muscles are very important and are linked to both shoulder muscles and spine-holding muscles; unfortunately, they are often overlooked. This drill develops the muscles of the back of the neck. Use a towel for protection and place your forehead on the side of the doorframe, but keep the rest of your body out of contact with it. Use your neck muscles to **push your forehead 'through' the frame.** Keep your maximum tension for 10 seconds while exhaling. Relax.

10.3.2.6 Back Neck Press

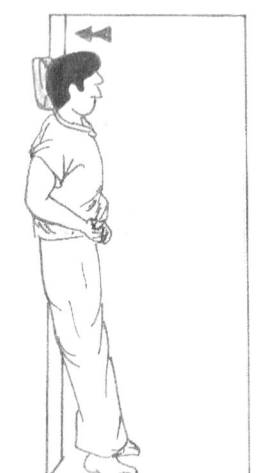

To drill the muscles of the frontal neck, place the back of your head, protected by a towel or a cushion on the door frame. Make sure you use only the muscles of the neck to **push back.** Once maximum tension is achieved, keep it for 10 seconds while exhaling. Relax.

10.3.2.7 One-arm Pectoral Drill

Place your elbow, at shoulder height, on the doorframe; you can use a towel to protect it if you want. Place your palms together and use the other arm **to push your elbow into the frame**. Make sure that you use your pectorals only, that your pushing arm is parallel to the ground, and that you do not use at all the muscles of the arm in contact with the frame (*It is the pecs of the other arm that are working*). Push as much as possible with the intent of moving the door frame. Keep maximum tension for 10 seconds while exhaling. Relax for a few seconds and switch sides.

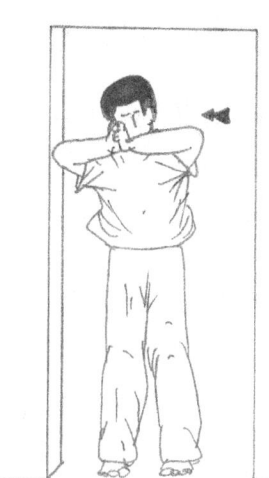

10.3.2.8 One-arm Side Press

This is a great overall drill for the pecs, the back and the shoulder muscles. It can only be done if the door frame is not too wide. Place a shoulder on the door frame and your other hand on the opposite side at shoulder height. This arm must be slightly bent. Use it **to push as strongly as possible,** *with the idea of widening the frame.* Make sure you only use the muscles of this side of the body and do not use the rest of your body to push away from the 'shoulder' side. Keep the maximum tension for 10 seconds while exhaling. Relax for a few seconds and switch sides.

10.3.2.9 Twin Arm Side Press

This is the same as the previous drill, but executed simultaneously on both sides. It saves time, but requires more concentration to benefit equally: it is more effective to focus on one side at a time. Place both palms on the door frames at shoulder height and **push to 'widen' the frame,** with both arms simultaneously. Keep maximal tension for 10 seconds while exhaling.

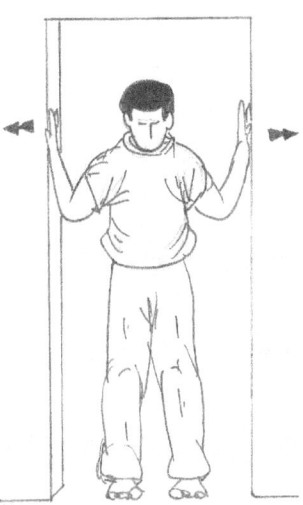

ISOMETRIC DRILLS

10.3.2.10 Door Pull-down

This drill for the back muscles can only be drilled on a *sturdy* door. Caution! Grip the top of an open door, while keeping your body slightly away. **Pull on your hands with your back muscles**; make sure you do not use your body weight and /or other muscles. *Imagine that you are trying to lower the door vertically into the ground.* Keep your maximum tension for 10 seconds while exhaling.

10.3.3 Chair Drills

10.3.3.1 Trapezius

Sit straight on a sturdy chair and grab the seat with both hands on the sides. Try to **lift your shoulders high** (towards your ears) **and back** (getting your shoulder blades together), but *resist any movement with your hands holding the chair*. Concentrate and make sure you only use your shoulder muscles (*Trapezius*). Keep the maximum tension for 10 seconds while exhaling. Relax

10.3.3.2 Back Squeeze

This Drill can also be done standing, but sitting helps the concentration on the back muscles. Sit with a straight back. Lift your arms bent at 90 degrees to shoulder height, parallel to the floor. Concentrate on **pulling you shoulder blades together by pulling your elbows back**; but of course you do not move. The move is similar to pulling a bar towards your chest, *but resisting*. Keep your maximal tension for 10 seconds while exhaling.

10.3.3.3 Back Pull against Leg

Sitting on a sturdy chair, lift one leg with both hands clasped below the thigh. Keep your back straight and use your back muscles **to pull your leg up**. Of course, *use your leg muscles to pull down* and keep everything immobile. Keep maximum tension for 10 seconds while exhaling. Relax for a few seconds and repeat with the other leg for symmetry.

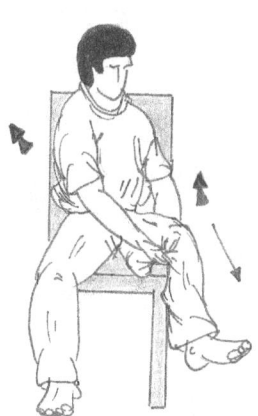

10.3.4 Wall Drills

Please remember that many 'Door Frame Drills' can be done on a wall as well!

10.3.4.1 High Wall Press

Stand about 5 inches from the wall, extend your arms up and place your palms on the wall as high as possible. **Press the wall** with the idea to push it back, *using your shoulders and back muscles*. Keep your maximum tension for 10 seconds while exhaling.

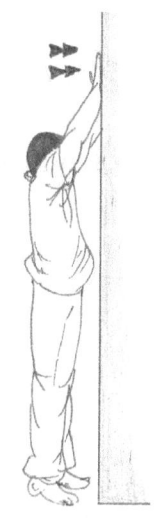

An oak is not felled at one blow.
~Spanish Proverb

ISOMETRIC DRILLS

10.3.5 Broomstick Drills

You can use a broomstick, a stick, an unweighted barbell,… Use your imagination.

10.3.5.1 Back Broom Pull

Take a half-squat position while holding a stick in the back of your knees. Keep your *back totally straight* and hold the stick with your palms upwards. **Pull the stick up against the back of your thighs,** while keeping the back straight. Nothing moves but you increase isometric tension to its maximum. Keep the maximal tension for 10 seconds while exhaling. Relax and move your hips around to release any lower back tension. *{This drill can easily be executed with the Isoplex Prop}*

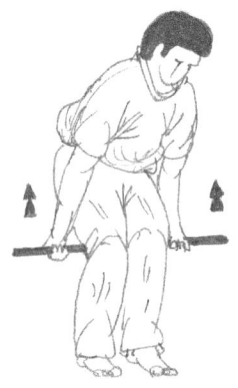

10.3.5.2 Upper Back Rowing Squeeze

Hold a stick with both hands at shoulder height. The arms are bent at 90 degrees. Pull the stick back **by getting your shoulder blades closer,** and resist to create tension. Keep the maximum tension for 10 seconds, and exhale.

Well done is better than well said.
~Benjamin Franklin

10.3.6 Doorway Bar (or Isometric Machine)

Doorway Hanging Bars (for suspension exercises) are available in any Sports Shop, or online. They are very easy to procure. They can be screwed out and they hold by tension. They can be placed at any height required. Of course, the ideal would be a full *Isometric Machine* as described earlier, with pre-drilled holes to place a bar at different heights.
Needless to mention that all these Drills can be executed with the proper set up of the '*Isometric Prop*'.

10.3.6.1 Shoulder Shrug

Place the bar in the doorframe at about groin level. Hold it with both hands and **use your shoulders to try to lift it,** by shrugging. *Aim at raising your shoulders towards your ears*. Hold the maximum tension for 10 seconds while exhaling.

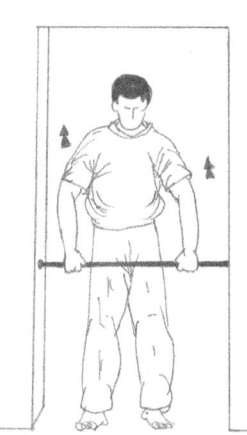

10.3.6.2 High Shoulder Pull-up

Place the bar in the doorframe at about pecs level. Hold the bar with your hands close to the middle and the elbows lifted upwards. **Pull the bar up by lifting your elbows** more and by using your shoulder muscles. Keep the maximum tension for 10 seconds and exhale.

10.3.6.3 Chin-level Shoulder Press

Place the bar in the door frame at chin level. **Push the bar up** in a classic military press exercise. Make sure you use only your *shoulder muscles*. At maximum tension, exhale for 10 seconds; then relax.

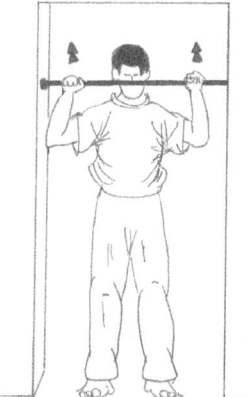

ISOMETRIC DRILLS

10.3.6.4 Sitting Military Press

Place the bar in the door frame at face level when sitting on a chair. Bar should be close to face, preferably to the forehead. **'Push' the bar up**, just like for a military press (lifting it above your head). Keep the maximum tension for 10 seconds while exhaling. *{The illustrations also show the same drill with the Isoplex Prop}*.

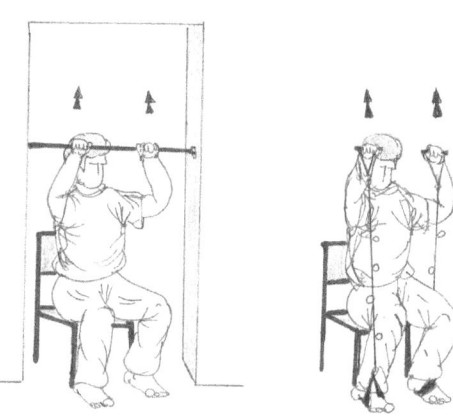

10.3.6.5 Dead-lift

Place the bar in the door frame at knee level. Bend the knees, keep the back straight, and grasp the bar with straight arms. Keep the arms straight and **use the lower back to 'pull' the immovable bar up,** in the way you would execute a deadlift. Do not move the knees or arms, keep the back straight and concentrate on using the lower back muscles only in the attempt to straighten up, deadlift-style. Keep the maximum tension for 10 seconds, then relax and move your hips and lower back to release the soreness. *{The Illustrations show how to use the Isoplex Prop for the same drill}*.

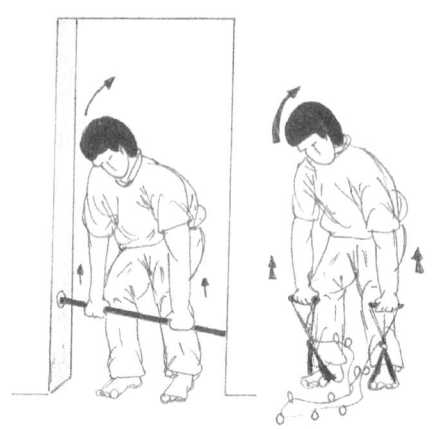

10.3.6.6 Biceps Curl

Place the bar in the door frame at about waist level. Grasp the bar with your palms up, just as if you were about to do a regular Biceps Curl. **Try to flex your arms and lift the bar up with your biceps muscles.** The back stays straight and the elbows stay in contact with your sides. Nothing moves but you achieve maximum tension by concentrating on the imaginary biceps curl. Keep the maximum tension for 10 seconds while exhaling. Relax. *{The Isoplex Prop can be easily used to execute this drill, as illustrated)*.

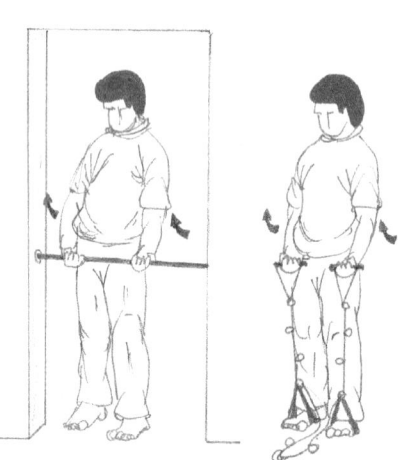

10.4 Lower Body No-props Isometrics

10.4.1 No props at all

10.4.1.1 Prone Leg Curls

You lie on the floor on your belly; it is best to be propped up on your elbows. Cross your ankles or feet and **try to bend your lower leg in a curling move**. Fully *resist the curl with your upper leg pushing down*. You lift and push down with as much power as possible, but nothing must move. At your maximum tension, you keep it up while exhaling during 10 seconds. Relax and switch legs.

10.4.2 Door Frame Drills

10.4.2.1 Legs & Shoulders Press

In this compounded exercise, you stand in the door frame while touching the top beam, but with both knees and arms slightly bent. If necessary use a step or a stool to achieve the position in the given frame. Tense all your body and imagine that you are trying to increase the size of the door frame, by pushing down with your legs (straightening the knees) and up with your shoulders (straightening the arms). Of course, nothing moves but you push as powerfully as possible both up and down. Keep the maximum tension for 10 seconds while exhaling.

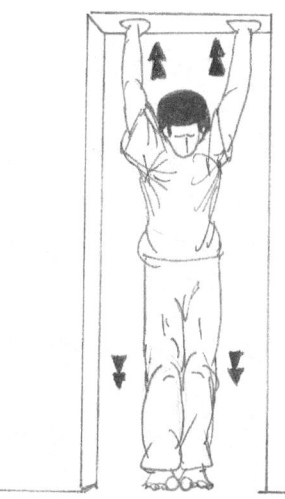

ISOMETRIC DRILLS

10.4.2.2 Toe Raise

This is an important drill, and it requires to concentrate on the calf muscles that we want to challenge; one easily drifts towards the use of the other muscles during the exercise. Standing in the doorframe with hands touching the upper beam, you **lift your heels as high as possible**. *You resist the move with your hands on the top* that will not allow any movement. Your heels should ideally be at half your maximum heel height during the drill. Concentrate on using your calves only and on keeping your arms and shoulders immobile. Keep the maximum tension for 10 seconds.

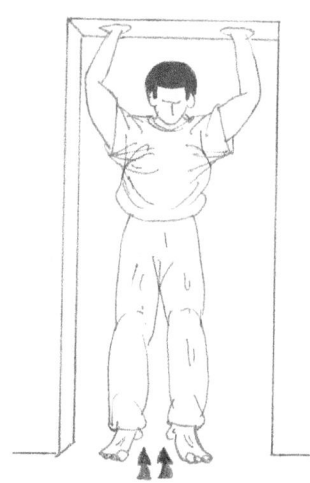

10.4.2.3 Outside Hip

Standing in the middle of the doorframe, lift one foot and press the lifted bent knee on the frame. **Try to push the side frame out** by opening your hip. Steady yourself to avoid any movement with your hands on both sides of the frame. *Concentrate on using your hip only*. Push as hard as possible, as if 'opening' your leg, and keep the maximum tension for 10 seconds while exhaling. Relax and repeat with the other leg. {*This drill can also be executed against a wall, with a steadying prop like a chair, as will be mentioned later*}

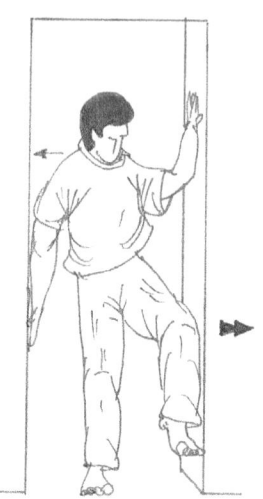

10.4.2.4 Back Kick

Standing in the middle of the doorframe, face on one side and place the sole of your foot back on the other frame, at knee level. Place your hands forward on the side frame to steady yourself and to resist your back push. **Push your foot back** as if to widen the frame, using your glutes and hamstrings. *Resist with your arms and body*, and make sure nothing moves. Push as hard as possible and keep the maximum tension for 10 seconds. Exhale. Relax and switch legs.

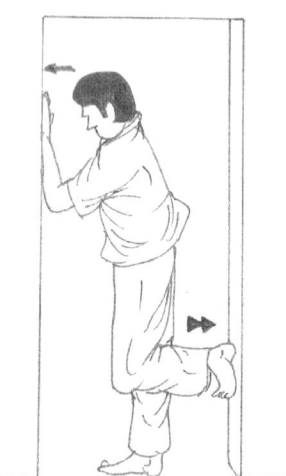

10.4.2.5 Front Push

Place your back on to one side frame and face the other. Place one foot on the other frame at mid-thigh level and **push**, as if to widen the doorframe. *Use your back to resist* and annul any movement. Push as hard as possible and keep the maximum tension for 10 seconds while exhaling. Relax and switch legs.

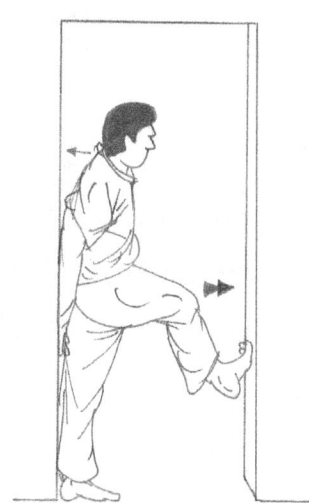

10.4.3 Chair Drills

10.4.3.1 Leg Extensions

Sitting straight on a sturdy chair, extend one leg and aim **to straighten it parallel to the floor**. But your *other leg crossed on top will resist the move and push down*. Grab the chair and achieve maximum tension. Keep it for 10 seconds while exhaling. Relax and switch legs.

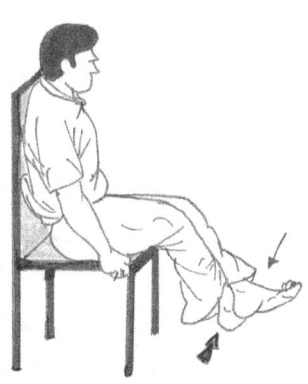

10.4.3.2 Inner Thigh Press

Sit on a chair with the feet on the ground, at hip width. Place the opposite hands on the inside knees in order to resist the closing of your knees. **Your hands push outside,** and *the knees push inside* as powerfully as possible. Resist and achieve maximum tension to be kept for 10 seconds while exhaling. Relax.

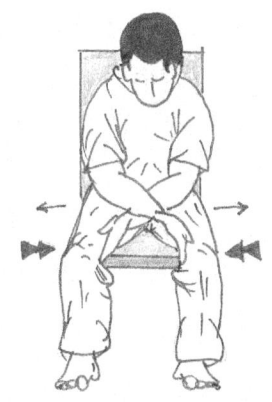

ISOMETRIC DRILLS

10.4.3.3 *Outer Thigh Press*

Sit on a chair with feet on the ground at hip width. Place your hands on your outer knees, and execute the opposite of the previous drill: **Try to open your knees by pushing them outside**, but *resist with your hands that push inside*. You do not move but achieve maximum tension. Keep it for 10 seconds while exhaling. Relax.

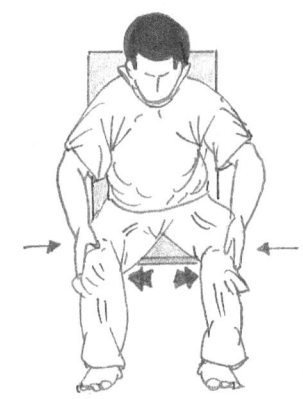

10.4.4 Wall drills

10.4.4.1 *Wall Squat*

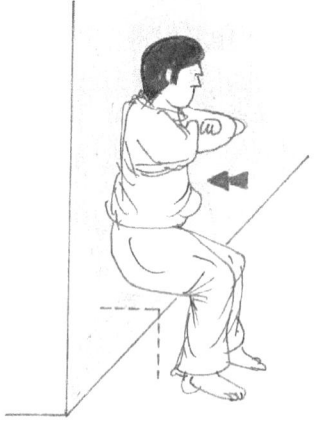

A very important exercise to be drilled often. Place your back on the wall and bend your knees at 90 degrees. Your back is straight against the wall, your lower legs parallel to the wall, your thighs parallel to the ground, and your feet flat on the floor. If you cannot assume the position, just bend the knees as much as you can. Cross your arms in order to avoid that they touch the wall and take part in the effort. You will now **push your back into the wall** and imagine that you are trying to push back the wall with all your might. Keep maximum tension for 10 seconds, and relax. This is a drill worth repeating, once you have become proficient. You can repeat by doing it while with the variations presented in the next paragraphs: you stand in the same position but on your toes (Heels off the floor – 10.4.4.2), or on your heels (Toes off the floor – 10.4.4.3).

10.4.4.2 Wall Squat on Toes

Same exercise as the previous one, but executed with the heels raised instead of with flat feet. Everything else is identical.

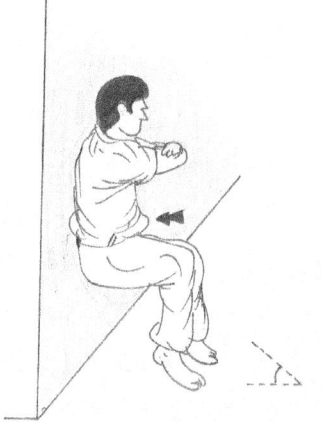

10.4.4.3 Wall Squat on Heels

Same exercise as before but executed on the heels, with toes raised. Everything else is identical.

10.4.4.4 Doorframe Drills Done on the Wall

The Illustrations show the 'wall' version of the previously encountered 'Doorframe Drills' *10.4.2.33* to *10.4.2.5*.

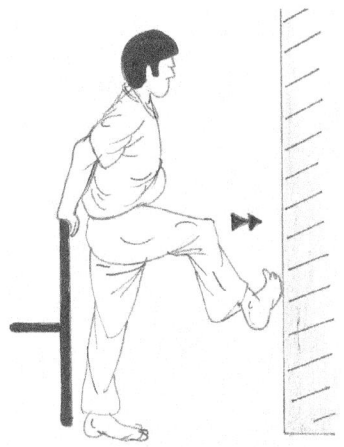  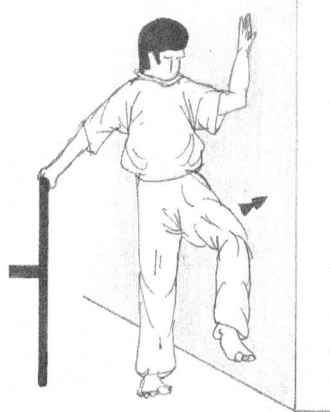

ISOMETRIC DRILLS 145

10.4.5 Doorway Bar or Isometric Machine

10.4.5.1 Squat

Place the Doorway Bar at the height suitable for your squat. For your longtime knee health, you should not squat lower than knees at 90 degrees. If you cannot squat that low, just simply go as low as comfortable for you. It is recommended to place something like a piece of wood to keep the heels lifted one or two inches, and *to never let the knees be further away than the straight line above your toes*. All this said, squat so as to have the bar held with your palms up, more or less at the level of your clavicles. Make sure you concentrate on using only your legs **to try to push the bar up.** Keep your maximum tension for 10 seconds while exhaling. Come out slowly out of the position and twist your hips and waist around to relax your back muscles. {*The Illustrations shows how to do the drill with the 'Isoplex Prop'*}.

One finds limits by pushing them.
~Herbert Simon

CHAPTER ELEVEN - THE ISOMETRIC 'MACHINES'

We have mentioned several times the "**Isometric Machine**", and what we meant by that was the stand in vogue in the Fifties and the Sixties, as illustrated. It was a kind of sturdy portal, in which a metal pole could be simply inserted through corresponding holes at the required height. The famous Actor and Martial Artist *Bruce Lee*, who had an incredible physique for his ectomorph-type frame, had one and he touted the use of *Isometrics* (He also had his own simpler and more transportable design). The big advantage of the **Isometric Machine** is the ease with which the height of the pole can be changed for multiple drills. This is certainly an excellent Prop for the serious Isometric trainee, who would be ready to build one, but it requires room and serious DIY skills.

The classic Isometric Machine

The 'portable' version

It should be noted that one could use the '*Squat and Chest Rack Cage*' at his local gym, if the design allows for **locking** the training bar safely in place for the relevant exercises. You could also load the bar with *so much weight* that it makes it an '**immovable**' object. Of course, that is true for all weight machines in your gym: stack enough weight, and it will become impossible to lift, push or pull, making it an ideal set up for an isometric exercise!

Squat Rack

Locking system

Overstacked gym machine becomes 'immovable'

148 THE ISOPLEX METHOD

Over the years, we have also seen many small trade-marked exercising gadgets based on *Isometrics*, but they were always limited to specific drills and muscles groups. Most were <u>excellent</u> props though and they can still be warmly recommended.

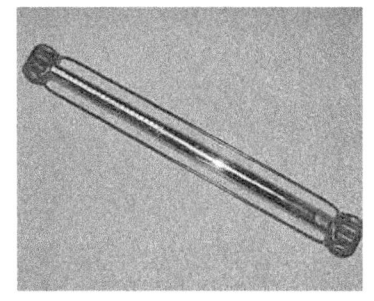

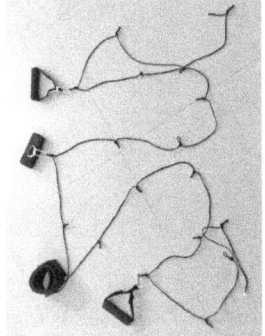

The Isoplex Prop

All in all, this is why we have designed a very simple apparatus, easy to carry on travel, easy to use, and as versatile as possible. The '*Isoplex Prop*' allows to drill most of the core Isometric Drills anywhere and easily. It lends itself to easy change to suit the next drill and to the adaptation of nearly all gym machine exercises. A length of nylon cable with loops at regular intervals allows to attach nearly anywhere either handles or feet belts. This will allow the trainee to choose a set up in which he can use one limb against another, or limbs against his own body weight. Moreover, additional handles allow to use a closed door at various heights, as resistance.

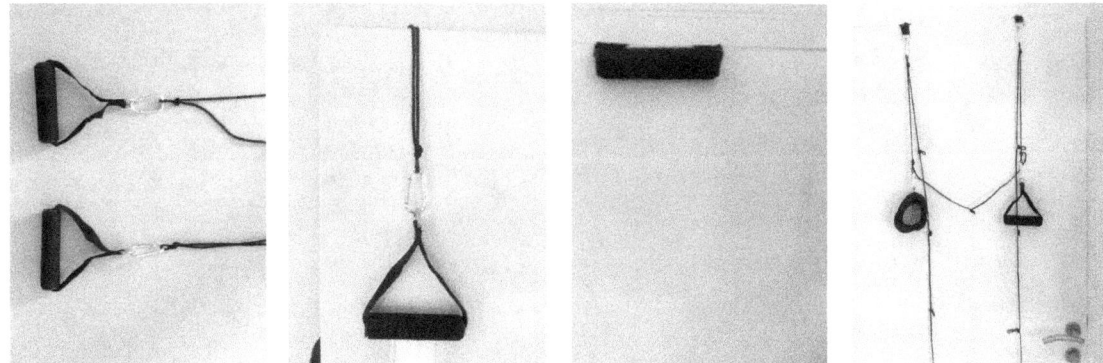

Additional Handles can be used to 'fix' the Prop high in a door

We have provided a few examples of Drills using the *Isoplex Prop*, and we shall add here a few ones. It should be clear that, just as Isometrics are a thing of the mind first and foremost, so is the use of the *Isoplex Prop*. Its versatility is only limited by the trainee's imagination. Good Luck!

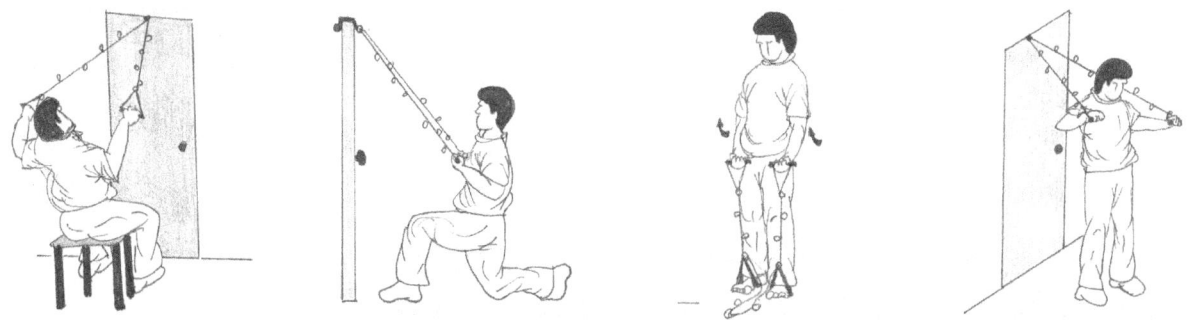

THE ISOMETRIC MACHINES

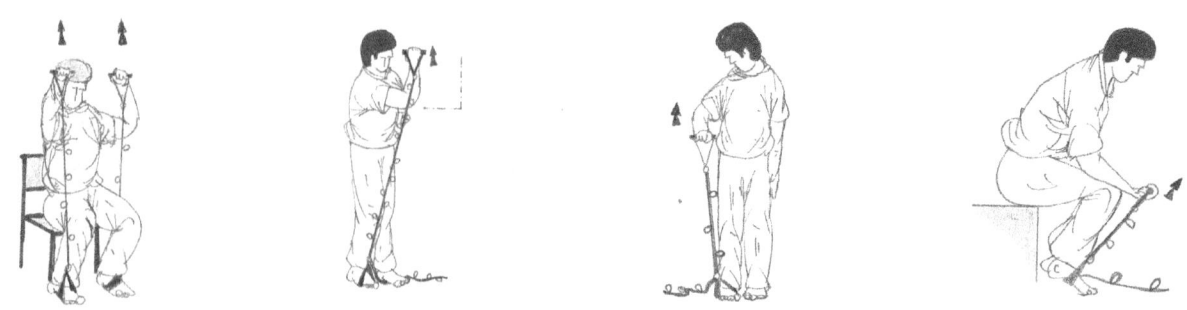

We are considering the commercialization of the **'Isoplex Prop'** and the interested reader is invited to contact us at *martialartkicks@gmail.com* to check on the progress of this plan.

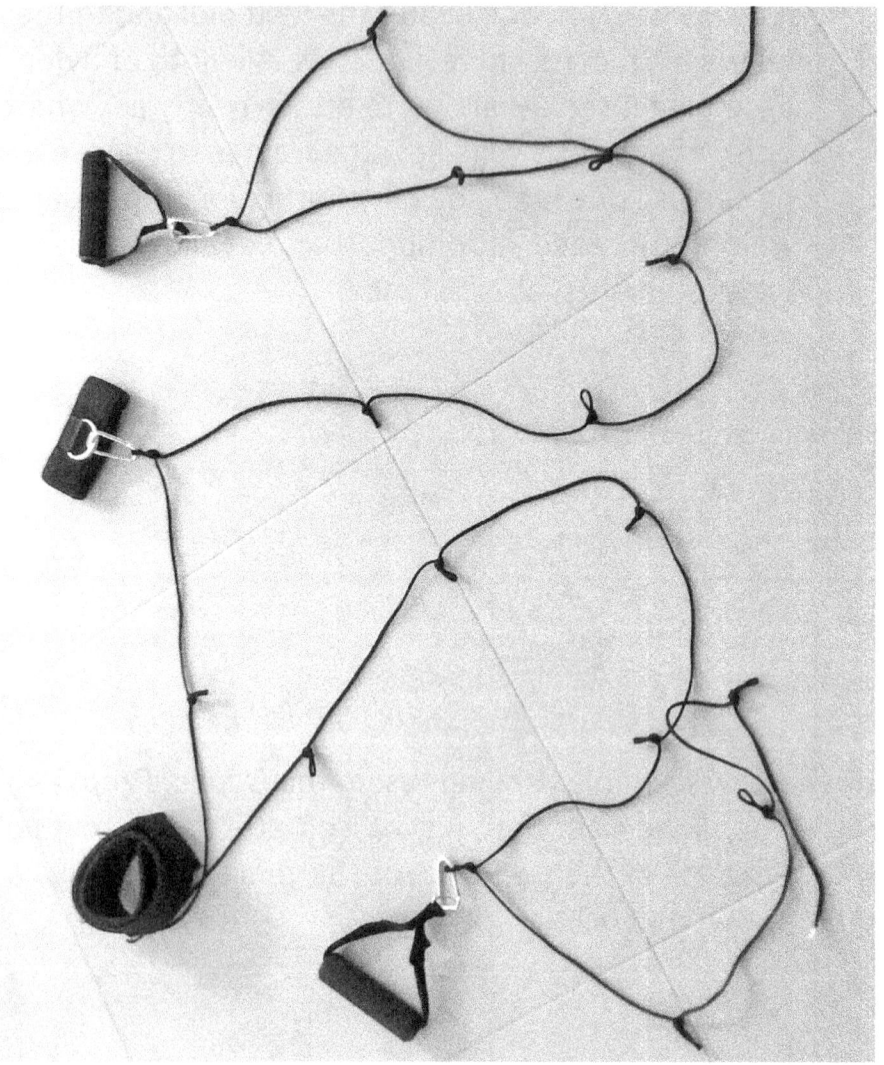

CHAPER TWELVE - THE PROGRAMS

Putting it all together...

12.1 Introduction

We remind the reader briefly of the **principles** on which the programs are based, as detailed before.

12.1.1　　The Isoplex programs are based on 6 sessions a week. One full day rest is a must for muscle growth and improvement.

12.1.2　　There should be a day hiatus between high impact Plyometric workouts. There should be a day hiatus between high impact Isometric workouts. Specific training cause specific muscle fiber damage that require time for healing.

12.1.3　　Low impact Plyometrics, Low impact Isometrics and light Stretching should be used for warming up. Abdominal exercises are particularly good at the warm-up stage, on top of building important core musculature.

12.1.4　　All training sessions should end with at least 10 minutes of intensive Flexiometrics. The trainee who has more time than an hour a day is invited to keep stretching.

12.1.5　　Progress within a program routine must be executed and measured: longer time in Isometric contractions, and more reps in Plyometric drills. In flexibility, it is simply about going gradually further in the stretch, while being careful and mindful of the body.

12.1.6　　You should switch programs every 3 months, to "fool" the body into progress and out of its comfort zone.

As a matter of principle, a weekly session would therefore generally look like this:

Day 1: 10 minutes Warm-up; 40 minutes Isometrics (Upper body emphasis); 10 minutes Flexiometrics (Upper body emphasis)

Day 2: 10 minutes Warm-up; 40 minutes Plyometrics (Lower body emphasis); 10 minutes Flexiometrics (Lower body emphasis)

Day 3: 10 minutes Warm-up; 30 minutes Isometrics (General); 20 minutes Intense Flexiometrics

Day 4: 10 minutes Warm-up; 40 minutes Plyometrics (Upper body emphasis); 10 minutes Flexiometrics (Upper body emphasis)

Day 5: 10 minutes Warm-up; 40 minutes Isometrics (Lower body emphasis); 10 minutes Flexiometrics (Lower Body emphasis)

Day 6: 10 minutes Warm-up; 30 minutes Plyometrics (General); 20 minutes intense Flexiometrics

And now we can finally go to the Programs themselves:

- The Beginner
- The Trainee
- The Intermediate
- The Advanced
- The Partner

Good Luck!

Perseverance, secret of all triumphs.
~Victor Hugo

12.2 FIRST PROGRAM: The Beginner

Even if you are a practicing sportsman, it is recommended that you start with this program. When you are familiar with it, you are invited to switch to the next ones faster, but *gradual* is always the right way in athletic performance.

12.2.1 DAY 1 — Iso and Upper body

1 Warm up 
High Knee March 8.1.1
2 minutes

2 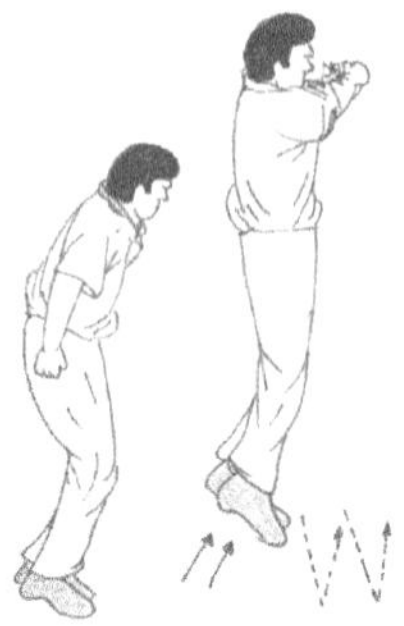
Low Hops 8.1.6
1 minute

3 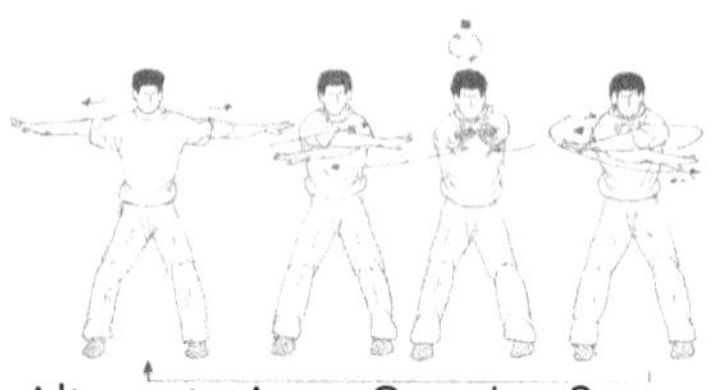
Alternate Arms Opening 8.1.10
2 minutes

4 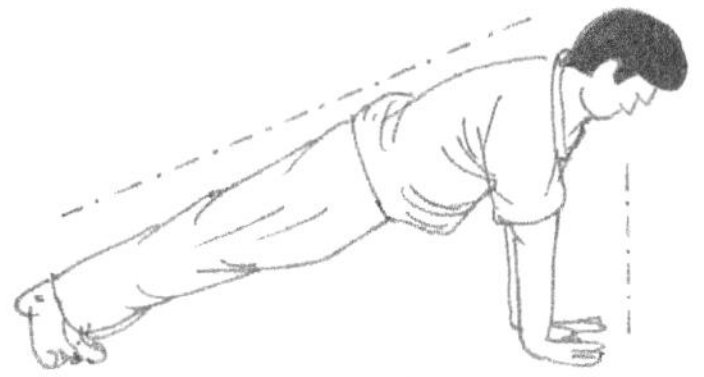
Plank Pose 10.1.2
1 minute

5 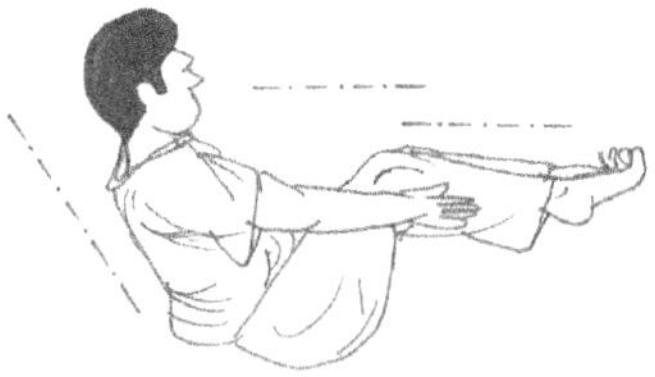
Half Boat Pose 10.1.5
1 minute

6 Isometrics 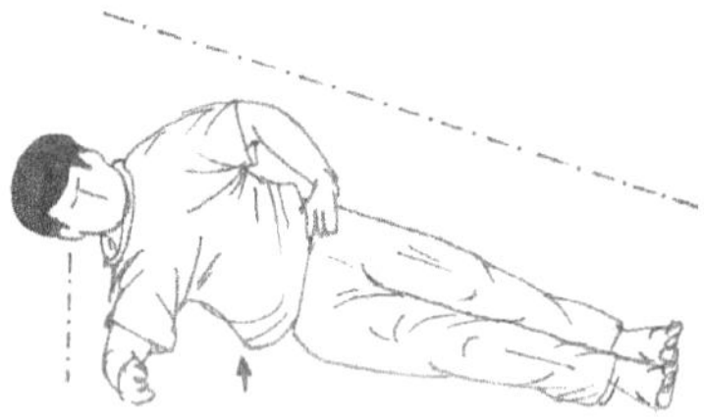
12 min
Side Plank on Elbow 10.1.7
1 minute, each side

7 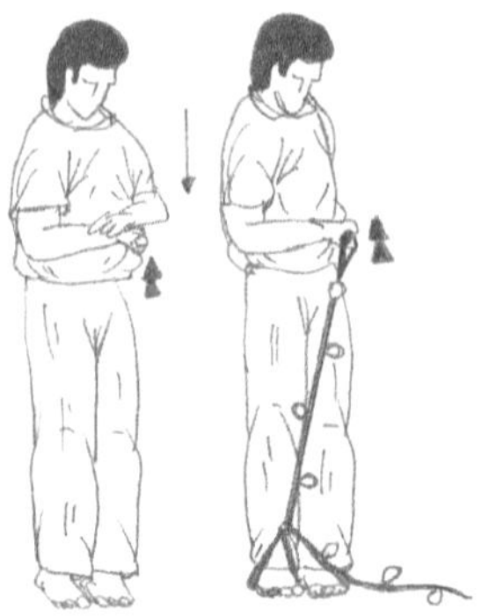
Biceps Curl 10.3.1.13
2 reps each side

8 
Abs-in 10.3.1.1
10 reps

9
21 min
Superman Pose 10.3.1.8
2 reps

154 THE ISOPLEX METHOD

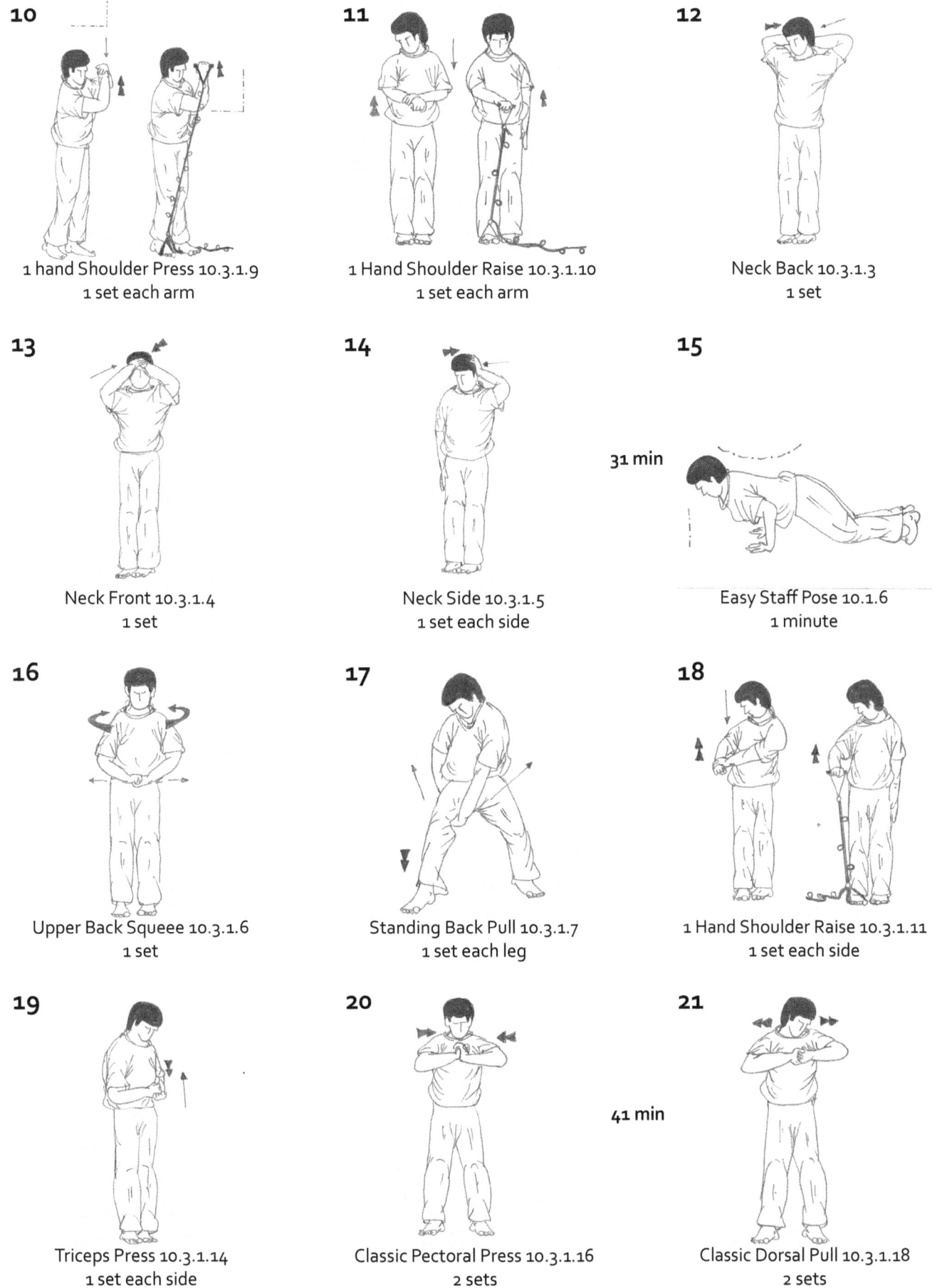

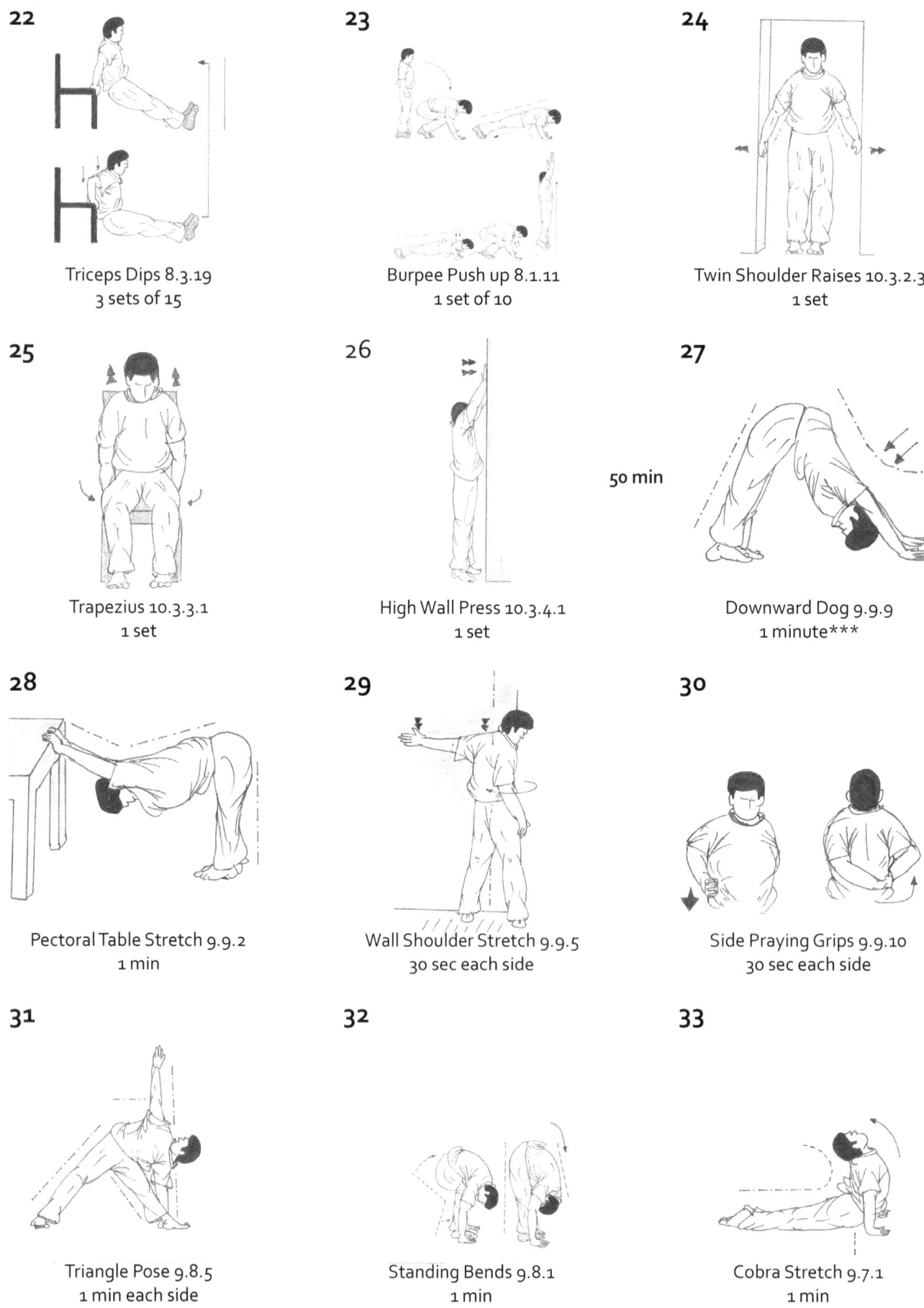

12.2.2 DAY 2

Plyo and Lower body

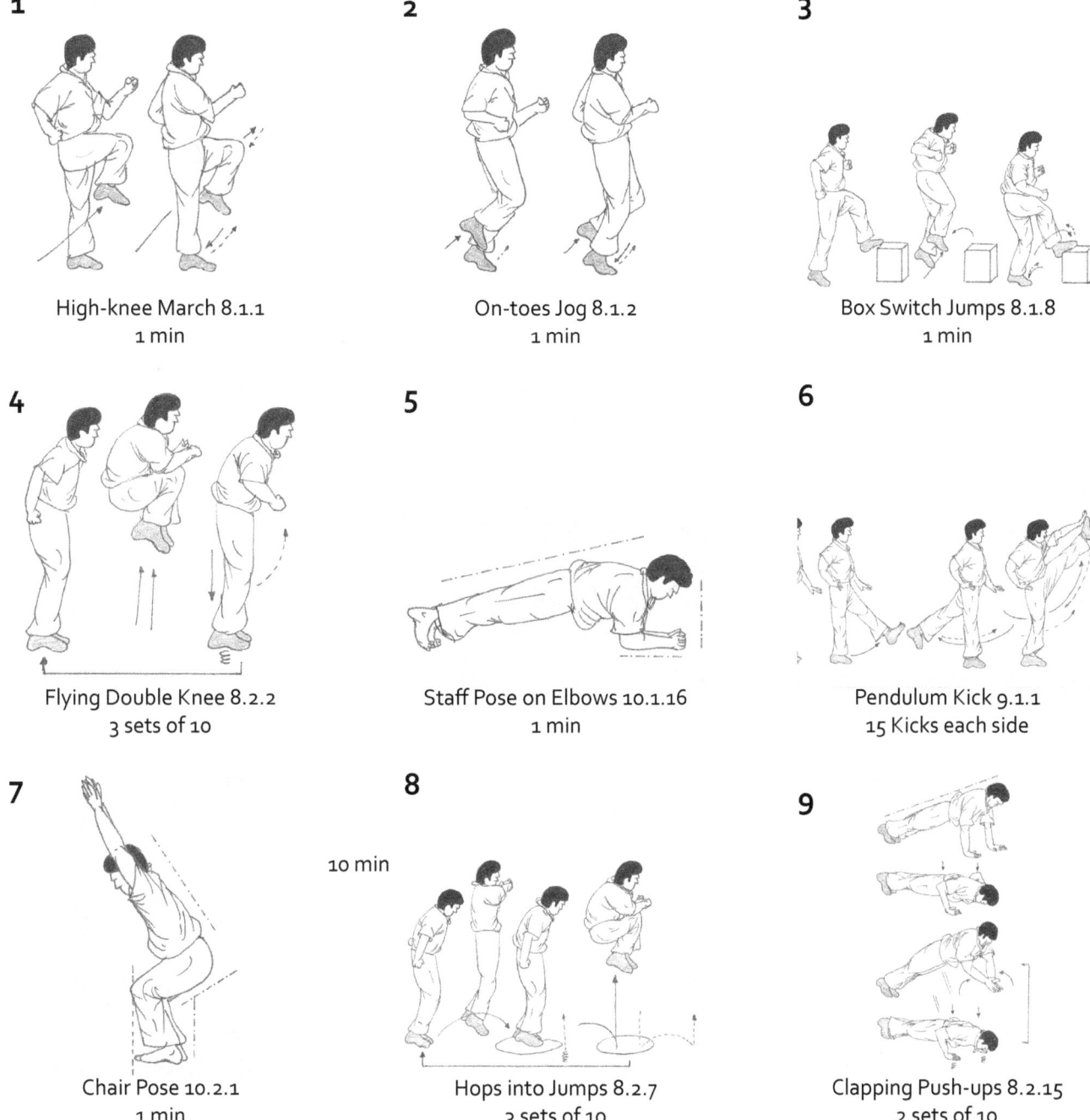

1. High-knee March 8.1.1 — 1 min
2. On-toes Jog 8.1.2 — 1 min
3. Box Switch Jumps 8.1.8 — 1 min
4. Flying Double Knee 8.2.2 — 3 sets of 10
5. Staff Pose on Elbows 10.1.16 — 1 min
6. Pendulum Kick 9.1.1 — 15 Kicks each side
7. Chair Pose 10.2.1 — 1 min
8. Hops into Jumps 8.2.7 — 3 sets of 10 (10 min)
9. Clapping Push-ups 8.2.15 — 2 sets of 10

22

On-box 1 leg Jumps 8.3.4
2 sets of 10 jumps per leg

23

Push up and Rotation 8.3.18
3 sets of 10

24
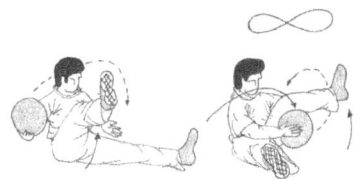
8 Abs Drill 8.7.2
10 'Eights' in each direction

25
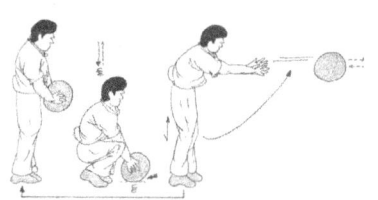
Squat to underhand Throw 8.7.4
3 sets of 10 Throws

26

Twisting Lunges 8.7.9
2 sets of 10 each side

27
50 min

Side Plank
1 min each side

28

Sitting Bends 9.3.1
2 min

29
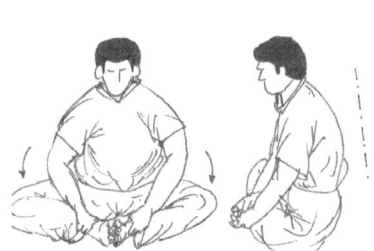
Cobbler Pose 9.4.1
1 min

30
Crossed-legs Bends 9.2.6
30 sec each side

31

Standing Quad Stretches 9.5.1
1 min each leg

32
Waist Twists 9.6.5
30 sec each side

33
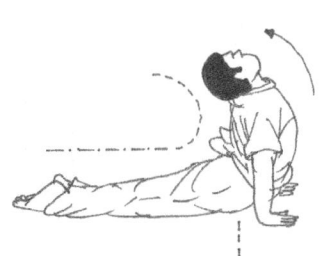
Cobra Stretch 9.7.1
1 min

PROGRAM 1

12.2.3 DAY 3
Iso and Flexio

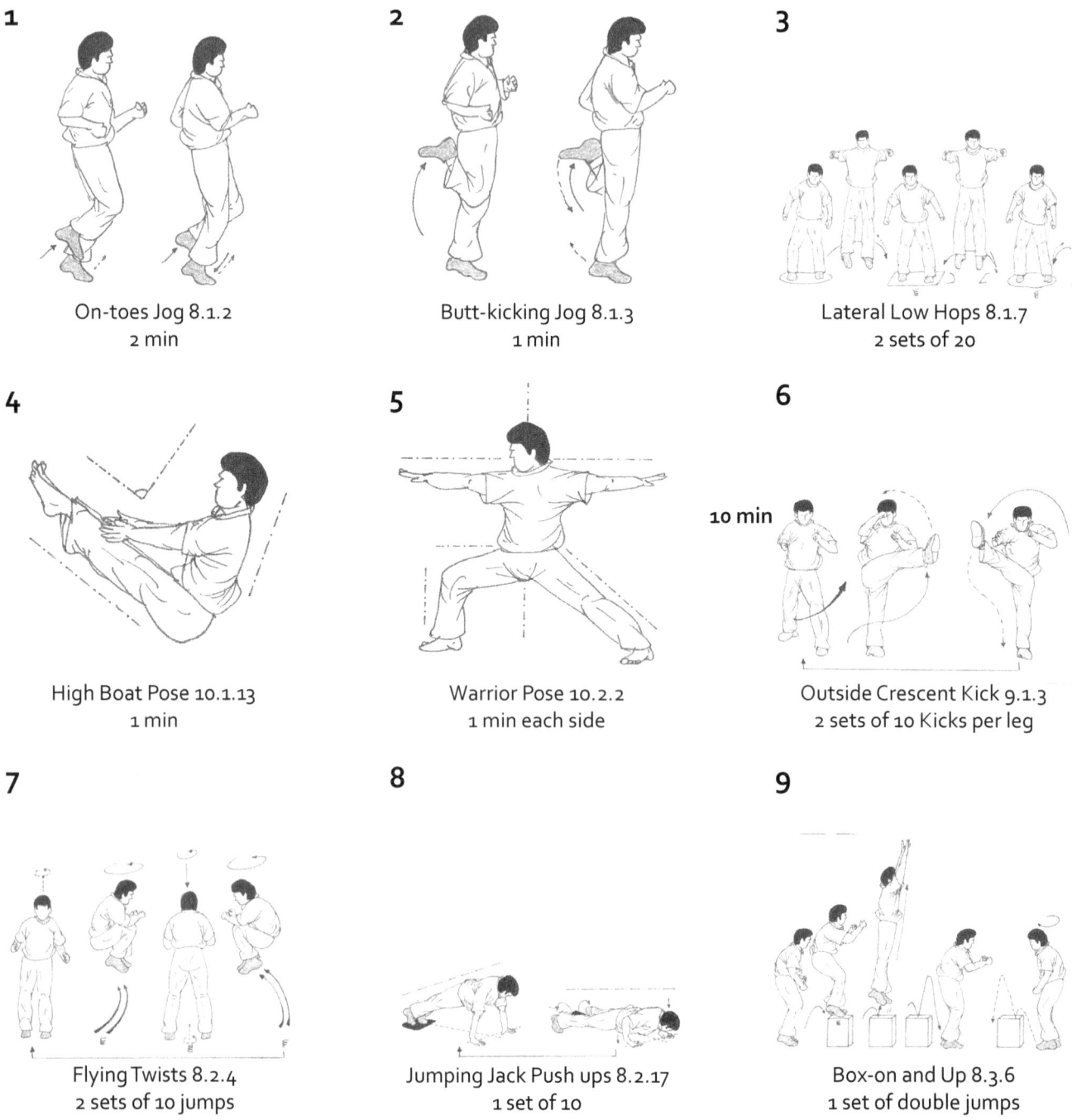

1. On-toes Jog 8.1.2 — 2 min
2. Butt-kicking Jog 8.1.3 — 1 min
3. Lateral Low Hops 8.1.7 — 2 sets of 20
4. High Boat Pose 10.1.13 — 1 min
5. Warrior Pose 10.2.2 — 1 min each side
6. Outside Crescent Kick 9.1.3 — 2 sets of 10 Kicks per leg (10 min)
7. Flying Twists 8.2.4 — 2 sets of 10 jumps
8. Jumping Jack Push ups 8.2.17 — 1 set of 10
9. Box-on and Up 8.3.6 — 1 set of double jumps

THE ISOPLEX METHOD

PROGRAM 1 DAY 3

12.2.4 DAY 4 — Plyos and Upper Body

1

Lateral Crosses 8.1.5
1 min

2

Inside Crescent Kick 9.1.2
2 sets of 10 reps per leg

3

Jumping Jacks 8.1.9
1 min

4
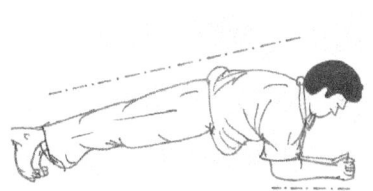
Staff Pose on elbows 10.1.16
1 min

5

Burpees 8.1.11
10 reps

7 min

6

Alternate Arms Opening 8.1.10
1 min

7
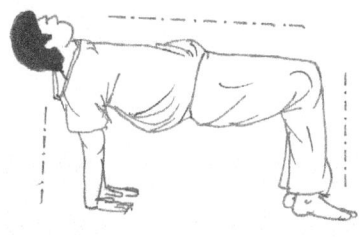
Upward Table Pose 10.1.3
1 min

8
Twin Arm Side Press 10.3.2.9
1 set

11 min

9

Pectoral Table Stretch 9.9.2
30 sec

PROGRAM 1 DAY 4

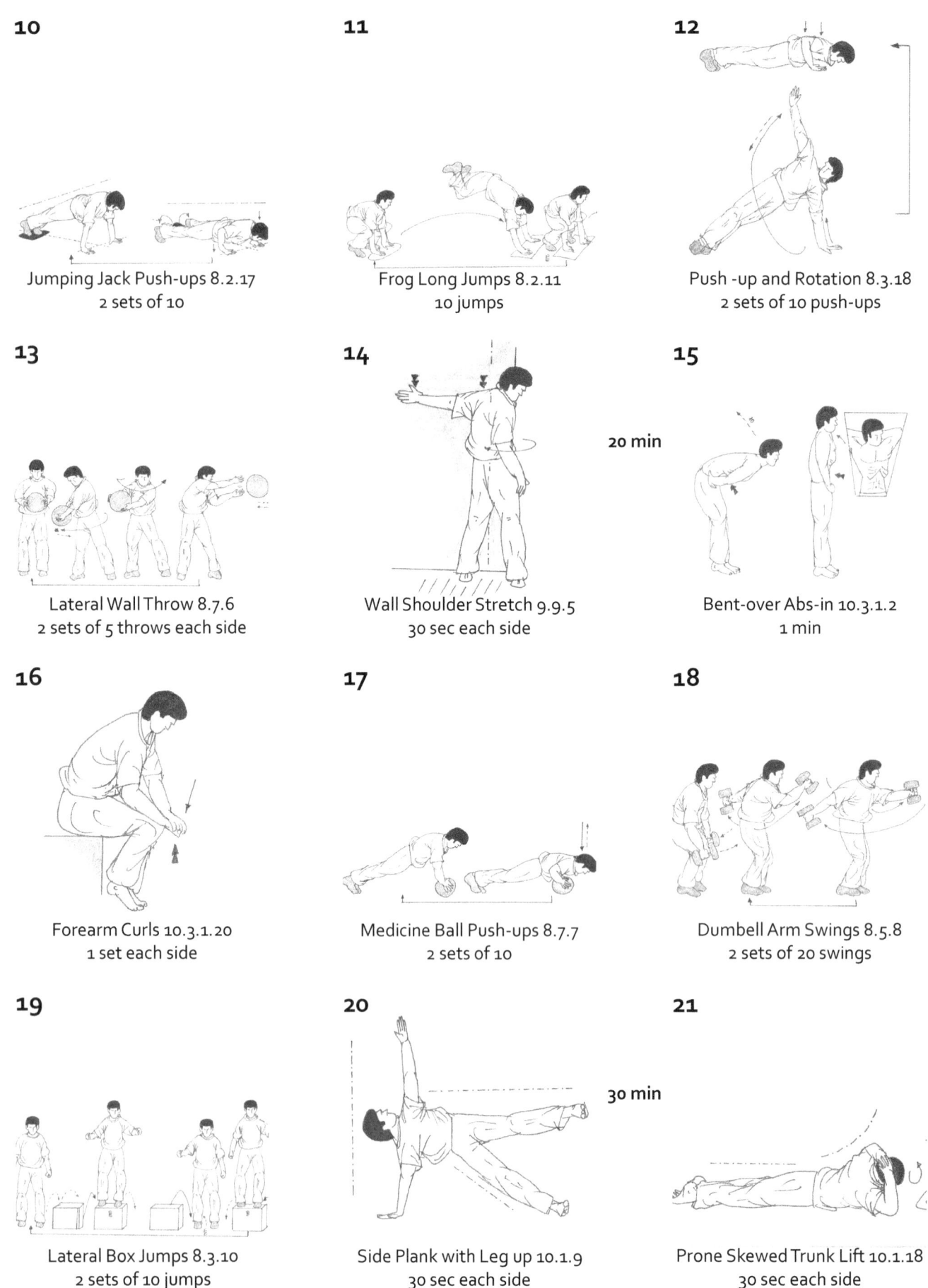

PROGRAM 1

34

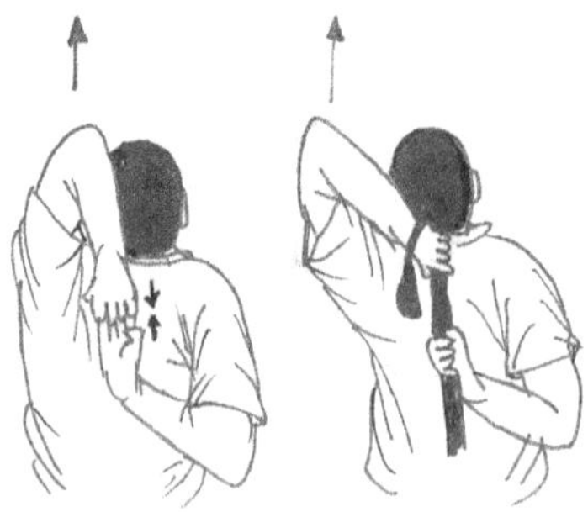

Cow's Face Grips 9.9.8
30 sec each side

35

Downward Dog Pose 9.9.9
1 min

36

Side Praying Grips 9.9.10
1 min each side

37

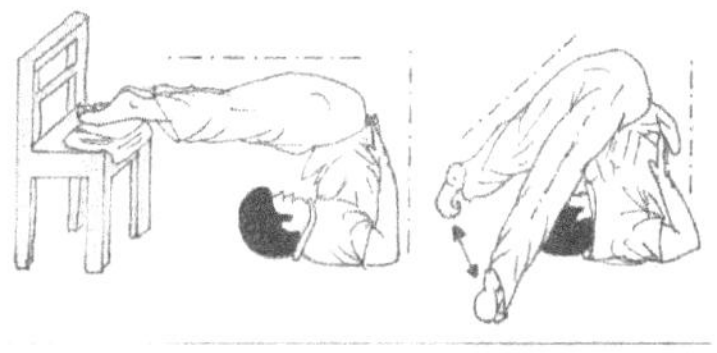

Plough Pose 9.8.2
1 min

38

Bow Pose 9.7.3
2 sets of 30 sec

39

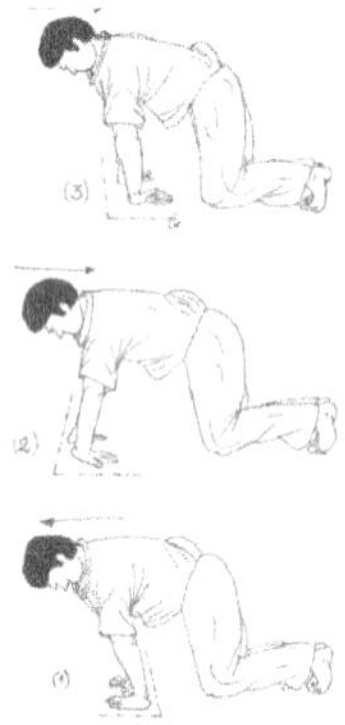

Wrist Stretches 9.9.15
30 sec each type

Set your goals high, and don't stop till you get there.
~Bo Jackson

12.2.5 DAY 5 — Iso and Lower Body

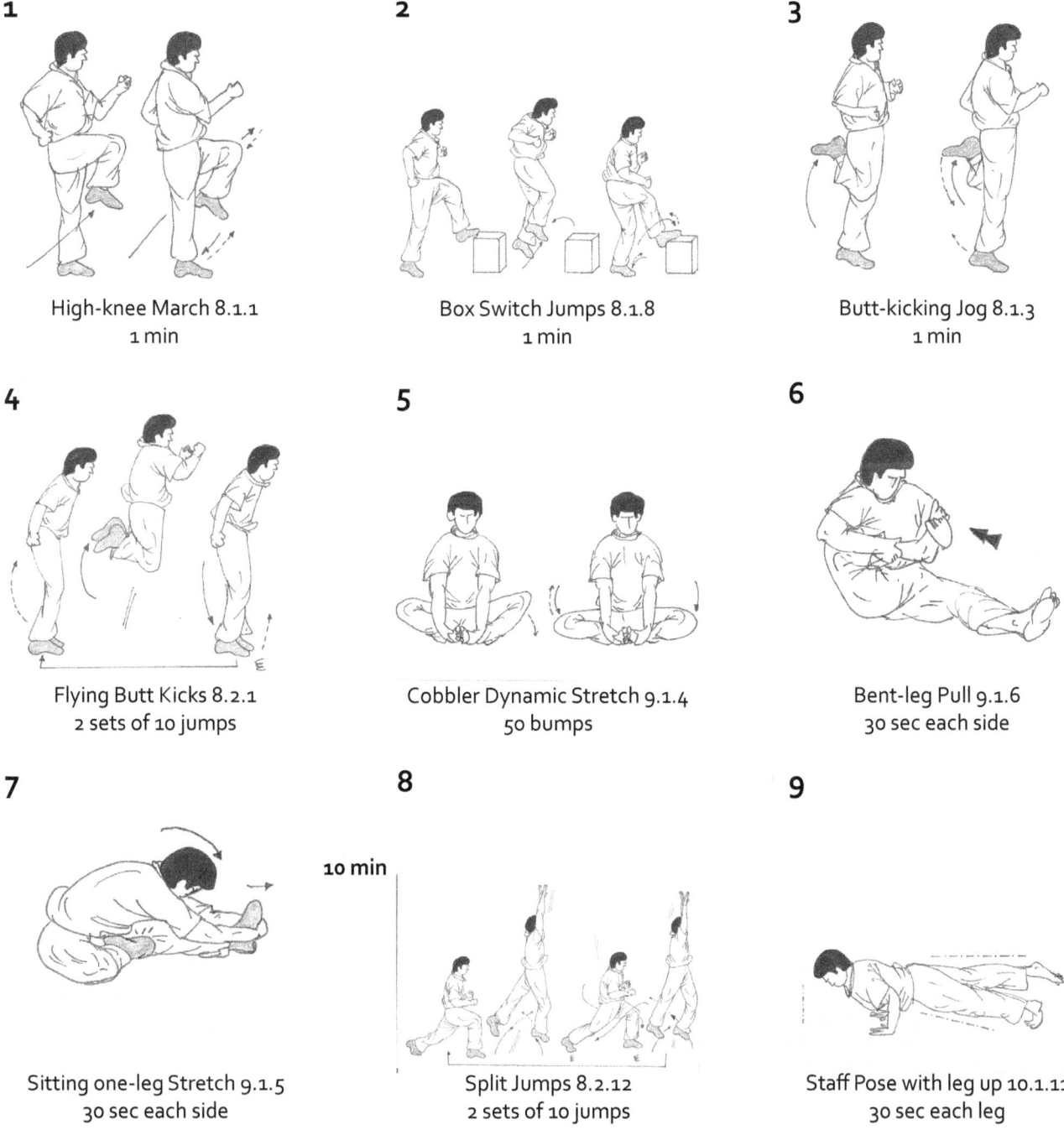

1. High-knee March 8.1.1 — 1 min
2. Box Switch Jumps 8.1.8 — 1 min
3. Butt-kicking Jog 8.1.3 — 1 min
4. Flying Butt Kicks 8.2.1 — 2 sets of 10 jumps
5. Cobbler Dynamic Stretch 9.1.4 — 50 bumps
6. Bent-leg Pull 9.1.6 — 30 sec each side
7. Sitting one-leg Stretch 9.1.5 — 30 sec each side
8. Split Jumps 8.2.12 — 2 sets of 10 jumps (10 min)
9. Staff Pose with leg up 10.1.11 — 30 sec each leg

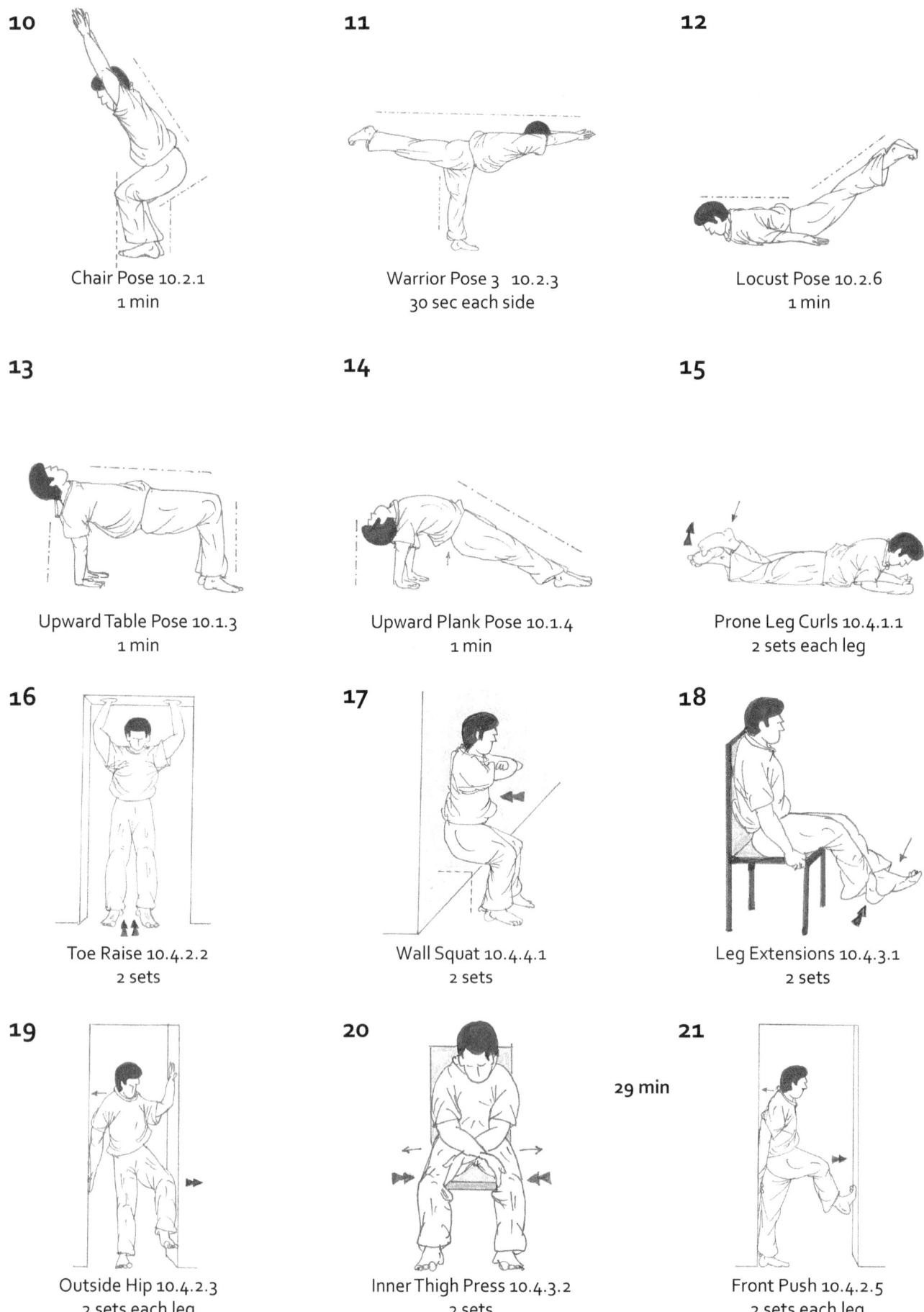

22

Lower Back Superman 10.3.1.8
30 sec

23

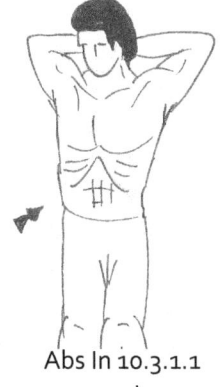

Abs In 10.3.1.1
2 sets

24

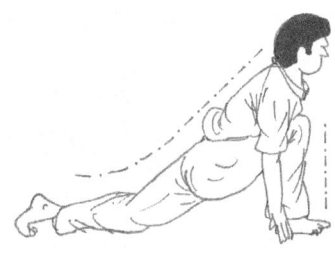

Low Lunge 10.2.7
1 min each side

25

Side Plank with leg up 10.1.9
30 sec each side

26

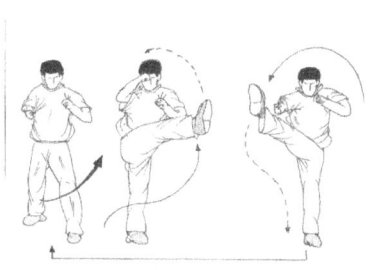

Outside Crescent Kick 9.1.3
2 sets of 10 per leg

27

Front Leg Stretch 9.2.4
1 min each side

28

Twisting Lunges 8.7.9
3 sets of 10

29

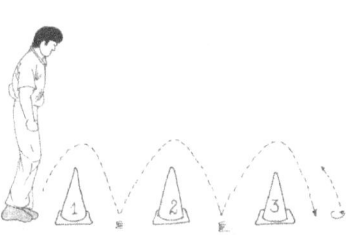

Cone Jumps in series 8.4.1
3 sets of 10 jumps

30

45 min

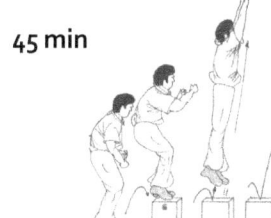

Box on and up 8.3.6
2 sets of 10 'double' jumps

31

Squats 10.4.5.1
2 sets

32

50 min

1-leg lateral hops 8.2.9
2 sets of 10 hops per leg

33

Forward Stretch Leg up 10.2.9
30 sec each side

PROGRAM 1

34

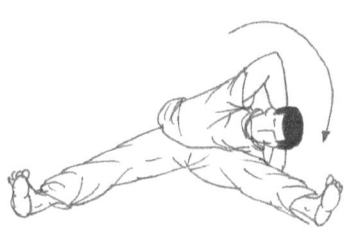

Sitting Side Bends 9.8.3
30 sec each side

35

Runner Stretches 9.6.7
30 sec each side

36

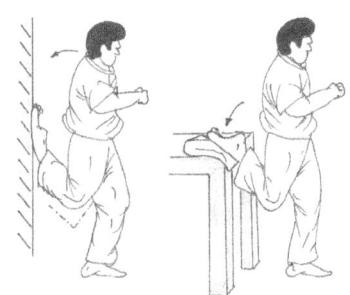

Quad Stretches 9.5.1
30 sec each side

37

Sitting Wide 1-leg 9.4.4
30 sec each side

38

Open legs Sitting Bends 9.3.2
1 min

39

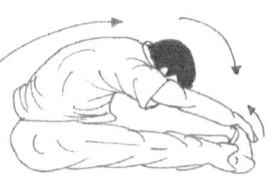

Sitting Stretch 9.2.5
1 min

40

Hero's Pose 9.2.2
2 min

Success is nothing more than a few simple disciplines, practiced every day.
~Jim Rohn

12.2.6 DAY 6 — *Plyo and Flexio*

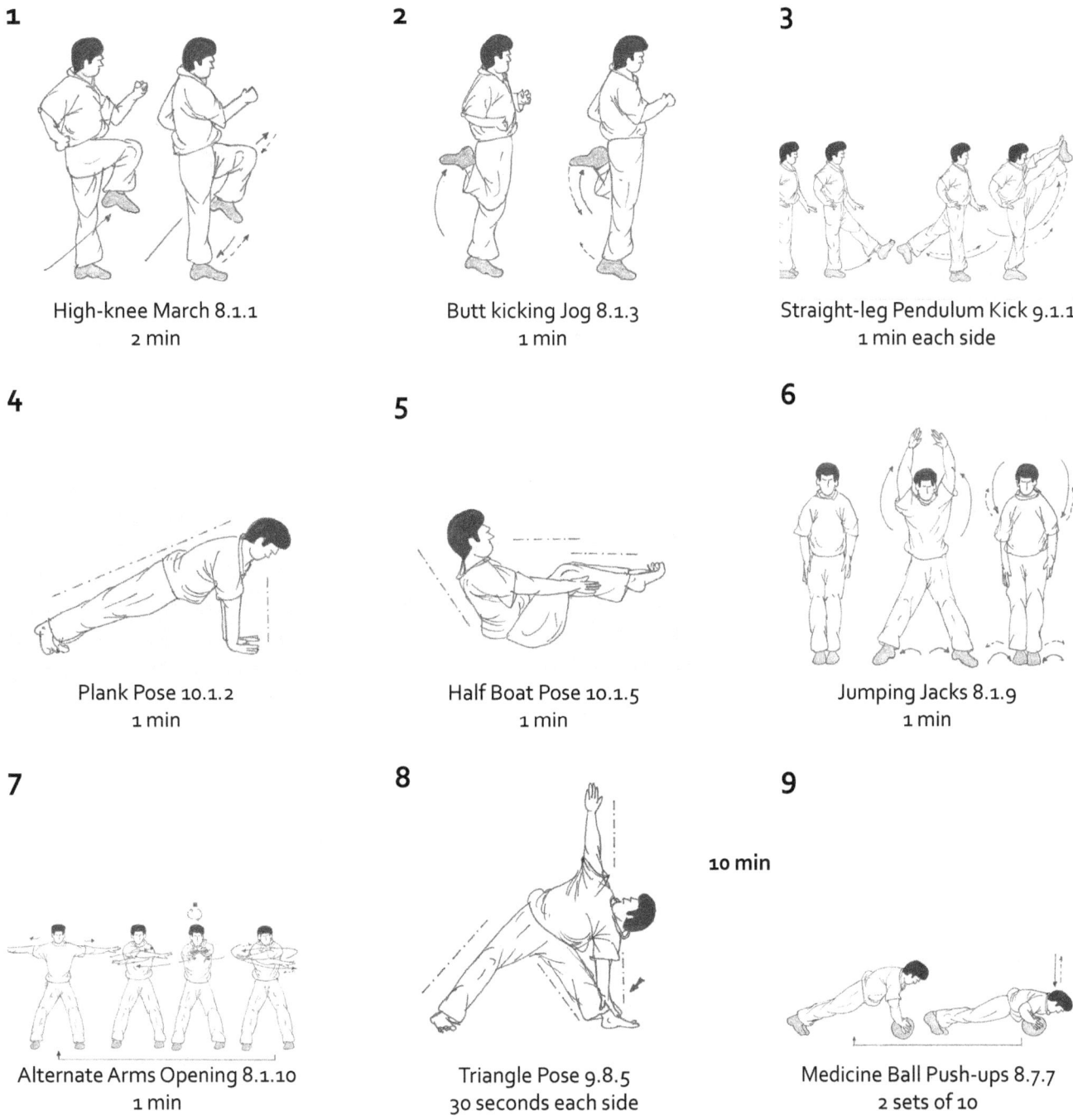

1. High-knee March 8.1.1 — 2 min
2. Butt kicking Jog 8.1.3 — 1 min
3. Straight-leg Pendulum Kick 9.1.1 — 1 min each side
4. Plank Pose 10.1.2 — 1 min
5. Half Boat Pose 10.1.5 — 1 min
6. Jumping Jacks 8.1.9 — 1 min
7. Alternate Arms Opening 8.1.10 — 1 min
8. Triangle Pose 9.8.5 — 30 seconds each side
9. Medicine Ball Push-ups 8.7.7 — 2 sets of 10

10 min

PROGRAM 1 DAY 6

10

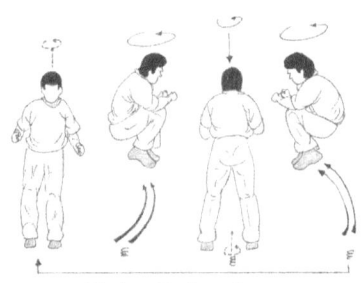

Flying Twists 8.2.4
2 sets of 10

11

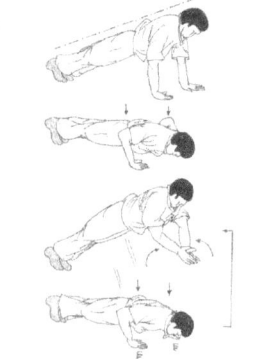

Clapping Push-ups 8.2.15
2 sets of 10

12

Frog Long Jumps 8.2.11
2 sets of 10 jumps

13

Box-on and Up 8.3.6
2 sets of 10 double jumps

14

Push-up and Rotation 8.3.18
2 sets of 10 on each side

15

Lateral Box jumps 8.3.10
2 sets of 10 jumps each side

16

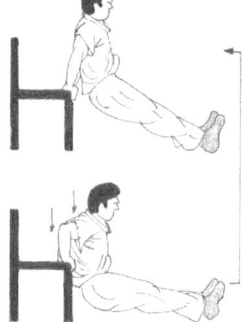

Triceps Dips 8.3.19
2 sets of 20

17

Front Cone Jumps in series 8.4.1
2 sets of 10 jumps

18

Squat to Underhand Throw 8.7.4
2 sets of 10

19

27 min

Box-off and Long 8.3.8
3 sets of 10 jumps

20

Dumbell Arm Swings 8.5.8
2 sets of 20

21

Bar Twist 8.5.6
2 sets of 50

THE ISOPLEX METHOD

22 Lateral Knee-up 8.6.4
2 sets of 10 on each side

23 On-box Jump 8.3.1
3 sets of 20

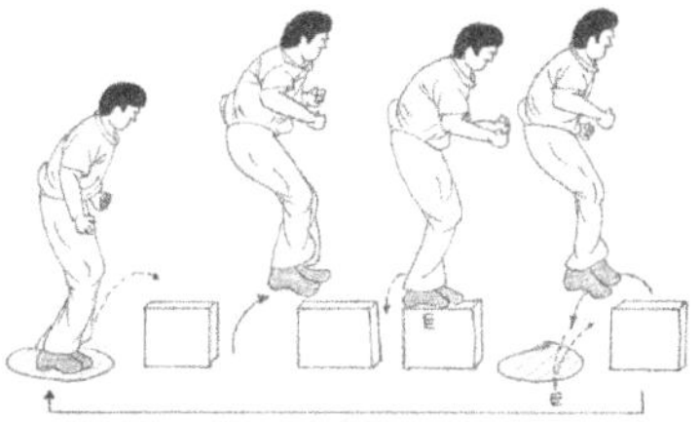

24 Trunk Rotation with Ball 8.7.3
3 sets of 10 in each direction

25 Squat Jumps with Ball 8.7.1
2 sets of 10

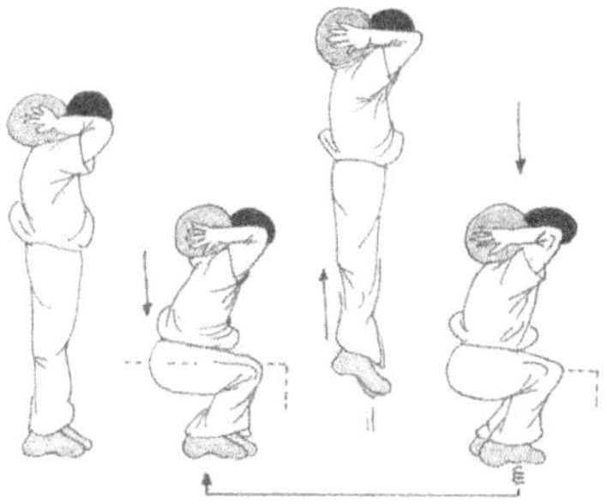

26 Upward Plank Pose 10.1.4
1 min

27 Prone Trunk Lift 10.1.17
3 sets of 20 sec

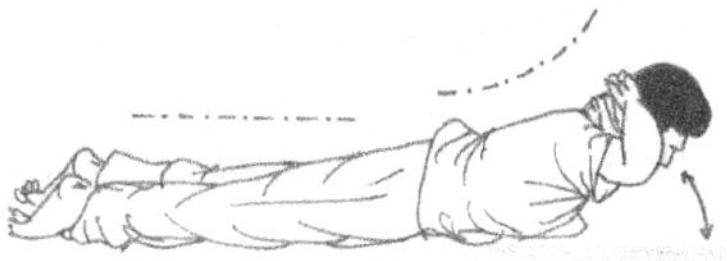

28 Joined legs Lateral Jumps 8.2.6
2 sets of 20 jumps

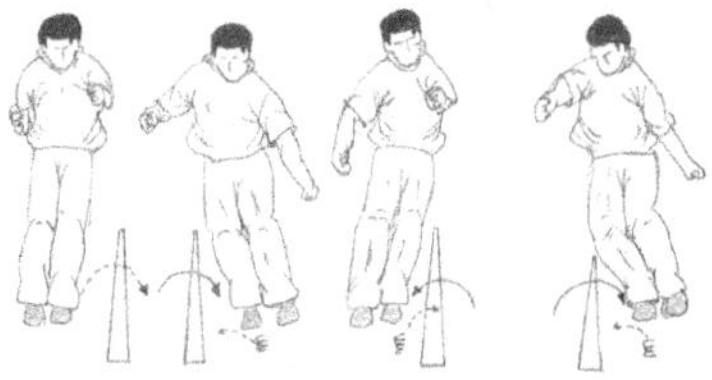

40 min

29 Cobbler Dynamic Stretch 9.1.4
50 bumps

30 2-legs Stretch 9.2.5
2 sets of 30 sec

31 Standing Side Bends 9.1.8
30 sec each side

32 Flexed Foot Front Leg 9.2.4
1 min each leg

49 min

33 Lying Leg Pull 9.3.3
1 min each leg

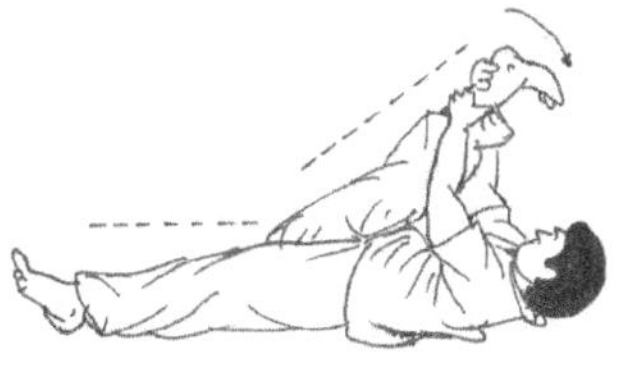

PROGRAM 1 DAY 6

34 Sitting Wide Stretch 9.4.5 — 1 min

35 Standing Quad Stretch 9.5.1 — 1 min each leg

36 Waist Twist 9.6.5 — 1 min each side

37 Side Praying Grips 9.9.10 — 1 min each side

38 Hero's Pose 9.2.2 — 1 min

This ends the presentation of the First Program for Beginners. If it was easy for you, it is still recommended to follow it for a full month before progressing to the Second Program. If it was not easy, keep at it for 3 months before going to the next one. Do what you can do, and keep your Ego out of it.

Patience and perseverance have a magical effect before which difficulties disappear and obstacles vanish.
~John Quincy Adams

12.3 SECOND PROGRAM: The Trainee

Now that you are familiar with the flow of Isoplex Training, it is time to start increasing the level gradually: more difficult and longer drills. Even if you feel advanced, do this program for a month before going to the next level.

12.3.1 DAY 1 — Iso and Upper body

1
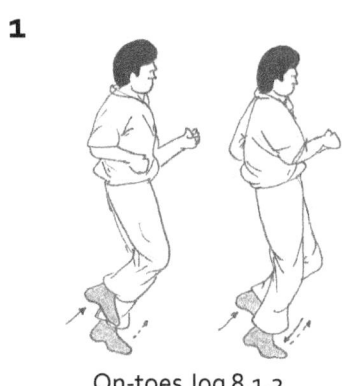
On-toes Jog 8.1.2
2 min

2
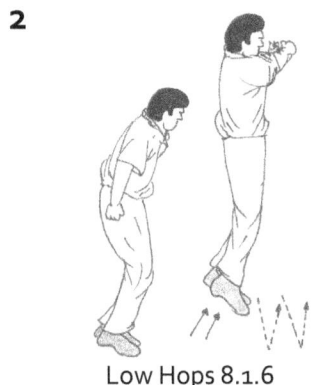
Low Hops 8.1.6
1 min

3
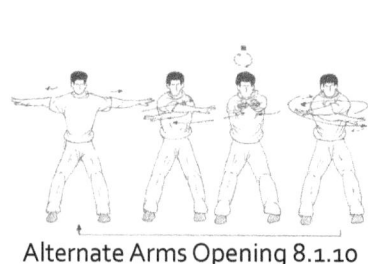
Alternate Arms Opening 8.1.10
1 min

4

Push-up Burpees 8.1.11
10 reps

5

Elbows Staff Pose 10.1.16
1 min

6
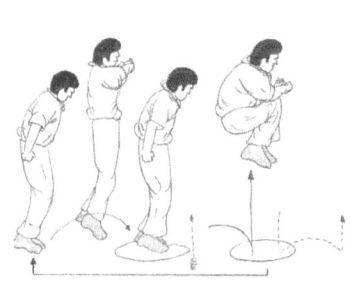
Hops into Jumps 8.2.7
2 sets of 10

7

Outside Crescent Kicks 9.1.3
2 sets of 10 each leg

8
10 min

Plank Pose 10.1.2
1 min

9
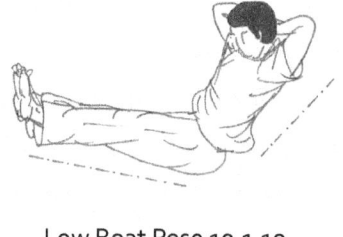
Low Boat Pose 10.1.10
1 min

PROGRAM 2 DAY 1

10

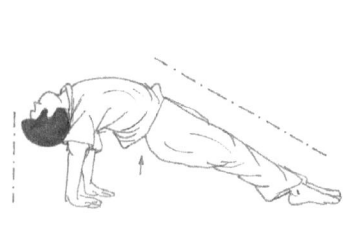

Medicine Ball Push ups 8.7.7
2 sets of 10

11

Upward Plank Pose 10.1.4
1 min

12

Abs-in 10.3.1.1
10 reps

13

Neck Front 10.3.1.4
1 rep

14

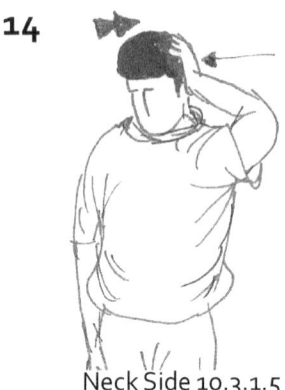

Neck Side 10.3.1.5
1 rep each side

15

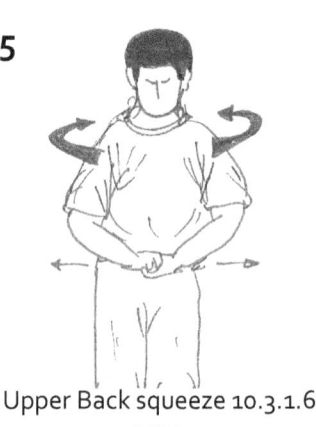

20 min

Upper Back squeeze 10.3.1.6
1 rep

16

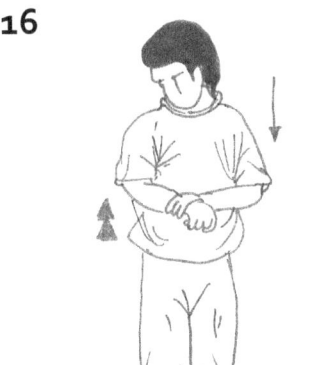

1 Hand Shoulder Front 10.3.1.10
1 rep each side

17

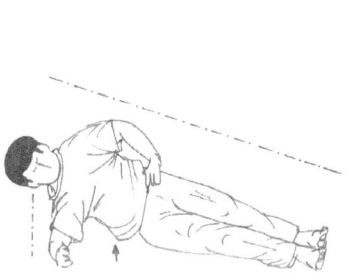

Side Plank on elbow 10.1.7
1 minute each side

18

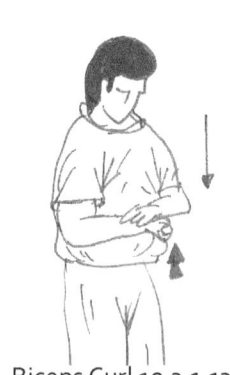

Biceps Curl 10.3.1.13
1 rep each side

19

Triceps Press 10.3.1.14
1 rep each side

20

25 min

Classic Pectoral Press 10.3.1.16
1 rep

21

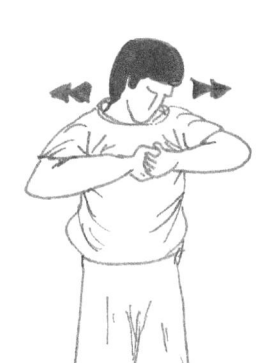

Classic Dorsal Pull 10.3.1.18
1 rep

THE ISOPLEX METHOD

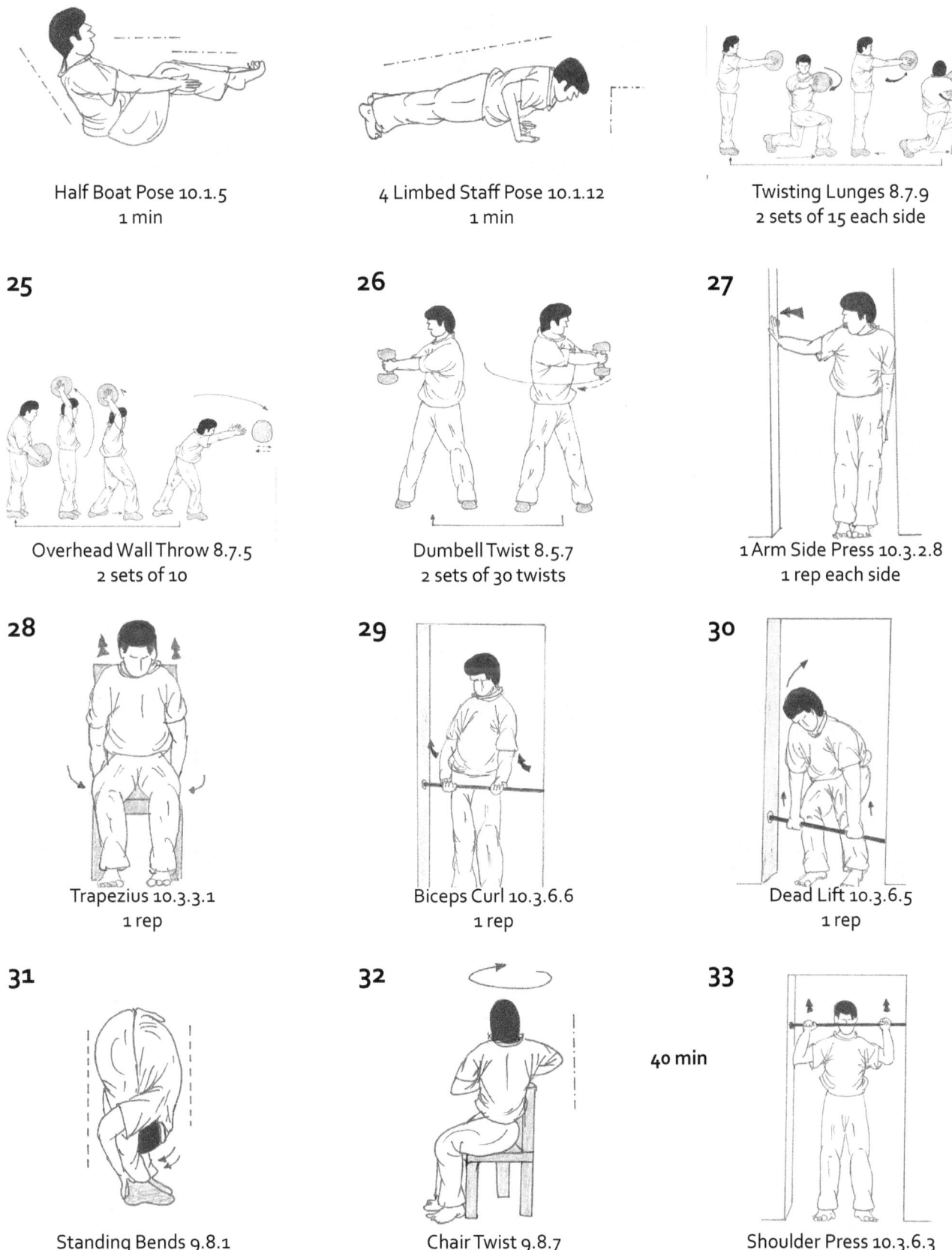

46

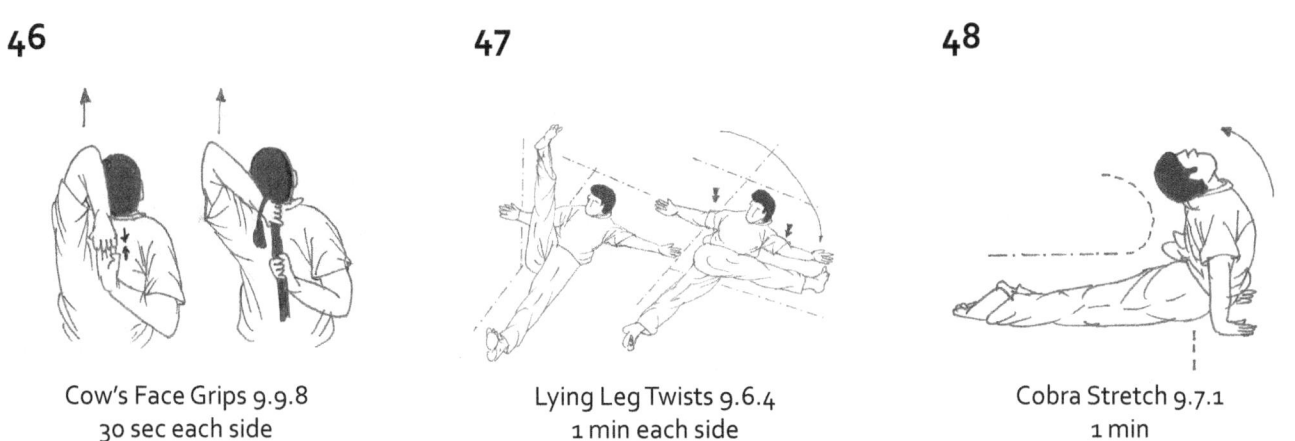

Cow's Face Grips 9.9.8
30 sec each side

47

Lying Leg Twists 9.6.4
1 min each side

48

Cobra Stretch 9.7.1
1 min

**Success isn't always about greatness. It's about consistency. Consistent hard work leads to success. Greatness will come.
~Dwayne Johnson**

PROGRAM 2

12.3.2 DAY 2 — Plyo and Lower body

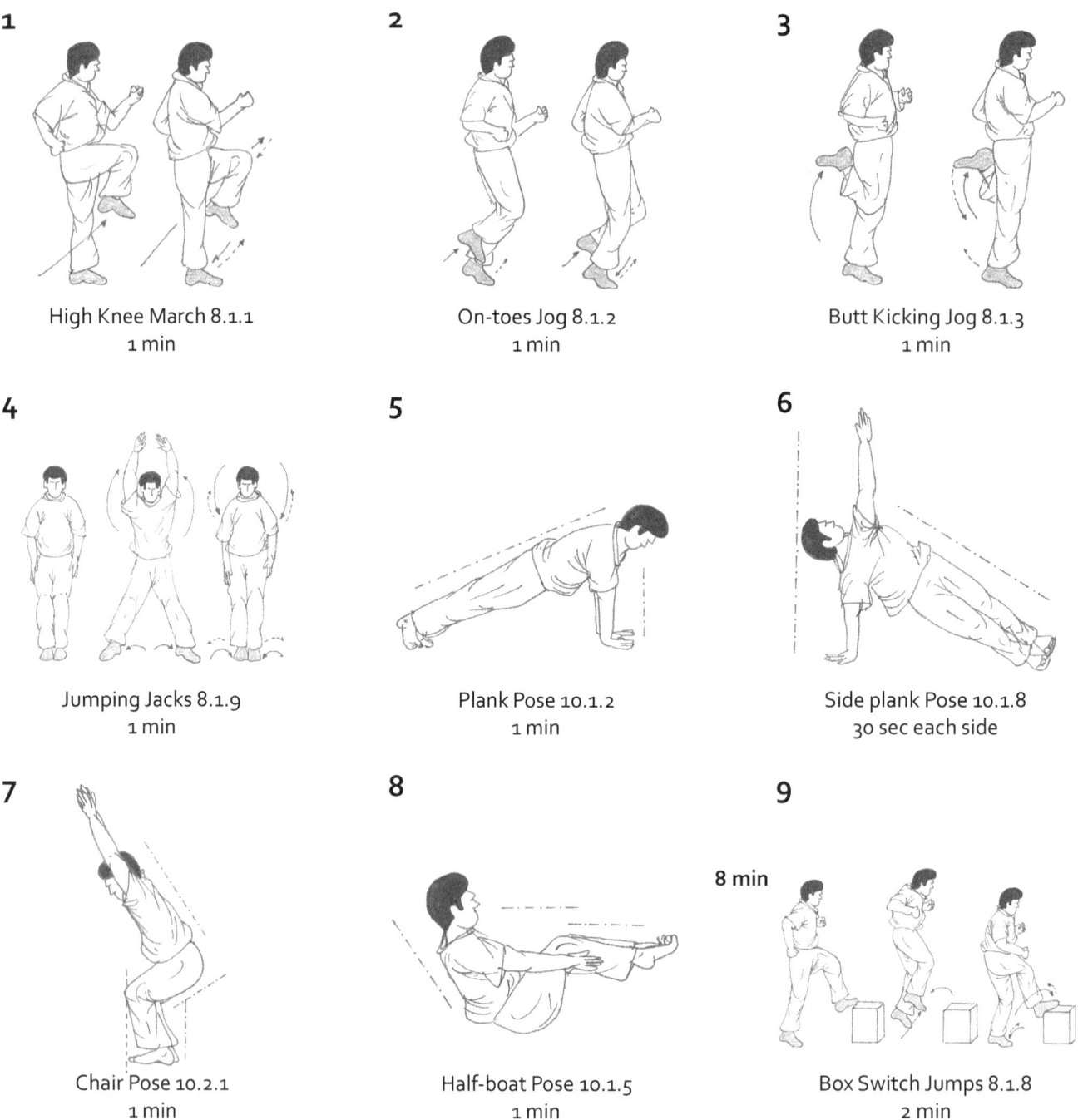

10

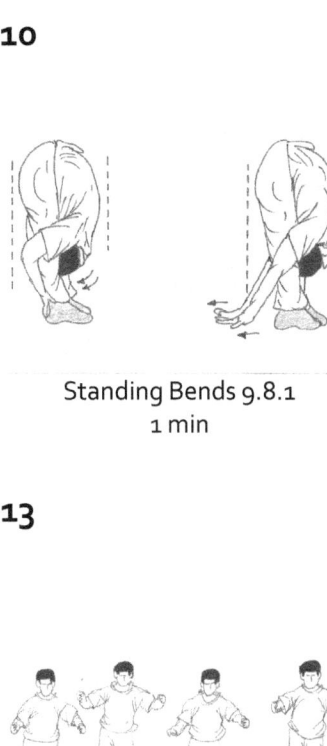

Standing Bends 9.8.1
1 min

11

Hop into Jumps 8.2.7
1 min

12

Frog Long jumps 8.2.11
2 sets of 10

13

1-leg Lateral jumps 8.2.8
3 sets of 5 each side

14

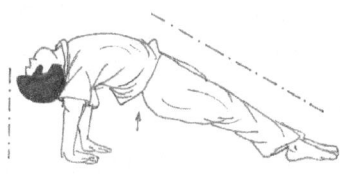

Upward Plank Pose 10.1.4
1 min

15

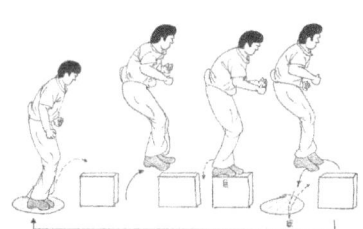

On-box jumps 8.3.1
3 sets of 20

16

On-box 1-leg Jumps 8.3.4
1 set of 10 each side

17

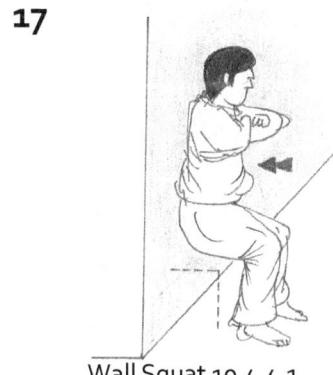

Wall Squat 10.4.4.1
2 sets

18

Crossed-legs Bends 9.2.6
30 sec each side

19

Lateral On-&Off-box 8.3.10
2 sets of 10 jumps each side

20

Box Cross-over jumps 8.3.9
3 sets of 10 jumps each direction

24 min

21

Dumbell Twist 8.5.7
3 sets of 30 twists

PROGRAM 2 DAY 2

22

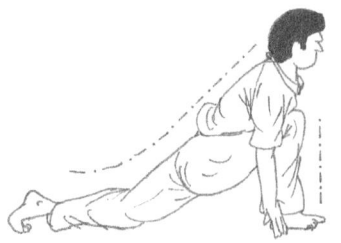

Low Lunge 10.2.7
30 sec each side

23

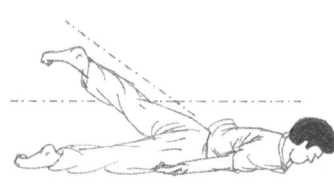

1-leg Locust 10.2.5
30 sec each leg

24

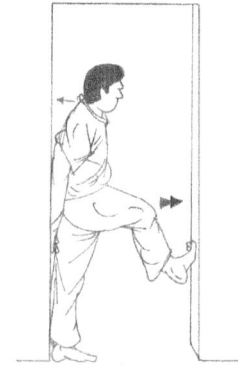

Front Push 10.4.2.5
1 set each leg

25

Back Kick 10.4.2.4
1 set each leg

26

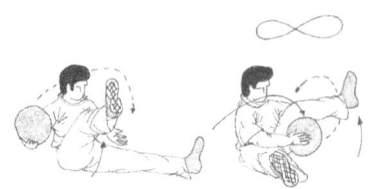

8 around legs Abs 8.7.2
1 set of 10 in each direction

27

Squat to Underhand Throw 8.7.4
2 sets of 10

28

Sitting Ball Rotation 8.7.3
2 sets of 20 circles each direction

29

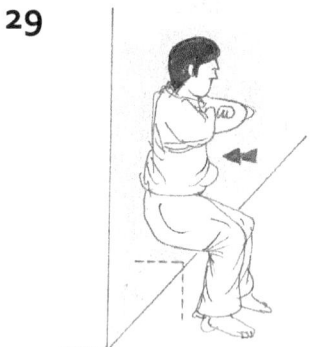

Wall Squat 10.4.4.1
1 rep (again)

30

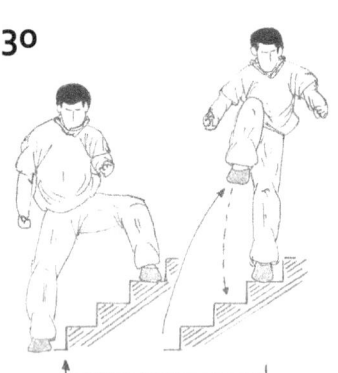

Lateral Stairs Knee-up 8.6.4
10 reps each side

31

Box-off and long 8.3.8
3 sets of 10 jumps

32

Push-ups Burpees 8.1.11
15 reps

43 min

33

Quad Stretch 9.5.1
1 min each leg

34
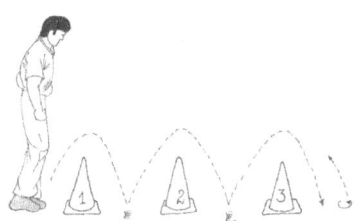
Front Cone jumps in series 8.4.1
4 sets of 10

35

On-box High Jumps 8.3.2
2 sets of 10

36

Split jumps 8.2.12
2 sets of 10 jumps

37
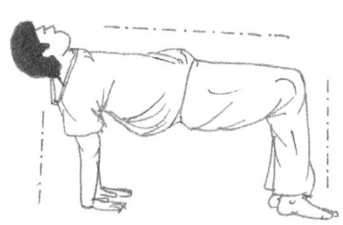
Upward Table Pose 10.1.3
1 min

38

Triangle Pose 9.8.5
1 min each side

39

Bow Pose 9.7.3
1 min

40

Bent-leg Pulls 9.6.6
1 min each side

41
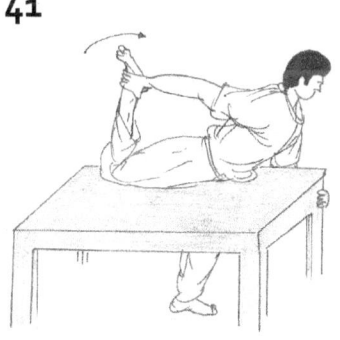
Lying Quad Stretch 9.5.4
30 sec each side

42
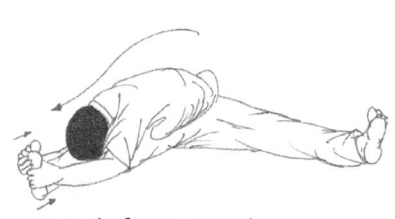
Wide front Stretch 9.4.4
30 sec each side

43
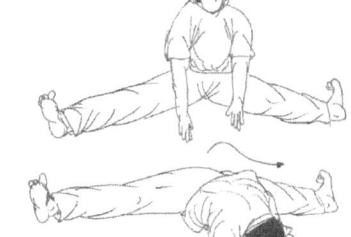
Wide Middle Stretch 9.4.5
1 min

44

Sitting Bends 9.3.1
2 min

PROGRAM 2 DAY 2

12.3.3 DAY 3

Iso and Flexio

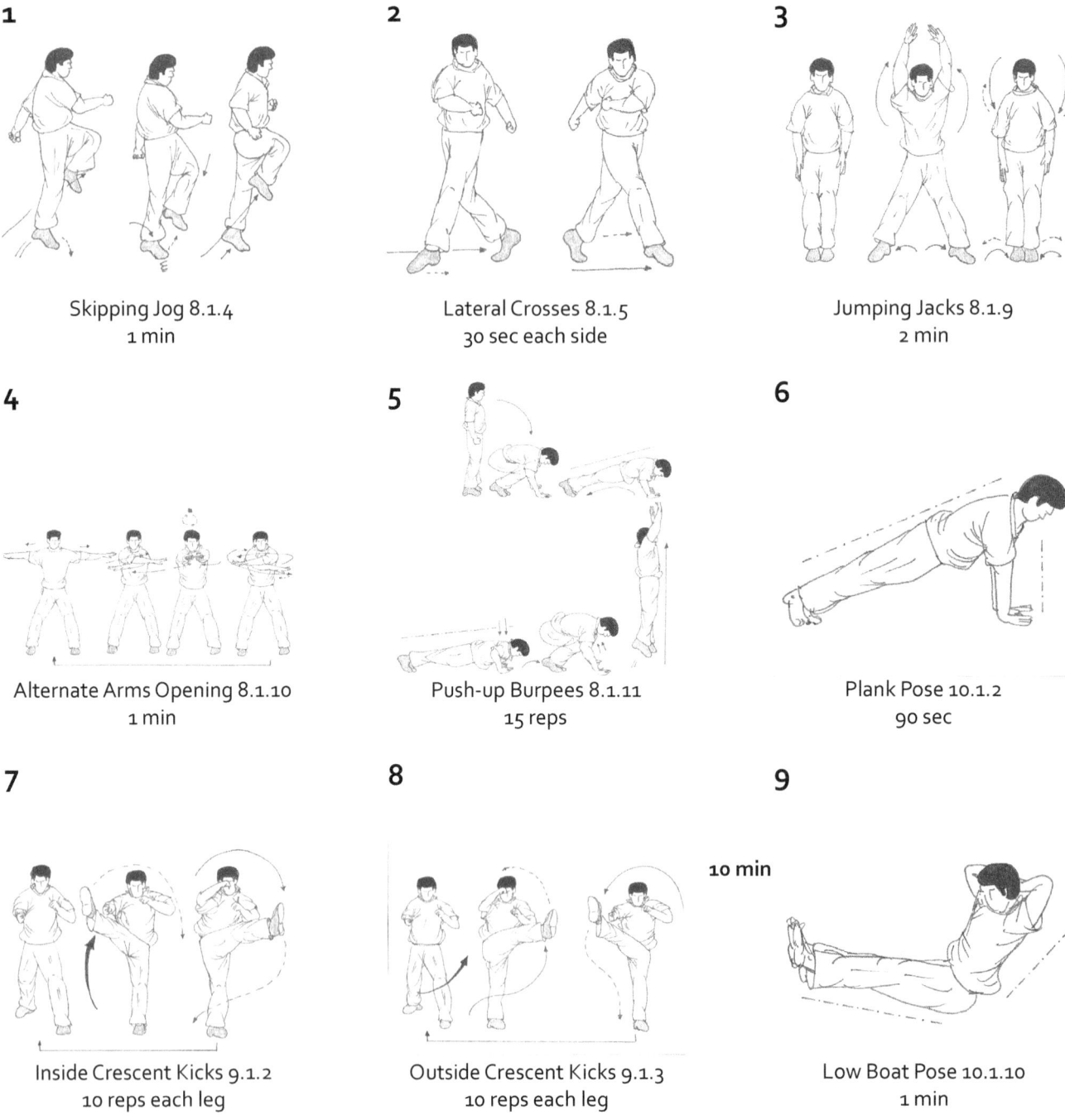

1. Skipping Jog 8.1.4 — 1 min
2. Lateral Crosses 8.1.5 — 30 sec each side
3. Jumping Jacks 8.1.9 — 2 min
4. Alternate Arms Opening 8.1.10 — 1 min
5. Push-up Burpees 8.1.11 — 15 reps
6. Plank Pose 10.1.2 — 90 sec
7. Inside Crescent Kicks 9.1.2 — 10 reps each leg
8. Outside Crescent Kicks 9.1.3 — 10 reps each leg
9. Low Boat Pose 10.1.10 — 1 min

10 min

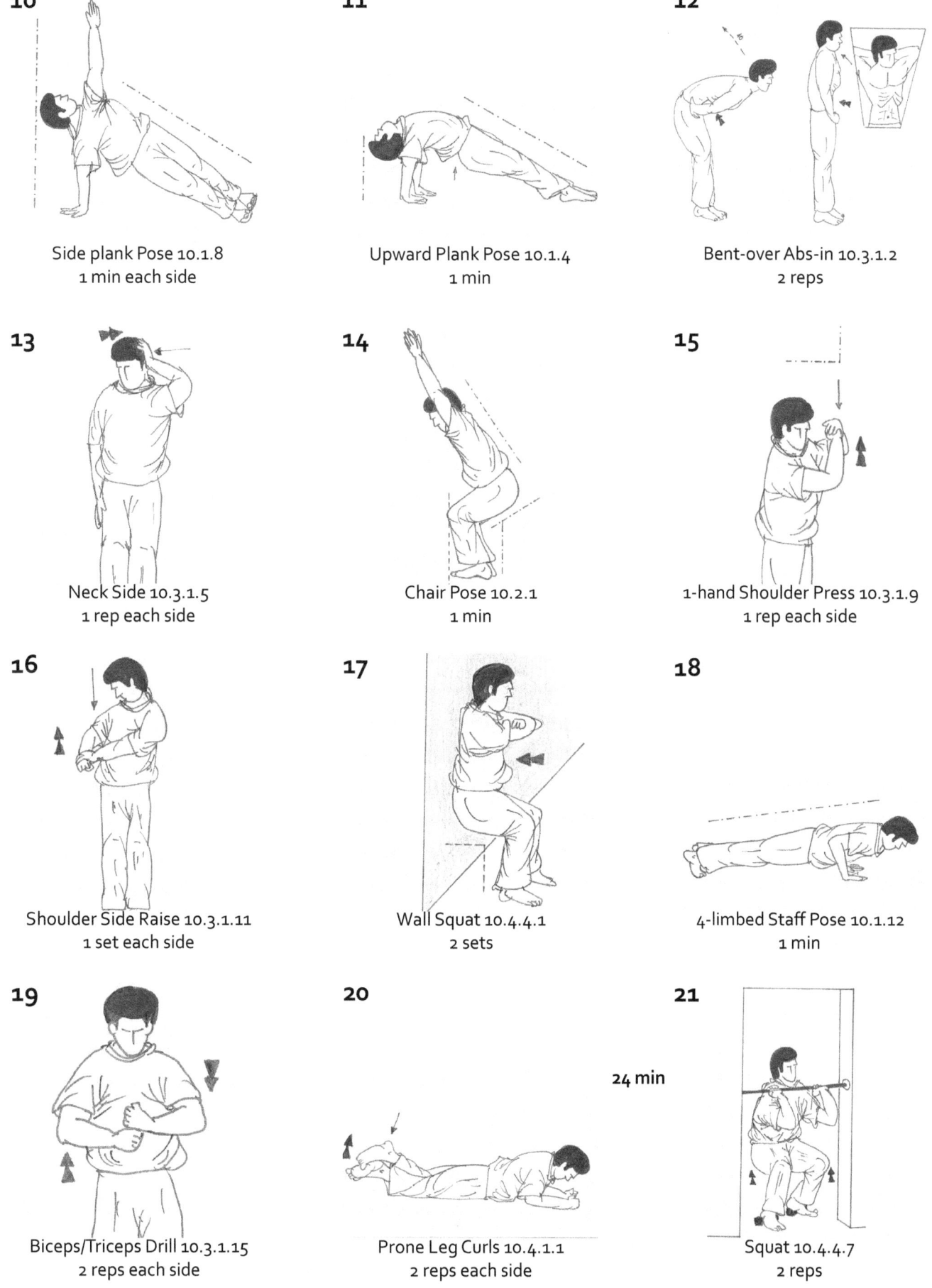

PROGRAM 2 DAY 3

34 High Wall Press 10.3.4.1 — 1 rep	**35** Biceps Curl 10.3.6.6 — 2 reps	**36** 1-leg Locust Pose 10.2.5 — 1 min each side
37 Buddhist Stupa Pose 10.2.4 — 1 min	**38** Front Leg Bends 9.3.5 — 1 min each side (40 min)	**39** Downward Dog Pose 9.9.9 — 1 min
40 Elbow Back Pull 9.9.4 — 1 min each side	**41** Crossed-leg Forward Bend 9.2.6 — 1 min each side	**42** Lying Leg Pulls 9.3.3 — 1 min each side
43 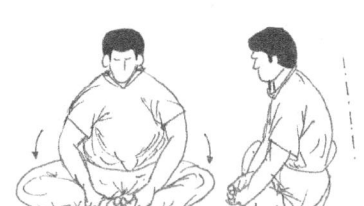 Cobbler Pose 9.4.1 — 1 min	**44**  Seated Twists 9.8.4 — 1 min each side	**45** 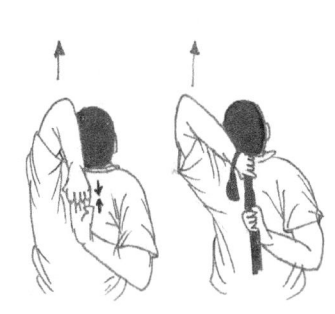 Cow's Face Grips 9.9.8 — 1 min each side (53 min)

PROGRAM 2 DAY 3

46

Camel Stretch 9.7.2
1 min

47

Kneeling Quad Stretch 9.5.2
1 min each side

48

Wide Side Stretch 9.4.3
1 min each side

Motivation is when your dreams put on work clothes.
~Benjamin Franklin

12.3.4 DAY 4 — *Plyos and Upper Body*

1

High-knee March 8.1.1
1 min

2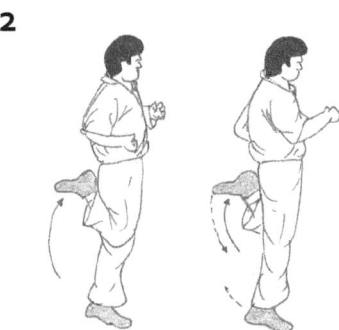

Butt-kicking Jog 8.1.3
1 min

3

Lateral low Hops 8.1.7
30 sec each side

4

Jumping Jacks 8.1.9
1 min

5

Alternate Arms Opening 8.1.10
1 min

6

Push-up Burpees 8.1.11
10 reps

7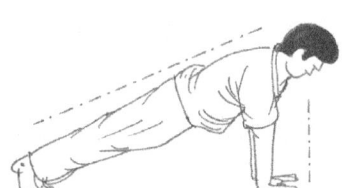

Plank Pose 10.1.2
1 min

8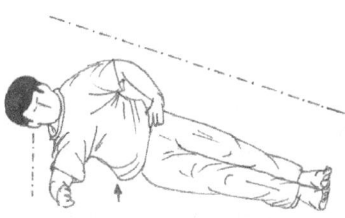

10 min

Side plank on Elbow 10.1.7
1 min each side

9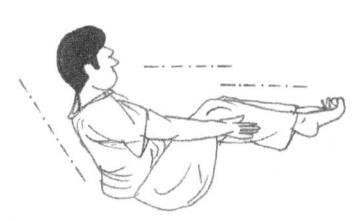

Half-boat Pose 10.1.5
1 min

PROGRAM 2 DAY 4

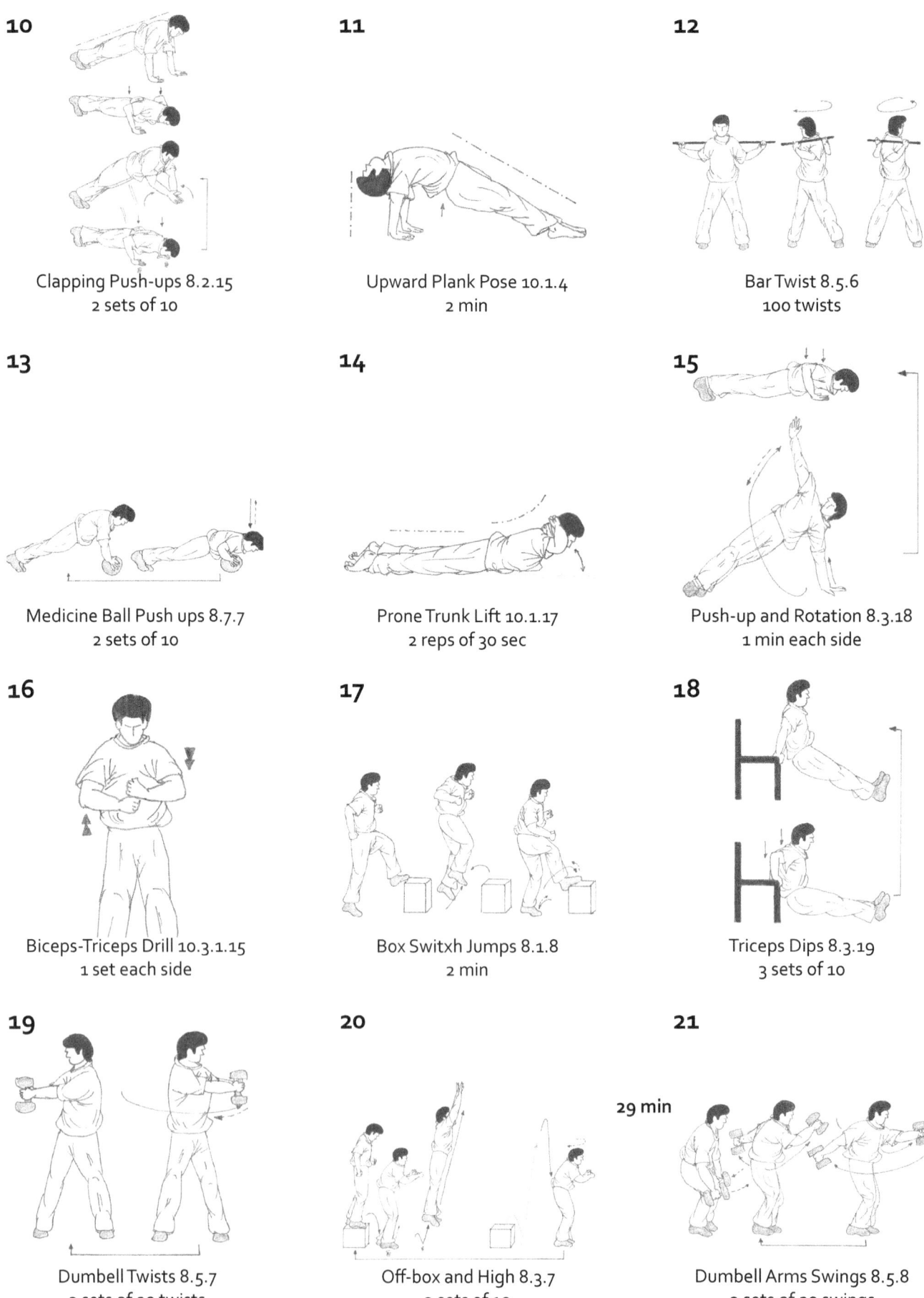

22
1-hand Side Raise 10.3.1.11
2 reps each side

23
Wall Shoulder Stretch 9.9.5
30 sec each side

24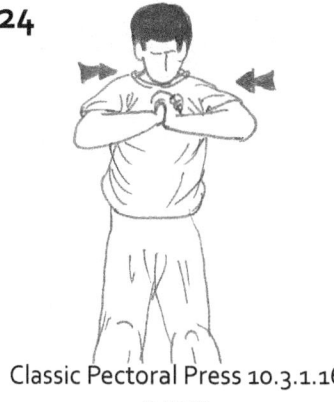
Classic Pectoral Press 10.3.1.16
2 reps

25
Chair Pose 10.2.1
1 min

26
Classic Dorsal Pull 10.3.1.18
2 reps

27
Assymetric Ball Push-ups 8.7.10
15 reps

28
Twisting Lunges 8.7.9
30 lunges

29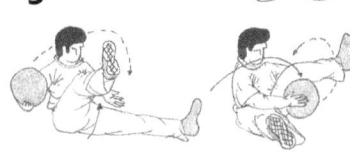
8 around Legs Ab-drill 8.7.2
2 sets of 10 in each direction

30
Overhead Wall Throw 8.7.5
2 sets of 10

31
Sitting Rotation with Ball 8.7.3
2 sets of 20 in each direction

32
44 min

Underhand Wall Throw 8.7.4
3 sets of 10

33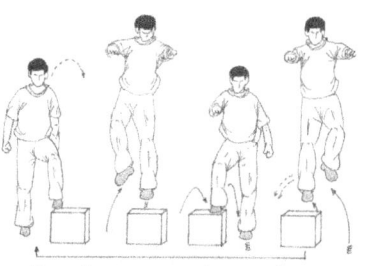
Box Cross-over Jumps 8.3.9
3 sets of 20 jumps

PROGRAM 2 DAY 4

34

AlternateArms Opening 8.1.10
2 min (again)

35

4-limbed Staff Pose 10.1.12
1 min

36

50 min

Pectoral Table Stretch 9.9.2
1 min

37

Downward Dog 9.9.9
1 min

38

Triangle Pose 9.8.5
30 sec each side

39

Inverted Triangle Pose 9.8.6
1 min each side

40

Plough pose 9.8.2
1 min

41

Back Namaste 9.9.7
1 min

42

Side Praying Grips 9.9.10
30 sec each side

43

Cobra Stretch 9.7.1
1 min

12.3.5 DAY 5 — Iso and Lower Body

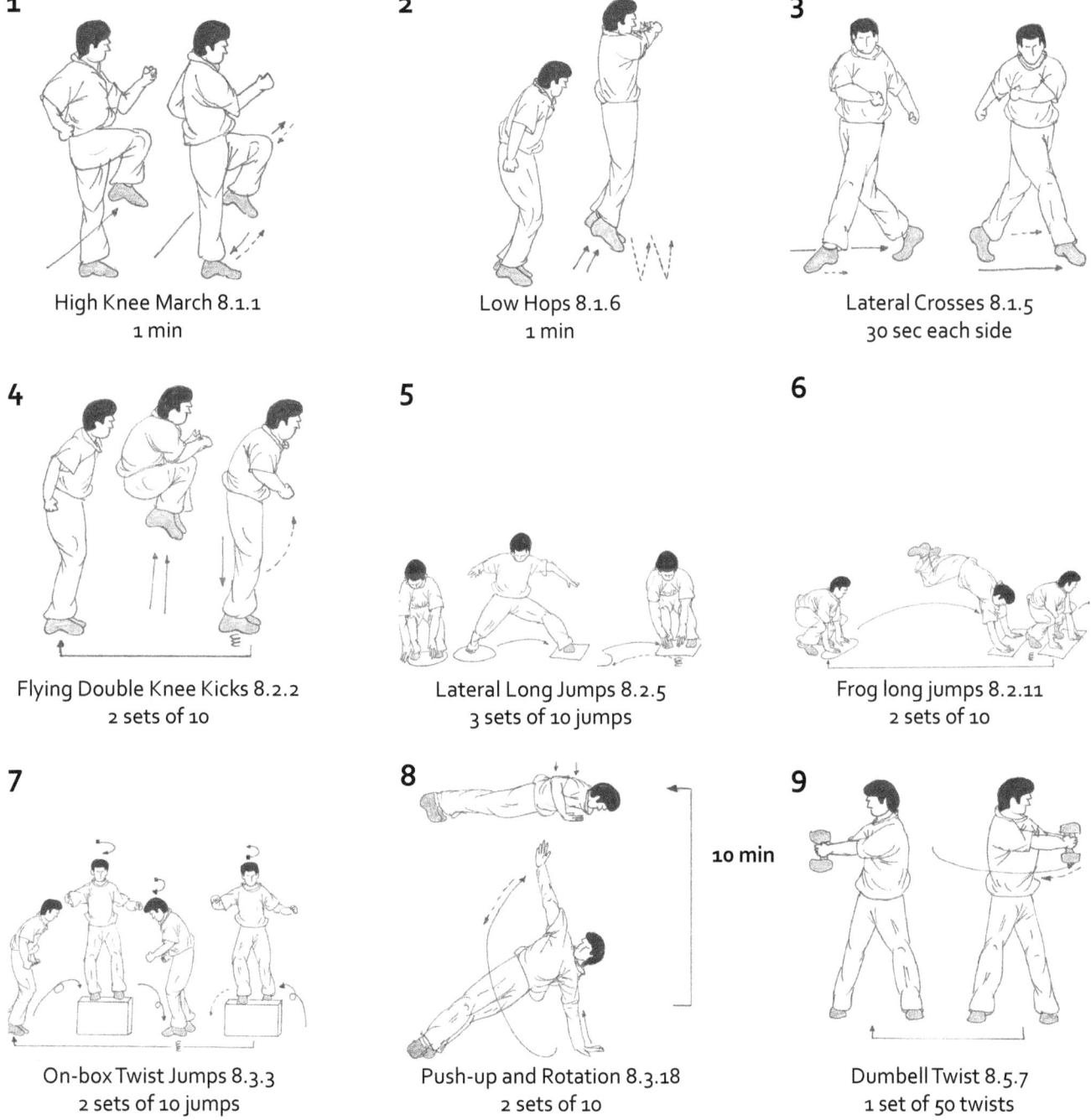

1. High Knee March 8.1.1 — 1 min
2. Low Hops 8.1.6 — 1 min
3. Lateral Crosses 8.1.5 — 30 sec each side
4. Flying Double Knee Kicks 8.2.2 — 2 sets of 10
5. Lateral Long Jumps 8.2.5 — 3 sets of 10 jumps
6. Frog long jumps 8.2.11 — 2 sets of 10
7. On-box Twist Jumps 8.3.3 — 2 sets of 10 jumps
8. Push-up and Rotation 8.3.18 — 2 sets of 10
9. Dumbell Twist 8.5.7 — 1 set of 50 twists

10 min

22
Twisting lunges 8.7.9
3 sets of 10

23
Squat Wall Throw 8.7.4
3 sets of 10

24
Stairs Knee-ups 8.6.4
2 sets of 15 each side

25
Standing Front Bend 9.1.7
1 min

26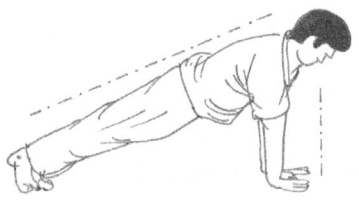
Plank Pose 10.1.2
1 min

27
Low Lunge 10.2.7
1 min each side

28
Prone Leg Curls 10.4.1.1
2 reps each side

29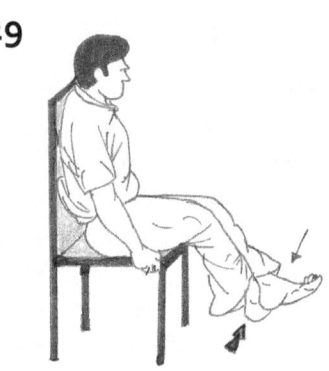
Leg Extensions 10.4.3.1
2 reps each side

30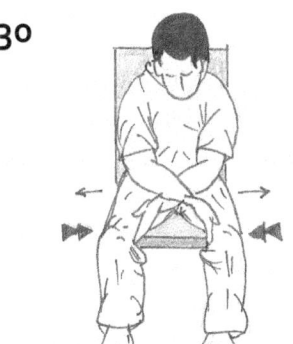
Inner Thigh Press 10.4.3.2
2 reps

31
Wall Squat on toes 10.4.4.2
3 reps

32
Lateral Wall Throw 8.7.6
2 sets of 5 each side

33 38 min
Squat 10.4.5.1
2 reps

PROGRAM 2 DAY 5

46

Sitting Wide Front Stretch 9.4.4
30 sec each side

47

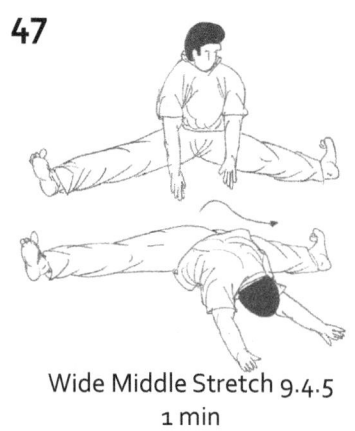

Wide Middle Stretch 9.4.5
1 min

48

Hero's Pose 9.2.2
1 min

**He who would arrive at the appointed end must follow a single road and not wander through many ways.
~Seneca**

12.3.6 DAY 6 — *Plyo and Flexio*

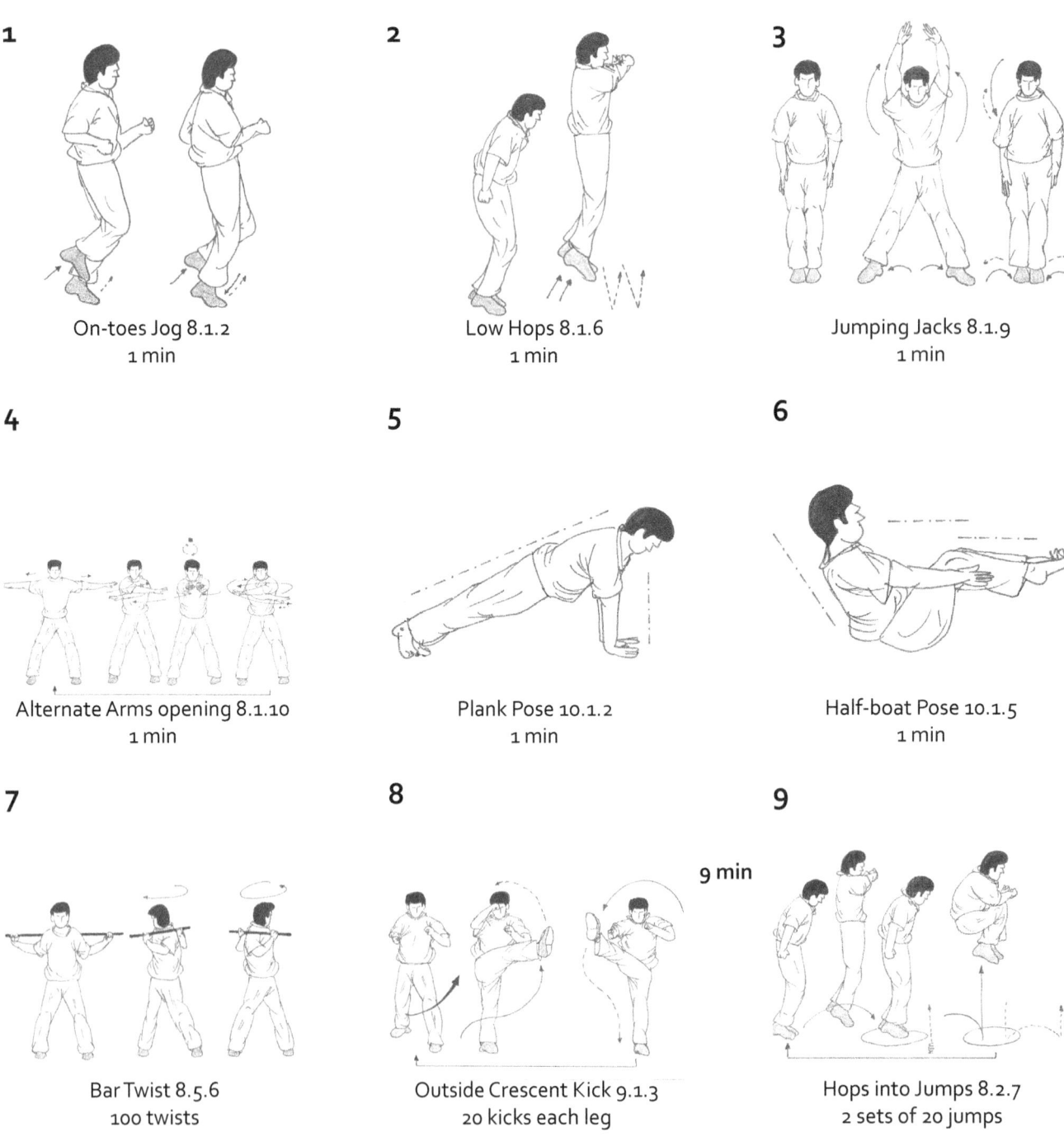

10

On-box Twist Jumps 8.3.3
2 sets of 20 jumps

11

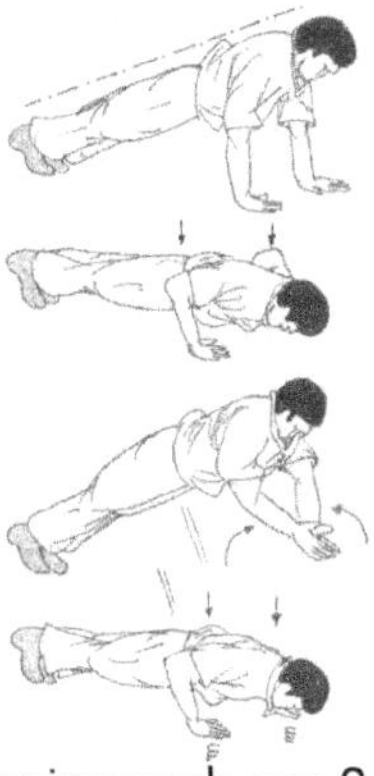

Clapping push-ups 8.2.15
3 sets of 10

12

Box-off and High 8.3.7
3 sets of 10

13

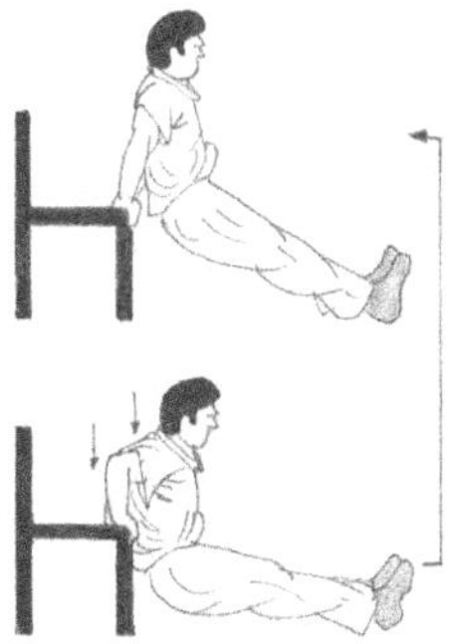

Triceps Dips 8.3.19
3 sets of 20

14

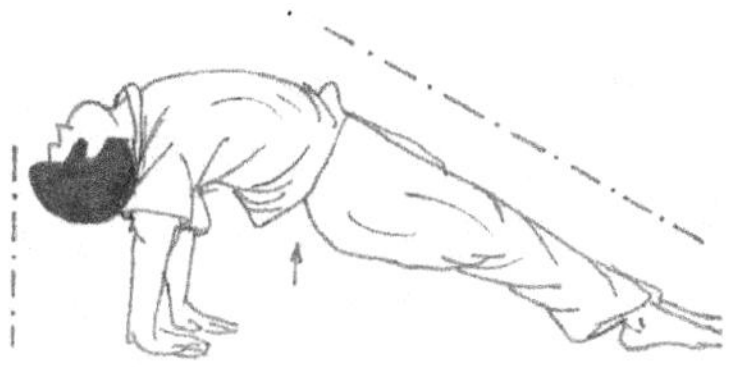

Upward Plank Pose 10.1.4
1 min

15

Box-off and Long 8.3.8
2 sets of 10

16

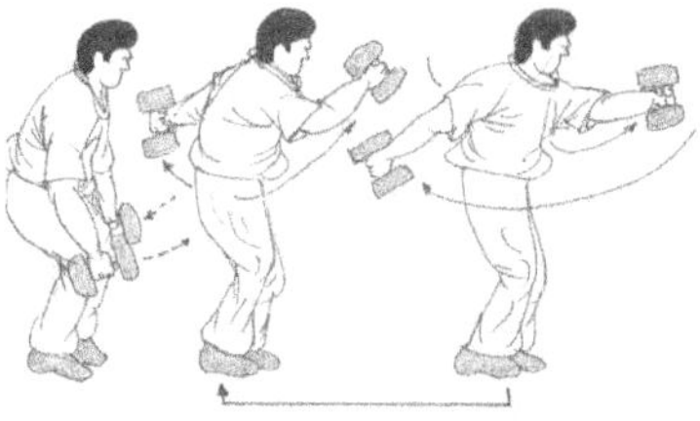

Dumbell Arms Swings 8.5.8
3 sets of 20 swings

17

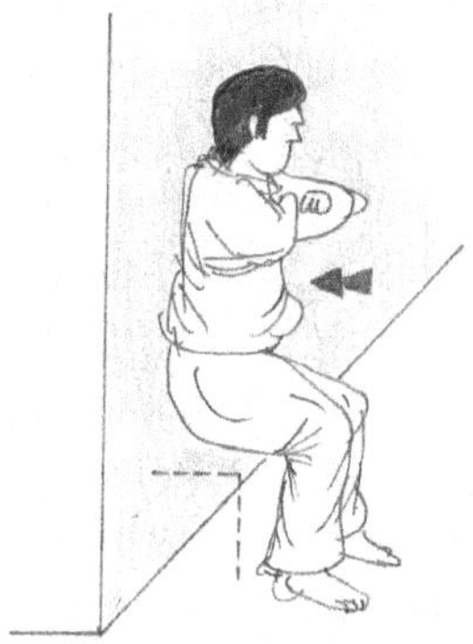

Wall Squat 10.4.4.1
2 sets

18

Flying Twists 8.2.4
3 sets of 10

19

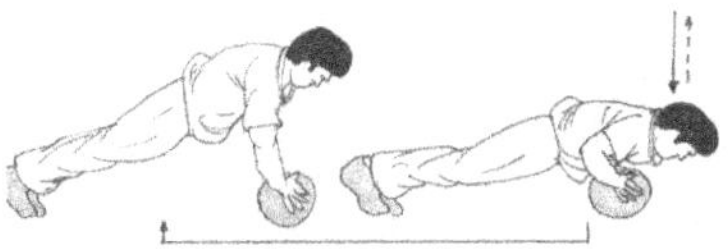

Medicine Ball Push-ups 8.7.7
2 sets of 10

20

On-box 1-leg Jumps 8.3.4
10 jumps per leg

22 min

21

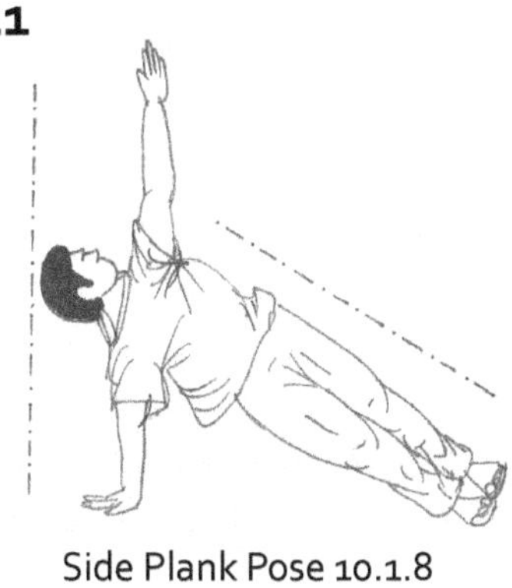

Side Plank Pose 10.1.8
1 min each side

PROGRAM 2 DAY 6

22

Twisting Lunges 8.7.9
3 sets of 10

23

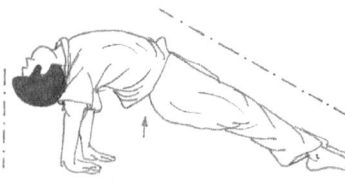

Upward Plank Pose 10.1.4
1 min

24

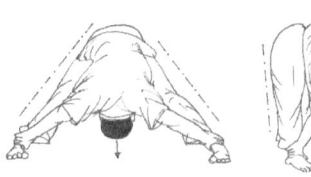

Open Legs Front Bends 9.3.7
1 min

25

Stairs Knee-up 8.6.4
2 sets of 10 climbs each side

26

Back Namaste 9.9.7
1 min

27

8 around Legs Abs Drill 8.7.2
20 "8" each side

28

Overhead Wall Throw 8.7.5
3 sets of 10

29

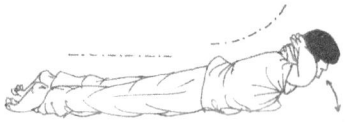

Prone Trunk Lift 10.1.17
2 sets of 30 sec

30

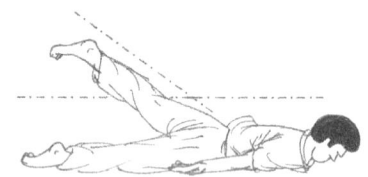

1-leg Locust Pose 10.2.5
30 sec each leg

31

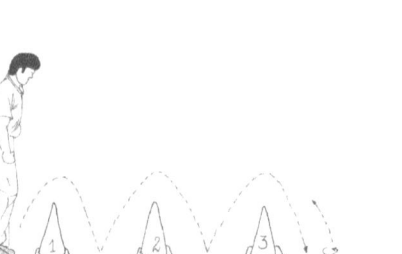

Cone Jumps in series 8.4.1
3 sets of 10 jumps

32

Push-up and Rotation 8.3.18
2 sets of 10 push-ups

33

38 min

Box Cross-over Jumps 8.3.9
3 sets of 20 jumps

12.4 THIRD PROGRAM: The Intermediate

Now that you are more familiar with Isoplex Training, it is time to keep increasing the level gradually: more difficult, longer drills *and less rest in-between*. Even if you it feel easy, do this program for a month before going to the next level.

12.4.1 DAY 1 — Iso and Upper body

1. High-knees March 8.1.1 — 1 min
2. Alternate Arms Opening 8.1.10 — 1 min
3. Jumping Jacks 8.1.9 — 2 min
4. Burpees 8.1.11 — 20 reps
5. Plank Pose 10.1.2 — 90 sec
6. Pendulum Kick 9.1.1 — 2 sets of 15 each leg
7. Clapping Push-ups 8.2.15 — 3 sets of 10
8. Hops into Jumps 8.2.7 — 1 min
9. Downward Dog 9.2.3 — 1 min

10 min

10

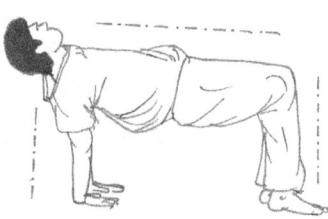

Upward Table Pose 10.1.3
90 sec

11

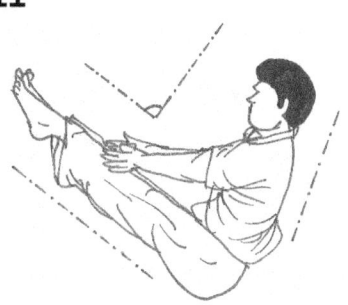

High Boat Pose 10.1.13
1 min

12

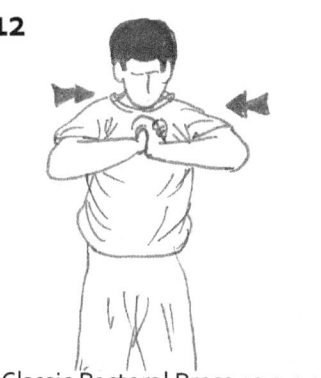

Classic Pectoral Press 10.3.1.16
2 reps

13

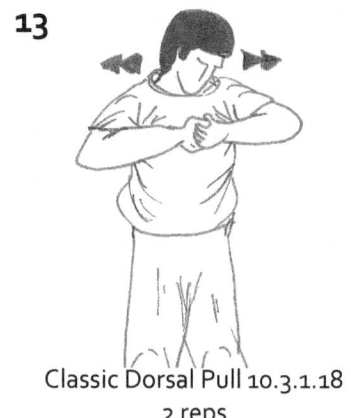

Classic Dorsal Pull 10.3.1.18
2 reps

14

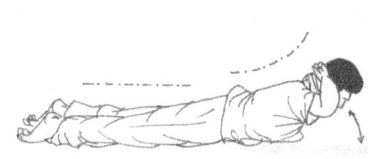

Prone Trunk Lift 10.1.17
1 min

15

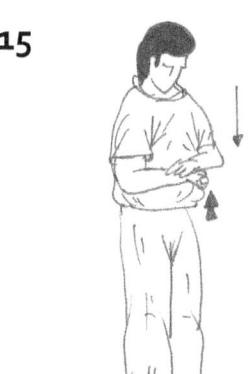

Biceps Curl 10.3.1.13
2 reps each side

16

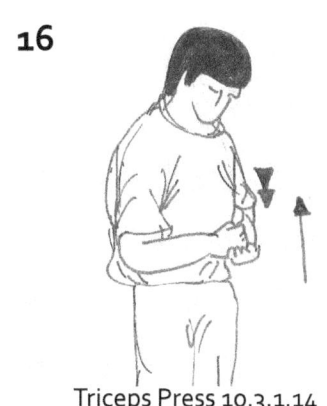

Triceps Press 10.3.1.14
2 reps each side

17

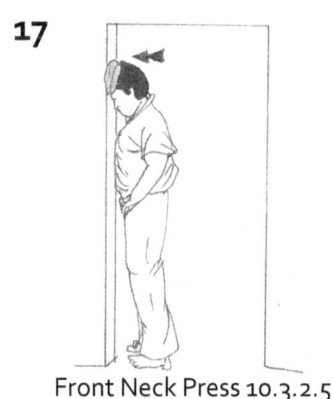

Front Neck Press 10.3.2.5
1 rep

18

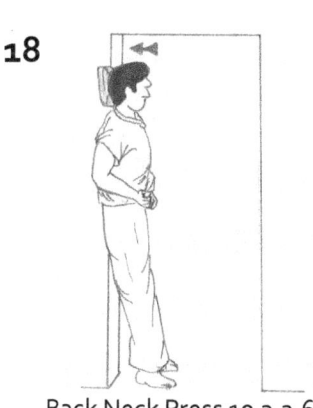

Back Neck Press 10.3.2.6
1 rep

19

Forearm Curls 10.3.1.20
1 rep each side

20

Forearm Reverse Curls 10.3.1.21
1 rep each side

21

22 min

4-limbed Staff Pose 10.1.12
1 min

PROGRAM 3 DAY 1

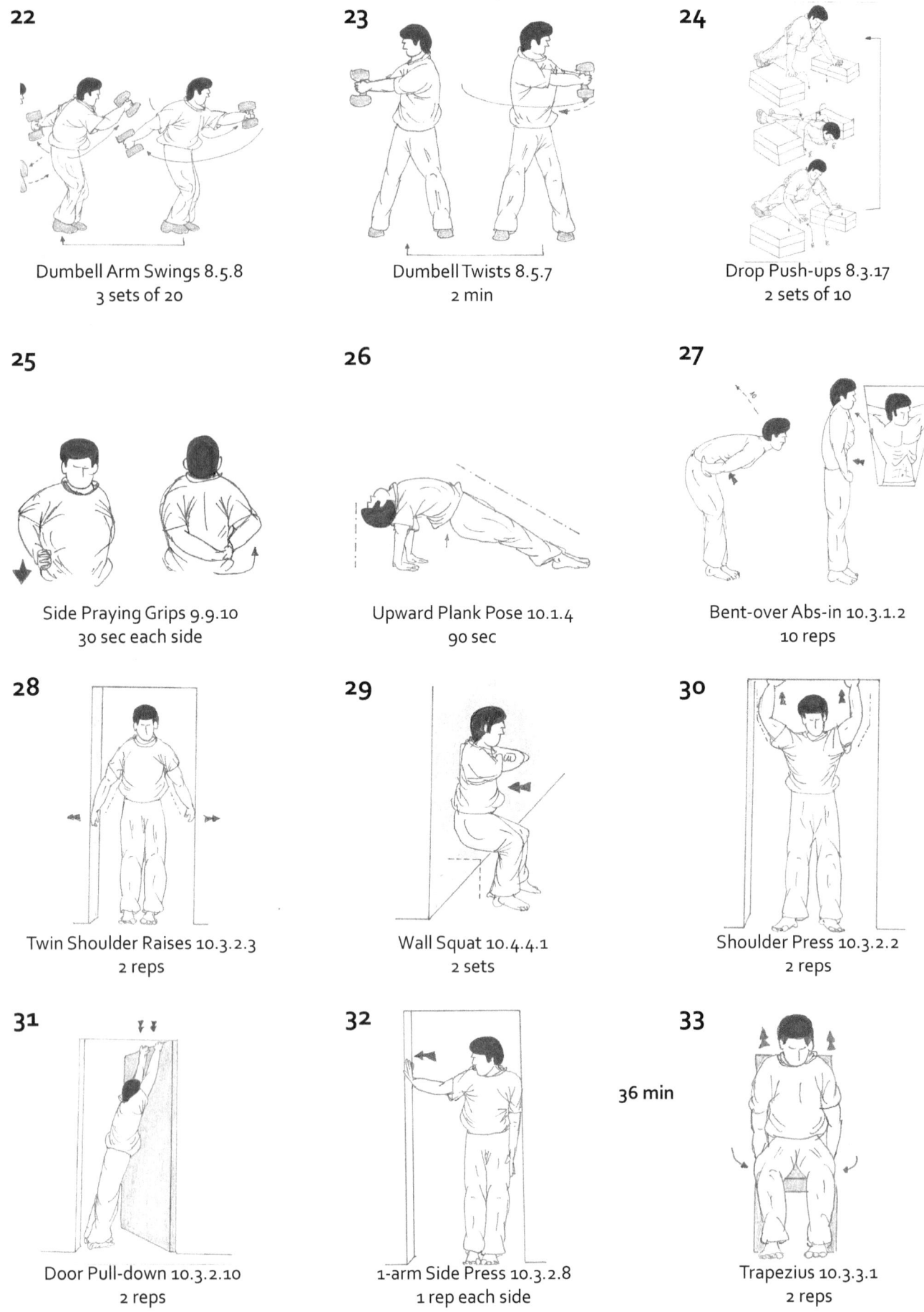

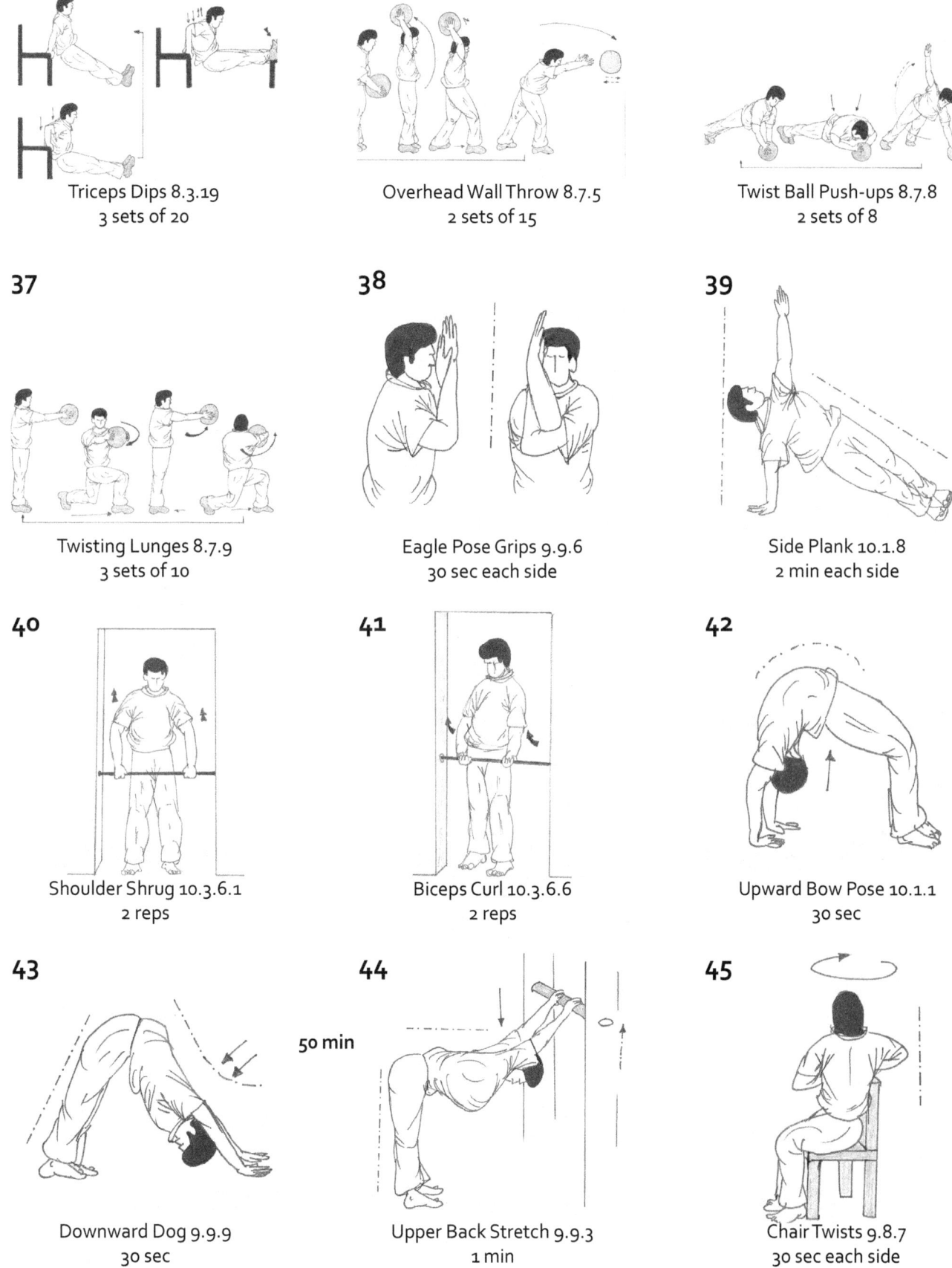

PROGRAM 3 DAY 1

| 46 Triangle Pose 9.8.5 — 30 sec each side |
| 47 Waist Twists 9.6.5 — 1 min each side |
| 48 Back Namaste 9.9.7 — 1 min |
| 49 Wide 1-leg Front Stretch 9.4.4 — 1 min each side |
| 50 Elbows Vise 9.9.11 — 1 min |
| 51 Crossed Side Bends 9.6.8 — 1 min each side |

Change your life today. Don't gamble on the future, act now, without delay.
~Simone de Beauvoir

12.4.2 DAY 2 — *Plyo and Lower body*

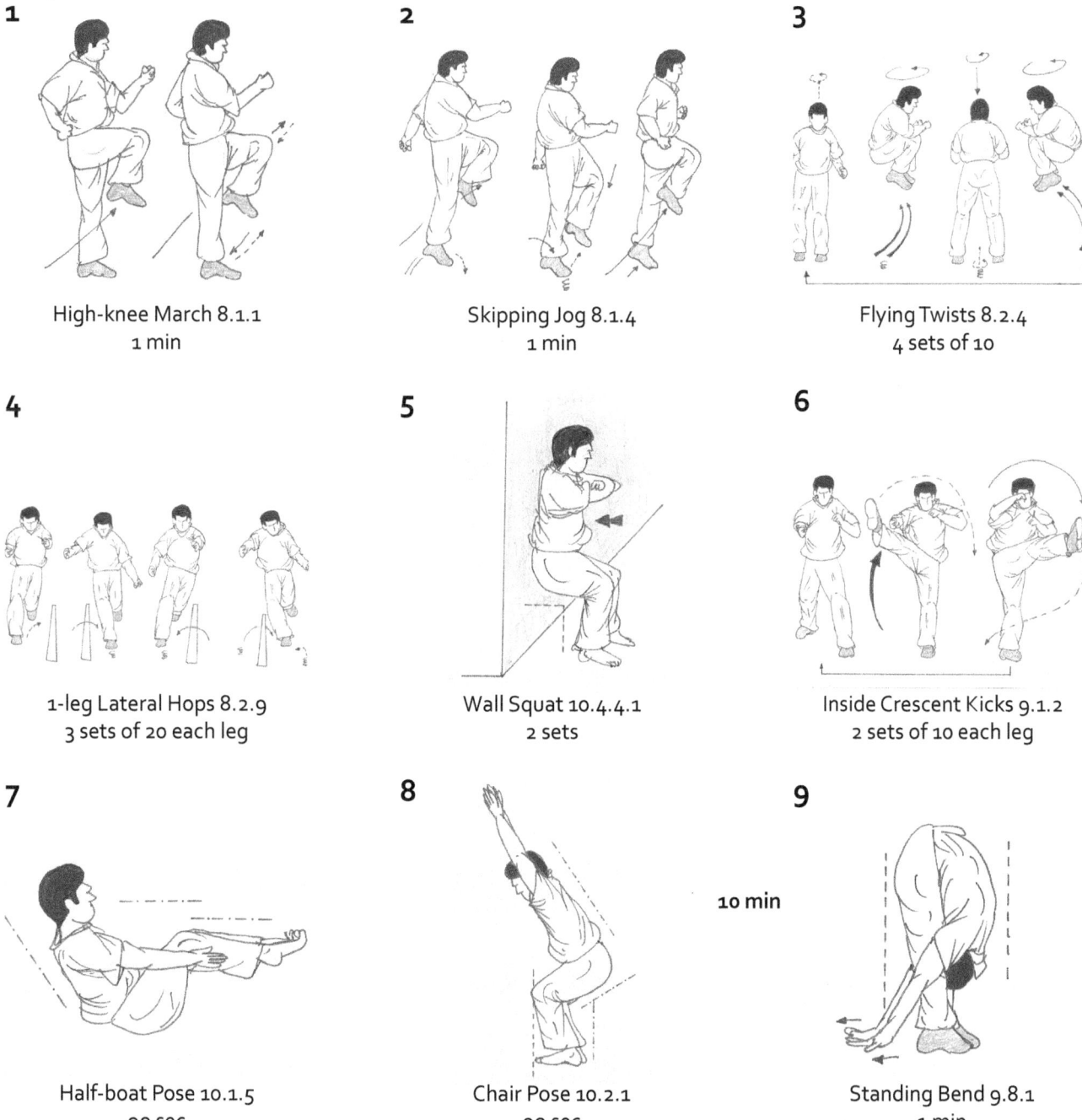

1. High-knee March 8.1.1 — 1 min
2. Skipping Jog 8.1.4 — 1 min
3. Flying Twists 8.2.4 — 4 sets of 10
4. 1-leg Lateral Hops 8.2.9 — 3 sets of 20 each leg
5. Wall Squat 10.4.4.1 — 2 sets
6. Inside Crescent Kicks 9.1.2 — 2 sets of 10 each leg
7. Half-boat Pose 10.1.5 — 90 sec
8. Chair Pose 10.2.1 — 90 sec
9. Standing Bend 9.8.1 — 1 min

10 min

PROGRAM 3 DAY 2

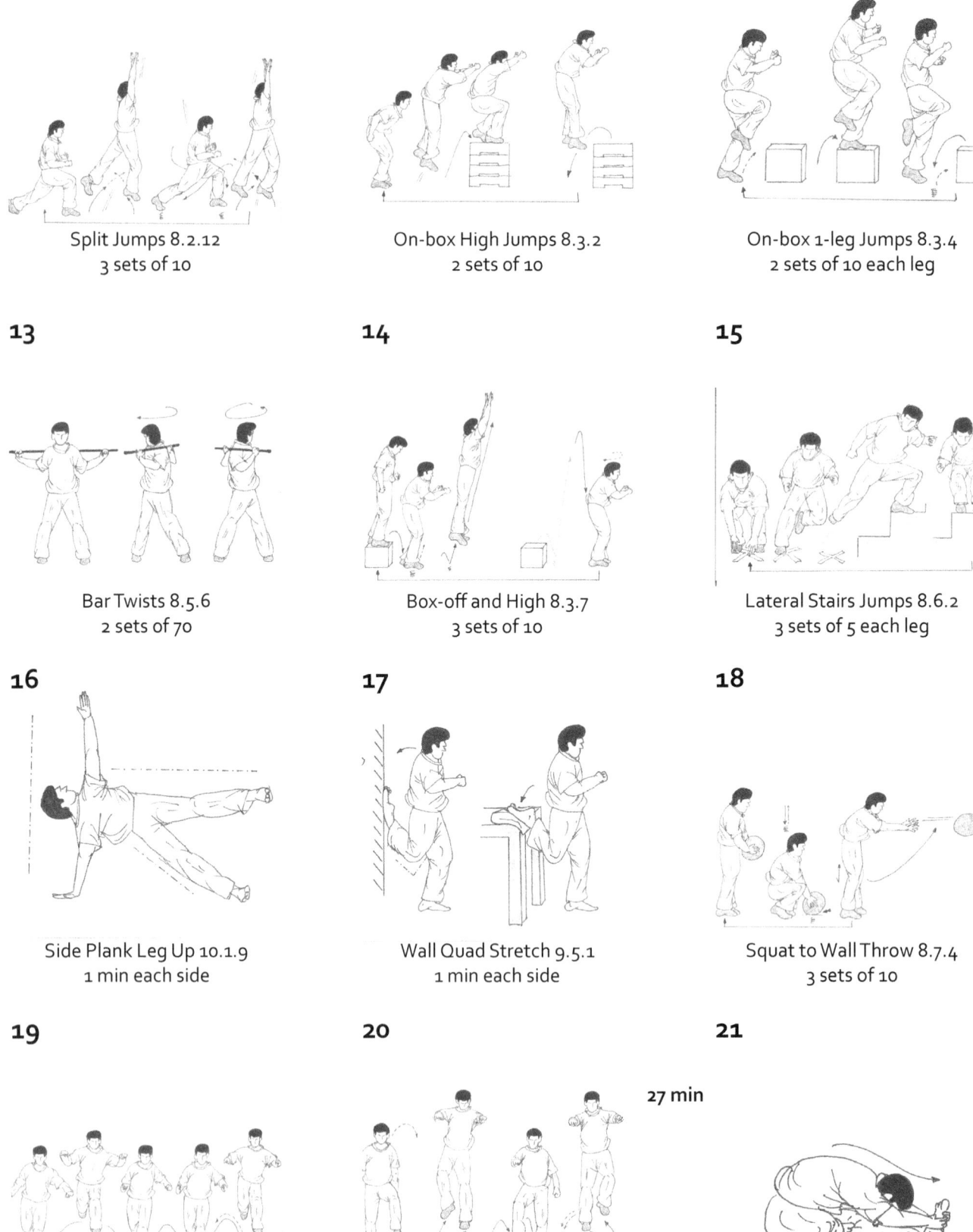

34

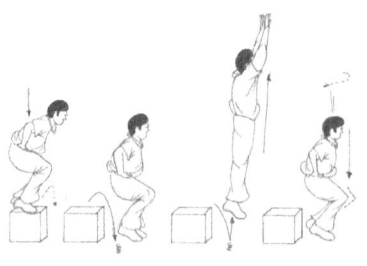

Off-box Squat to High 8.3.13
2 sets of 10

35

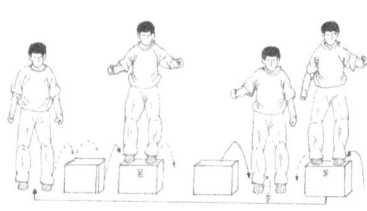

Lateral On/Off-box 8.3.10
3 sets of 5 each side

36

Off-box and Long 8.3.8
3 sets of 10

37

Standing Side Bends 9.1.8
30 sec each side

38

Front Push 10.4.2.5
1 set each leg

49 min

39

Back kick 10.4.2.4
2 sets each side

40

Forward Bend Leg-up 10.2.9
30 sec each side

41

Inverted Triangle 9.8.6
1 min each side

42

Lying Leg Twists 9.6.4
1 min each side

43

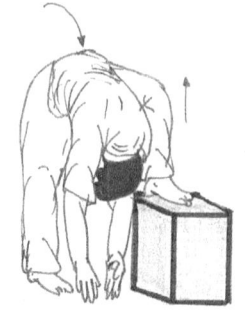

1-leg Chair Bends 9.4.9
1 min each side

44

Wide Middle Stretch 9.4.5
2 min

45

Wide Side Stretch 9.4.3
1 min each side

12.4.3 DAY 3

Iso and Flexio

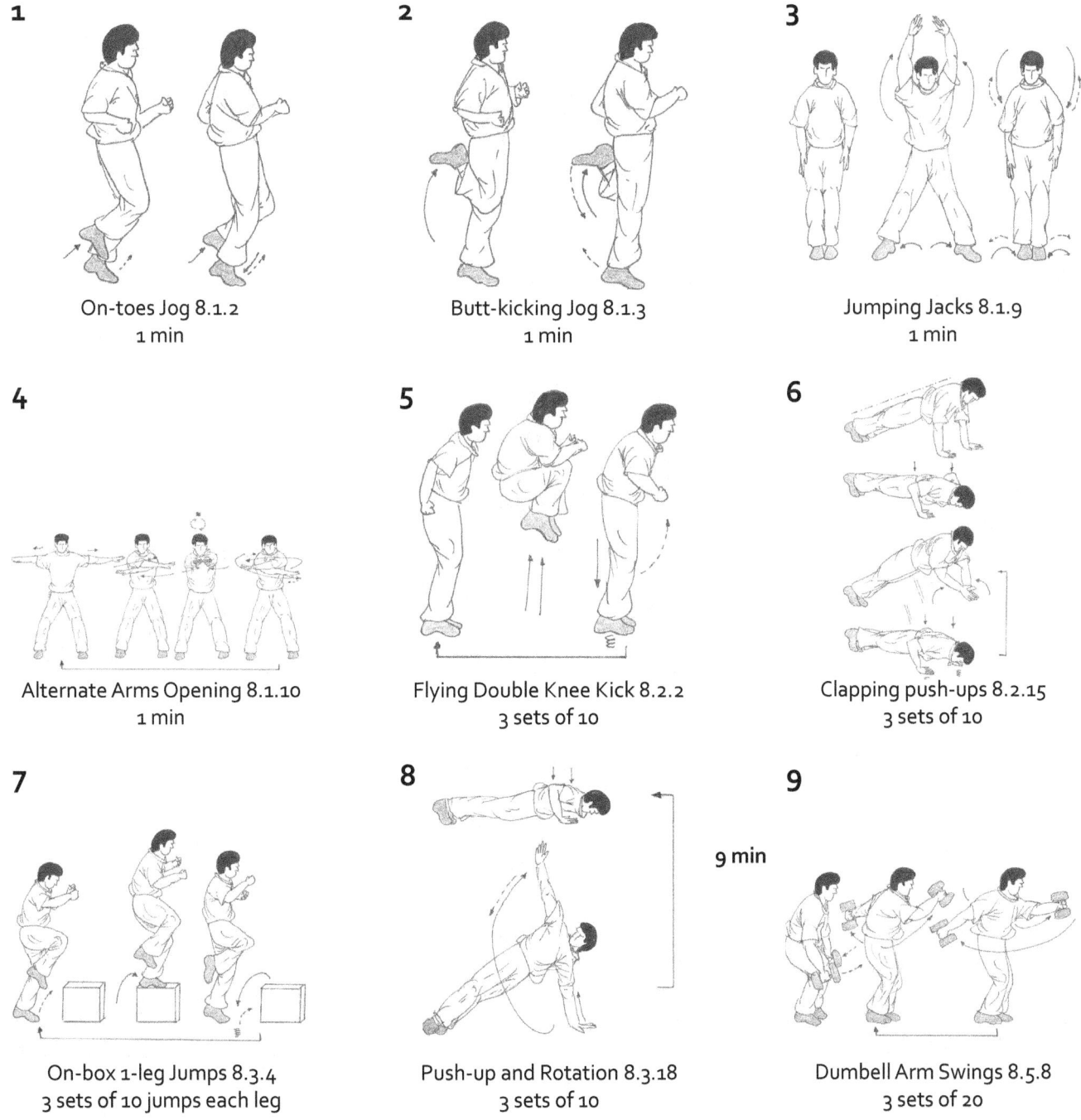

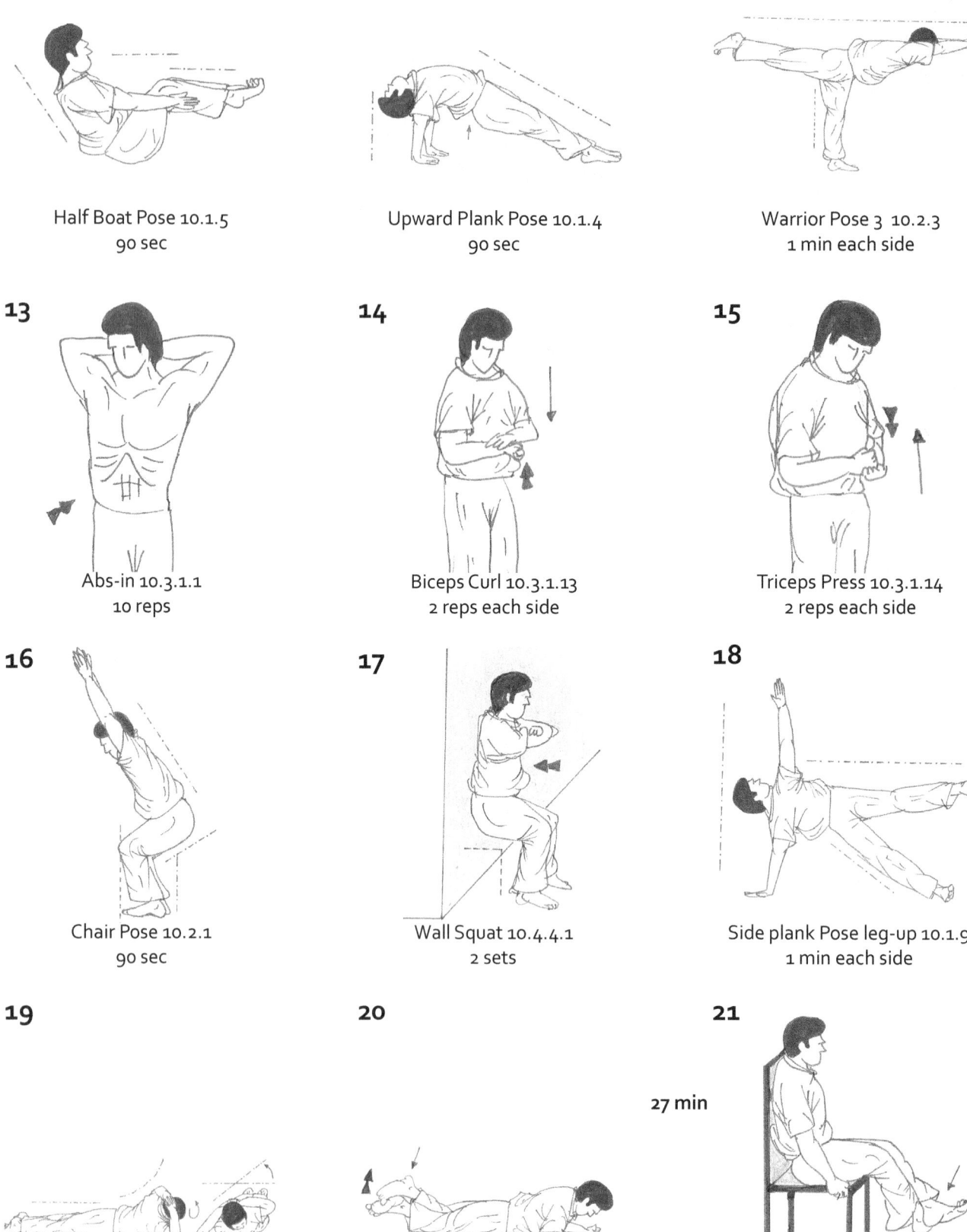

PROGRAM 3 DAY 3

46

Cow's Face Grips 9.9.8
1 min each side

47

Cobbler's Pose 9.4.1
1 min

48

2-legged Stretch 9.2.5
1 min

12.4.4 DAY 4 — *Plyos and Upper Body*

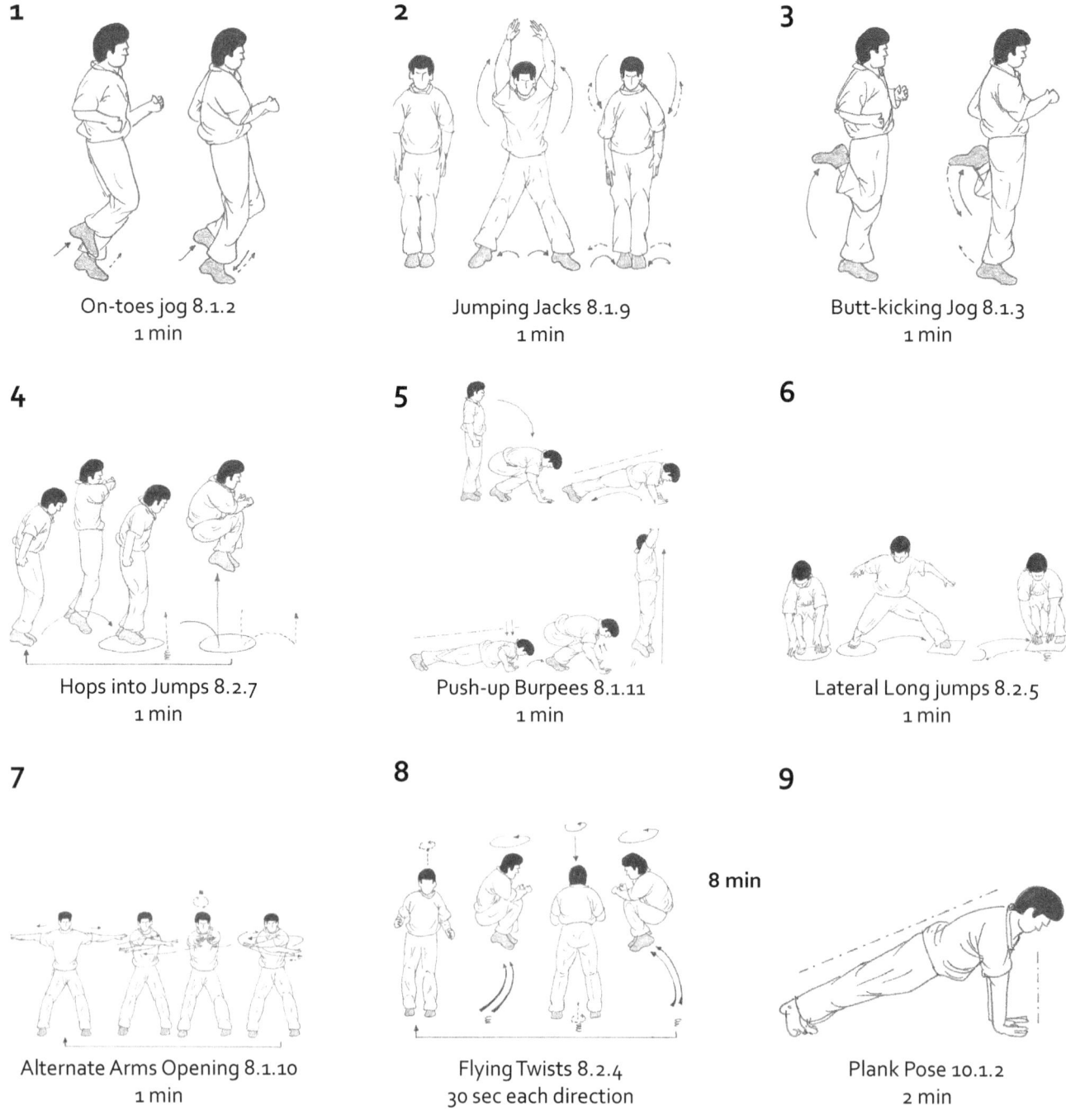

10

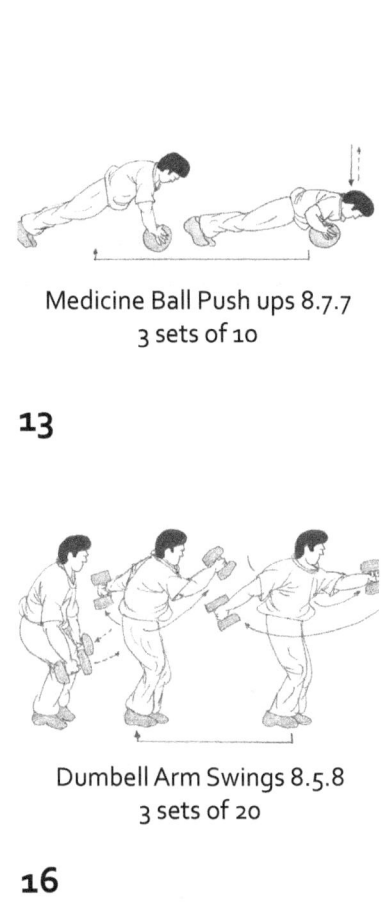

Medicine Ball Push ups 8.7.7
3 sets of 10

11

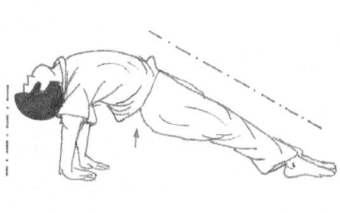

Upward Plank Pose 10.1.4
90 sec

12

Twisting lunges 8.7.9
4 sets of 10

13

Dumbell Arm Swings 8.5.8
3 sets of 20

14

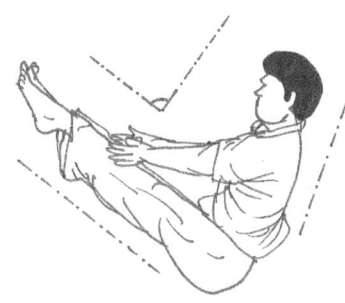

High Boat pose 10.1.13
1 min

15

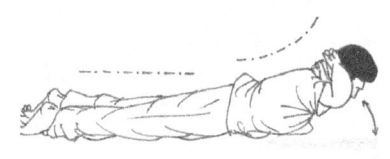

Prone Trunk Lift 10.1.17
1 min

16

Overhead Wall Throw 8.7.5
3 sets of 10

17

Lateral Wall Throw 8.7.6
3 sets of 10

18

Sitting Trunk Rotation 8.7.3
5 sets of 20

19

Assymetric Ball Push-ups 8.7.10
3 sets of 10

20

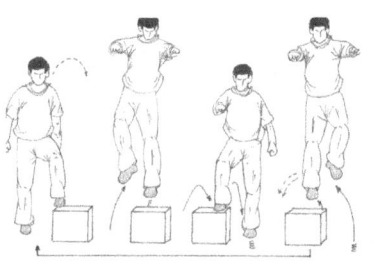

Box Cross-over Jumps 8.3.9
1 min

21

26 min

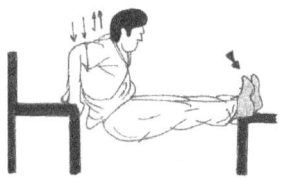

High-feet Triceps Dips 8.3.19
4 sets of 20

PROGRAM 3 DAY 4

22

Side Praying Grips 9.9.10
1 min each side

23

Downward Dog Pose 9.9.9
1 min

24

Side plank Leg-up 10.1.9
1 min each side

25

Twist and Switch Push-ups 8.7.8
2 sets of 10

26

Squat to Underhand Throw 8.7.4
3 sets of 10

27

Back Namaste 9.9.7
1 min

28

Bar Twist 8.5.6
2 min

29

42 min

Clapping Depth push-ups 8.3.16
3 sets of 10

30

Lateral Neck Stretches 9.9.12
30 sec each side

31

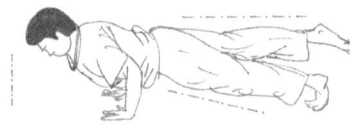

Leg-up Staff pose 10.1.11
1 min each side

32

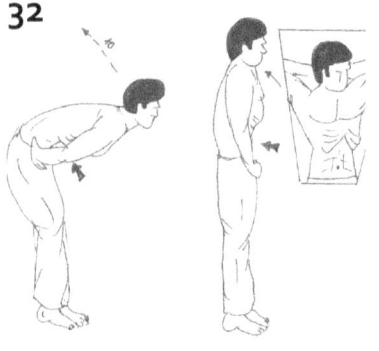

48 min

Bent-over Abs-in 10.3.1.2
10 reps

33

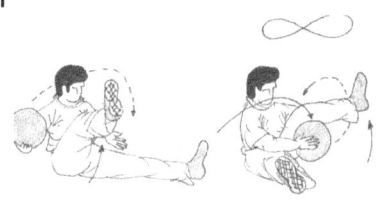

8-around Legs Abs 8.7.2
2 sets of 20

218 **THE ISOPLEX METHOD**

**Success isn't always about greatness; it's about consistency. Consistent hard work gains success. Greatness will come.
~Dwayne 'The Rock' Johnson**

PROGRAM 3 DAY 4

12.4.5 DAY 5 — Iso and Lower Body

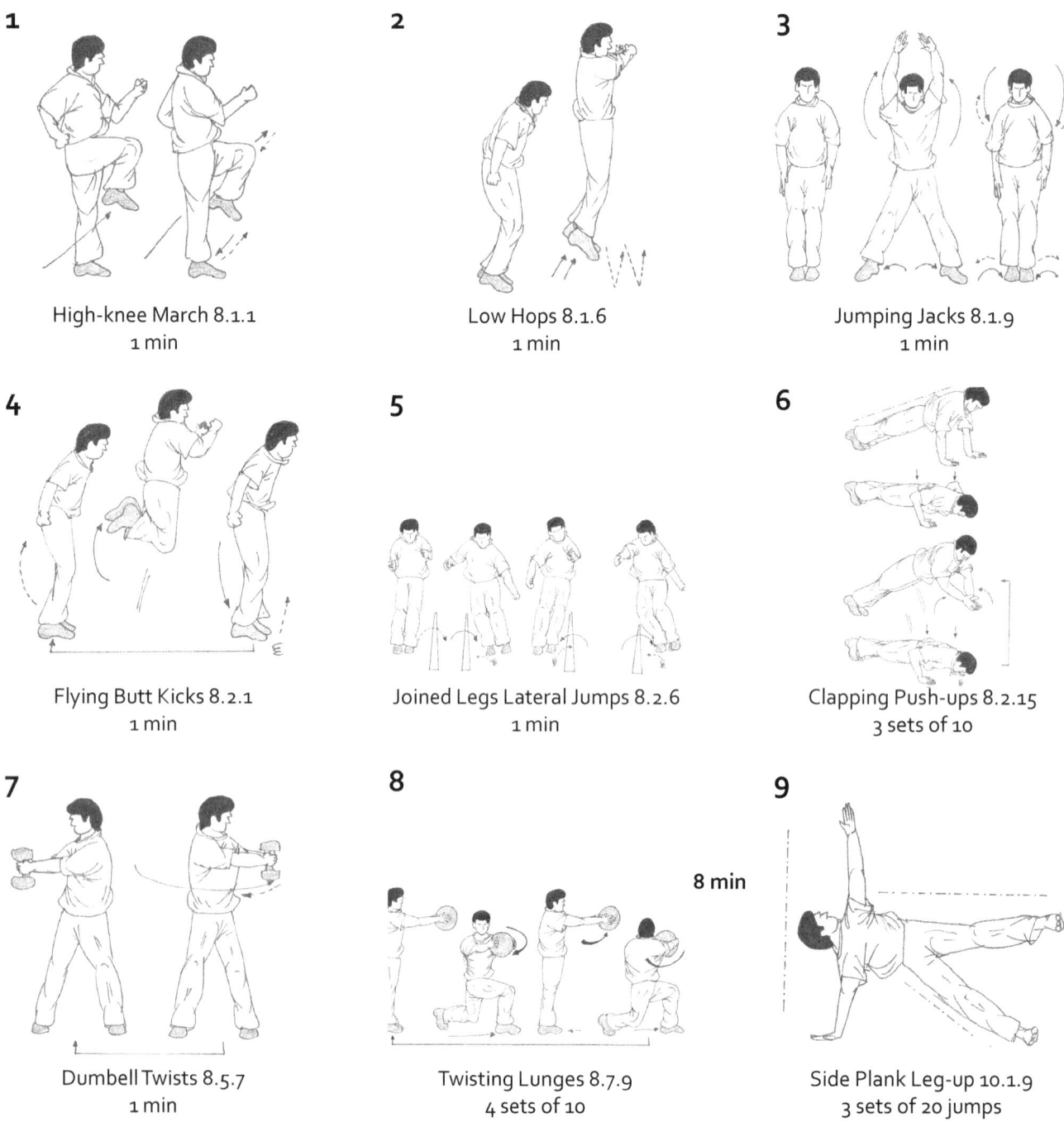

1. High-knee March 8.1.1 — 1 min
2. Low Hops 8.1.6 — 1 min
3. Jumping Jacks 8.1.9 — 1 min
4. Flying Butt Kicks 8.2.1 — 1 min
5. Joined Legs Lateral Jumps 8.2.6 — 1 min
6. Clapping Push-ups 8.2.15 — 3 sets of 10
7. Dumbell Twists 8.5.7 — 1 min
8. Twisting Lunges 8.7.9 — 4 sets of 10
9. Side Plank Leg-up 10.1.9 — 3 sets of 20 jumps

8 min

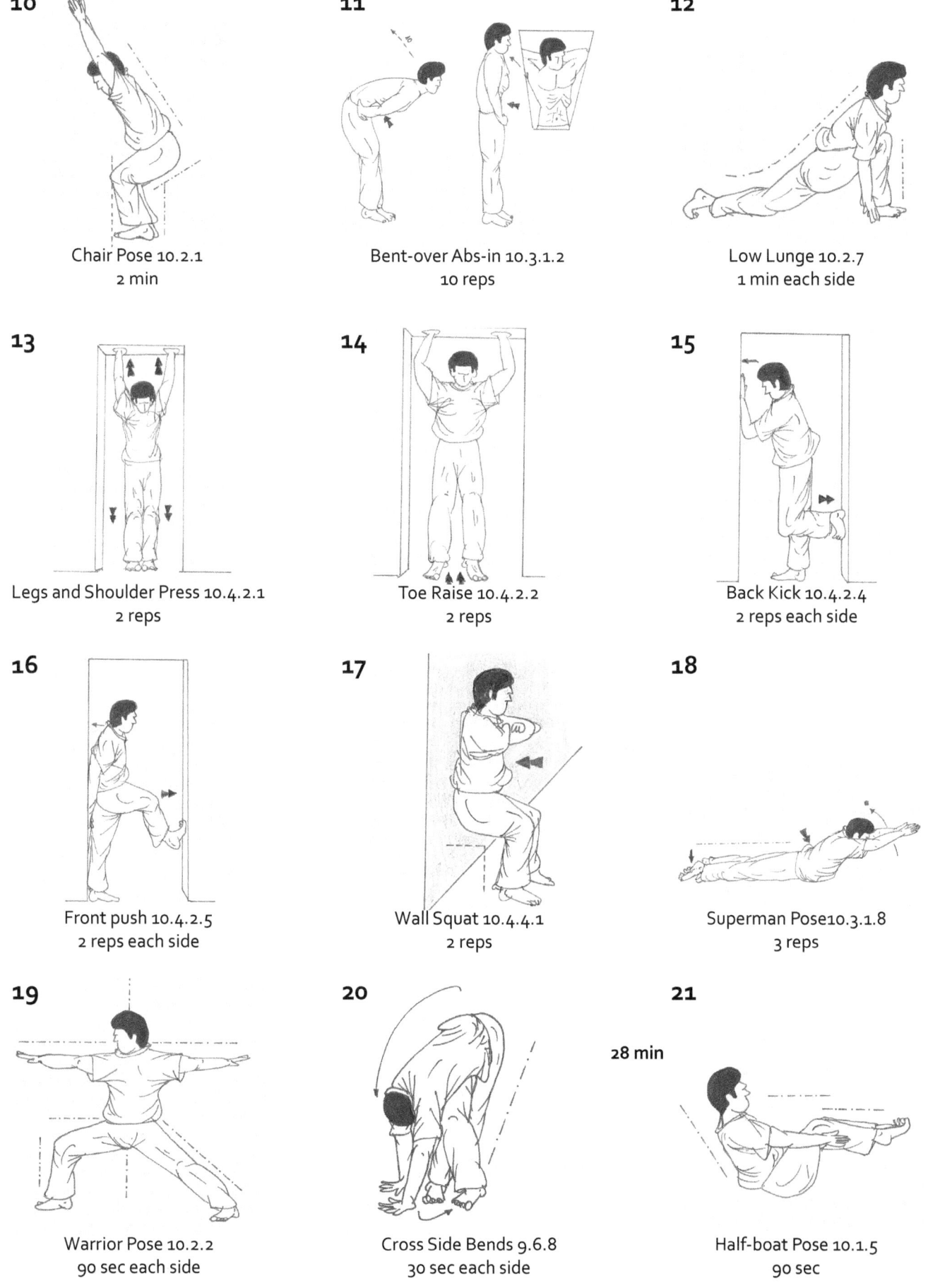

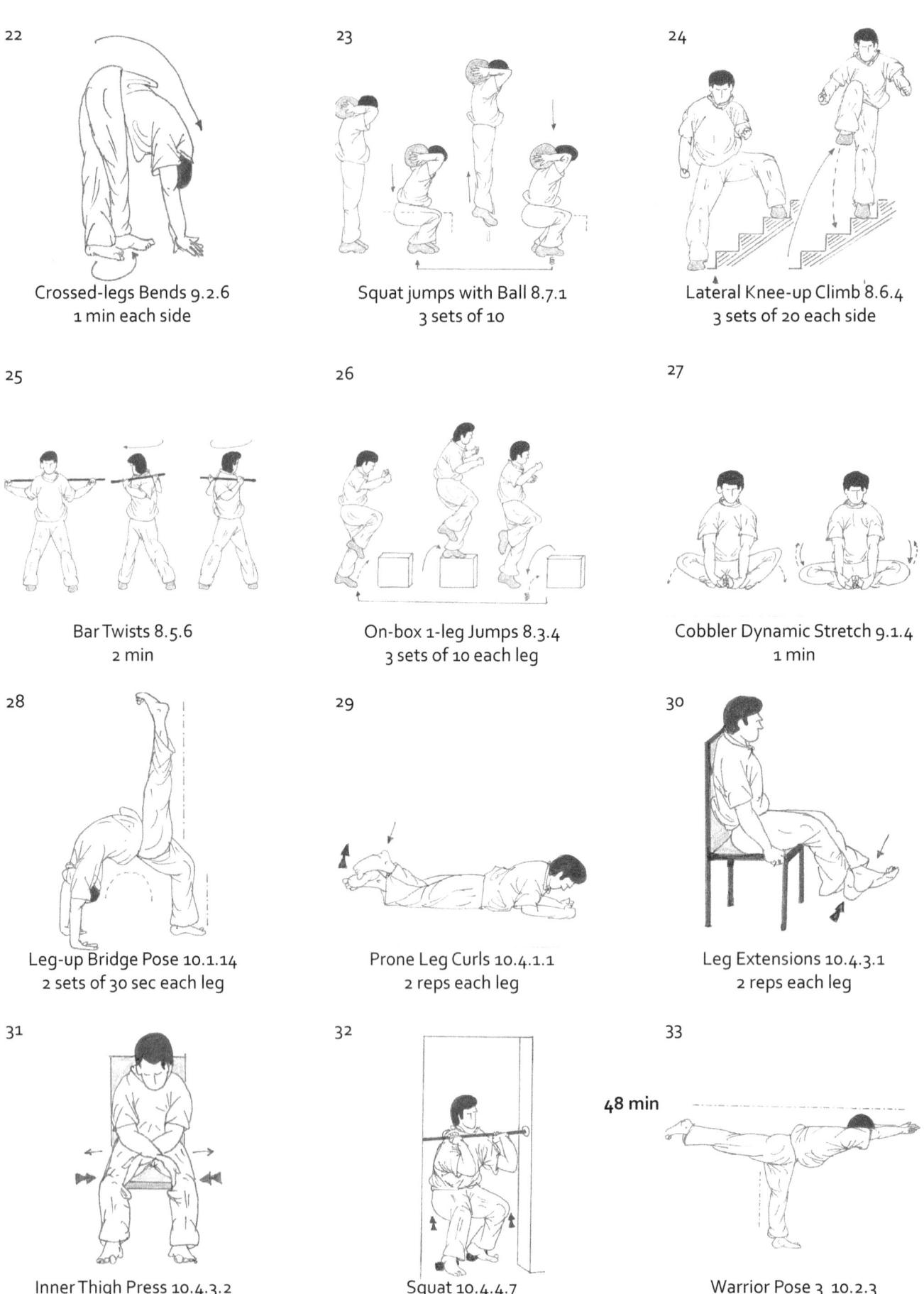

34
Downward Dog Pose 9.9.9
1 min

35
Sitting Side Bends 9.8.3
1 min each side

36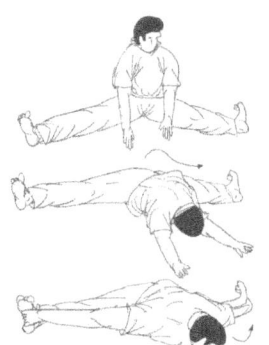
Wide Middle Stretch 9.4.5
90 sec

37
Wide 1-leg Front Stretch 9.4.4
1 min each side

38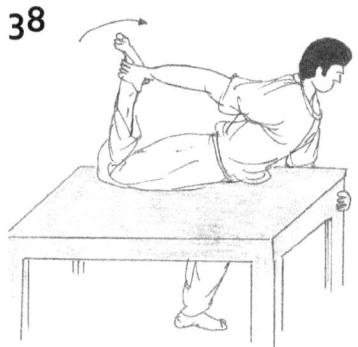
Lying Quad Stretches 9.5.4
1 min each side

39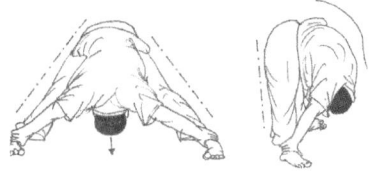
Open-legs Front Bend 9.3.7
1 min

12.4.6 DAY 6 — *Plyo and Flexio*

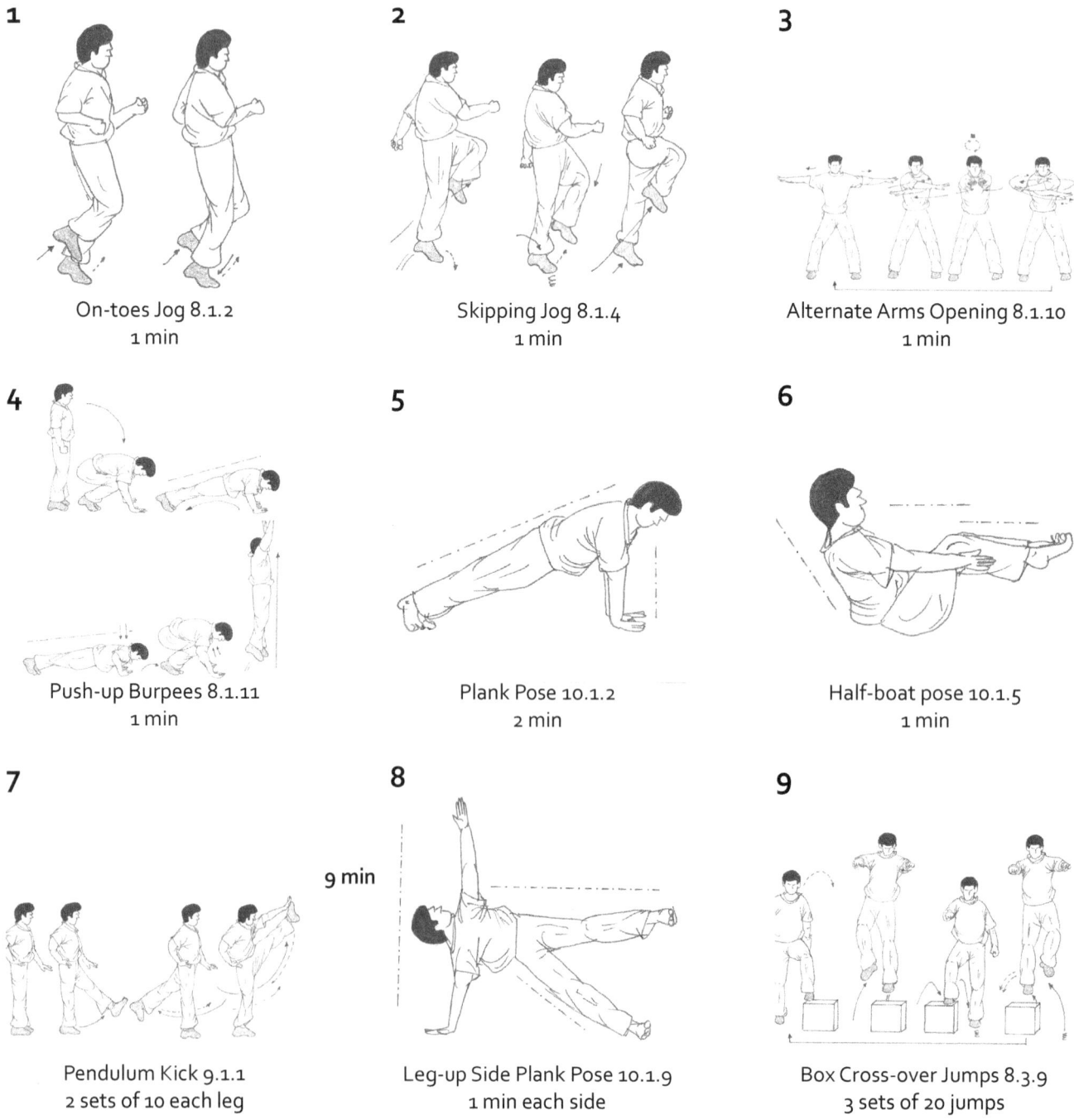

1. On-toes Jog 8.1.2 — 1 min
2. Skipping Jog 8.1.4 — 1 min
3. Alternate Arms Opening 8.1.10 — 1 min
4. Push-up Burpees 8.1.11 — 1 min
5. Plank Pose 10.1.2 — 2 min
6. Half-boat pose 10.1.5 — 1 min
7. Pendulum Kick 9.1.1 — 2 sets of 10 each leg
8. Leg-up Side Plank Pose 10.1.9 — 1 min each side
9. Box Cross-over Jumps 8.3.9 — 3 sets of 20 jumps

9 min

10

On-box High Jumps 8.3.2
3 sets of 10

11

Push-up and Rotation 8.3.18
3 sets of 10

12

On-box 1-leg Jumps 8.3.4
2 sets of 10 each leg

13

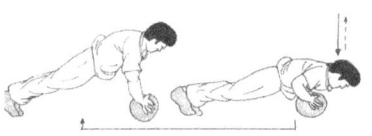

Medicine Ball Push ups 8.7.7
3 sets of 10

14

Twisting lunges 8.7.9
5 sets of 10

15

Flexed Foot Leg Stretch 9.2.4
30 sec each side

16

Box-on and Up 8.3.6
3 sets of 10

17

Box-off and High 8.3.7
3 sets of 10

18

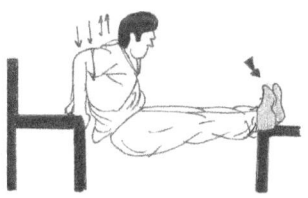

Elevated Triceps Dips 8.3.19
4 sets of 15

19

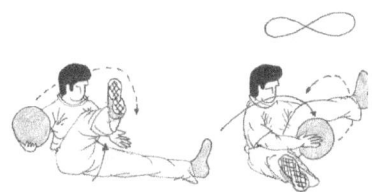

8 aroundLegs Abs Drill 8.7.2
2 sets of 10 each direction

20

Sitting Trunk Rotation 8.7.3
3 sets of 10 in each direction

28 min

21

Asymmetric Push-ups 8.7.10
3 sets of 13

PROGRAM 3 DAY 6

34 Lying Knee twist 9.6.3
1 min each side

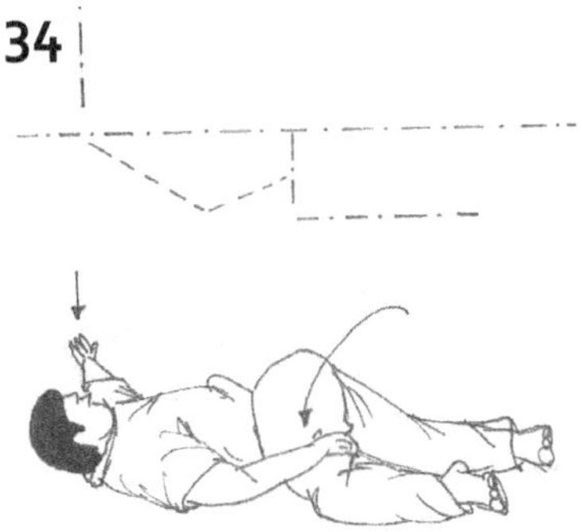

35 Reclining Hero 9.5.3
1 min each side

36 Wide 1-leg Side Stretch 9.4.3
1 min each side

37 Wide 1-leg Front Stretch 9.4.4
1 min each side

38 Wide Middle Stretch 9.4.5
1 min

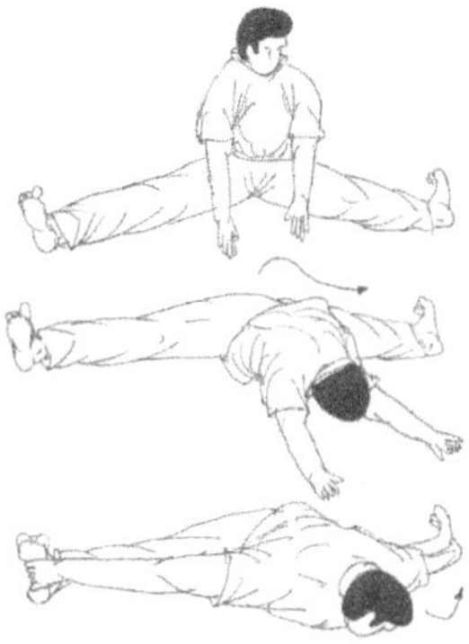

39 Hero's Pose 9.2.2
2 min

12.5 FOURTH PROGRAM: The Advanced

Even if you are in shape, do not start this program before you complete at least one month of the previous one. Once you become familiar and proficient in the Advanced Program, start working faster and resting less. You can also start replacing drills by others from the book and go your own way towards fitness, while respecting the guiding principles of Isoplex.

12.5.1 DAY 1   *Iso and Upper body*

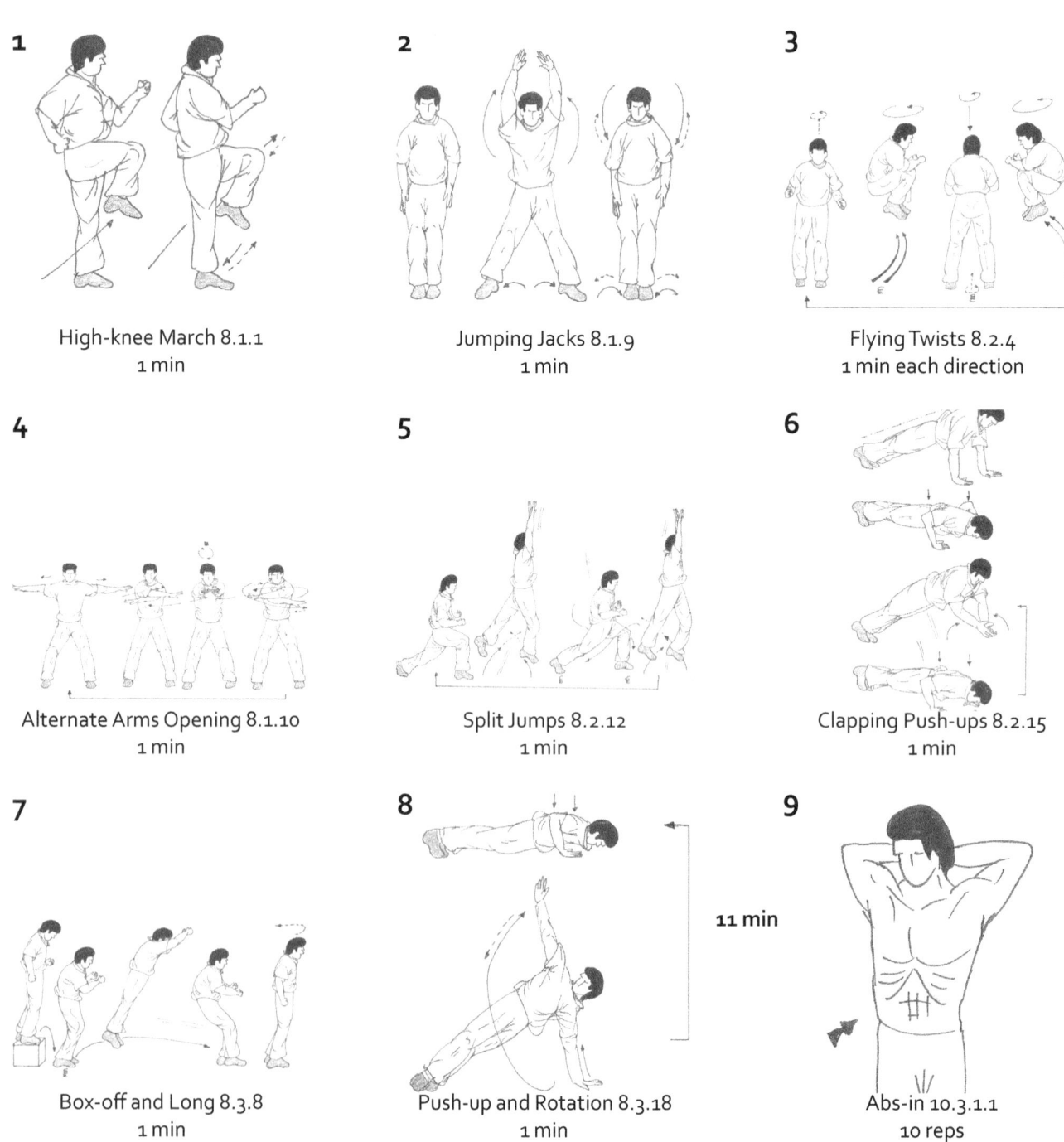

1. High-knee March 8.1.1 — 1 min
2. Jumping Jacks 8.1.9 — 1 min
3. Flying Twists 8.2.4 — 1 min each direction
4. Alternate Arms Opening 8.1.10 — 1 min
5. Split Jumps 8.2.12 — 1 min
6. Clapping Push-ups 8.2.15 — 1 min
7. Box-off and Long 8.3.8 — 1 min
8. Push-up and Rotation 8.3.18 — 1 min
9. Abs-in 10.3.1.1 — 10 reps

11 min

10

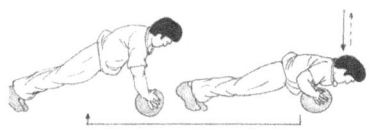

Medicine Ball Push ups 8.7.7
3 sets of 10

11

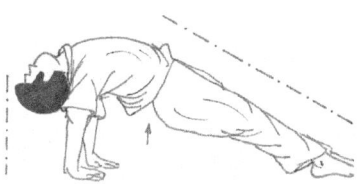

Upward Plank Pose 10.1.4
2 min

12

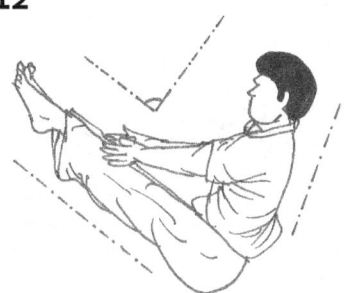

High Boat Pose 10.1.13
90 sec

13

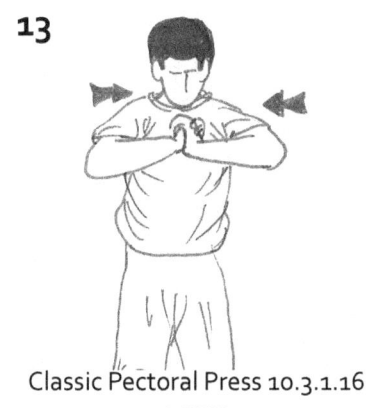

Classic Pectoral Press 10.3.1.16
3 reps

14

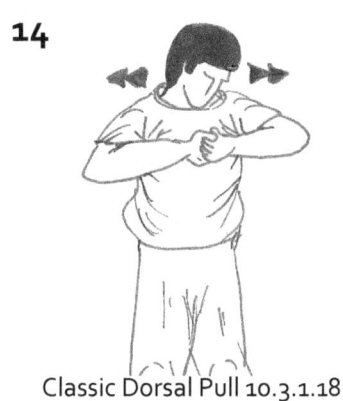

Classic Dorsal Pull 10.3.1.18
3 reps

15

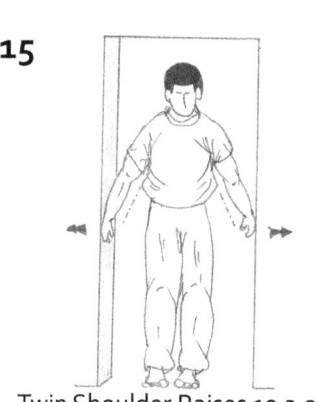

Twin Shoulder Raises 10.3.2.3
3 reps

16

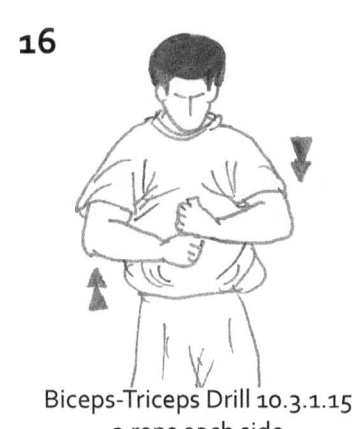

Biceps-Triceps Drill 10.3.1.15
2 reps each side

17

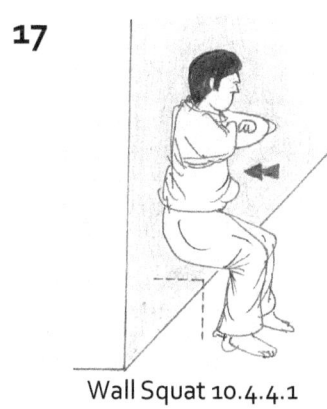

Wall Squat 10.4.4.1
3 reps

18

Door pull-down 10.3.2.10
3 reps

19

Plank Pose 10.1.2
2 min

20

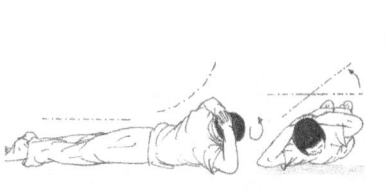

Prone Skewed Trunk Lift 10.1.18
2 sets of 30 sec each side

21

27 min

Leg-up Side Plank 10.1.9
1 min each side

PROGRAM 4 DAY 1   **229**

22 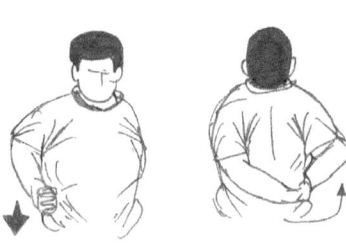 Side Praying Grips 9.9.10 1 min each side	**23** 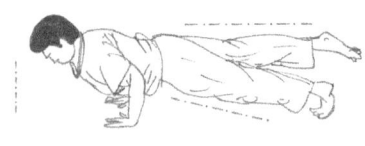 Leg-up Staff pose 10.1.11 1 min each side	**24**  Biceps Curl 10.3.6.6 3 reps
25  Dead Lift 10.3.6.5 3 reps	**26** 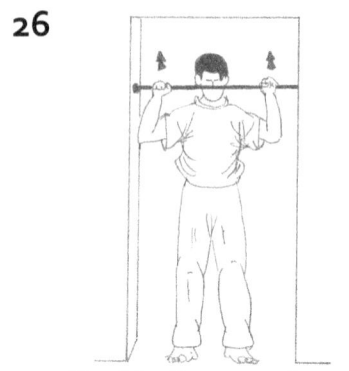 Shoulder Press 10.3.6.3 3 reps	**27** 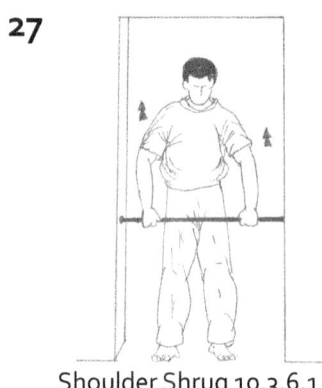 Shoulder Shrug 10.3.6.1 3 reps
28  Pectoral Plane Press 10.3.1.19 3 reps	**29**  Warrior Pose 3 10.2.3 90 sec each side	**30** 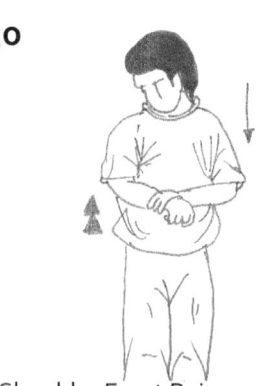 Shoulder Front Raise 10.3.1.10 2 reps each side
31 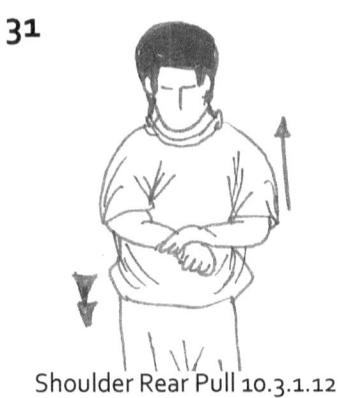 Shoulder Rear Pull 10.3.1.12 2 reps each side	**32**  Leg-up Bridge Pose 10.1.14 1 min each side	**33** 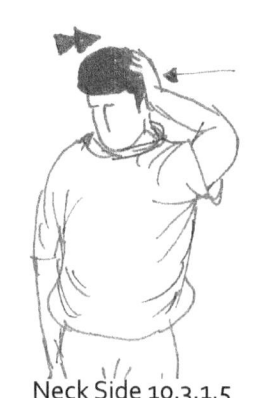 Neck Side 10.3.1.5 2 reps each side

47 min

34 Twisting Lunges 8.7.9
5 sets of 10

35 Cow's Face Grips 9.9.8
1 min each side

36 Bow Pose 9.7.3
90 sec

37 Elbows Vise 9.9.11
1 min

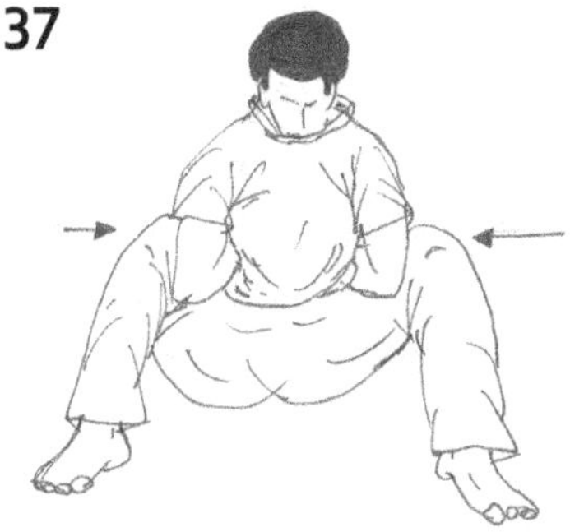

38 Open-legs Front Bend 9.3.7
1 min

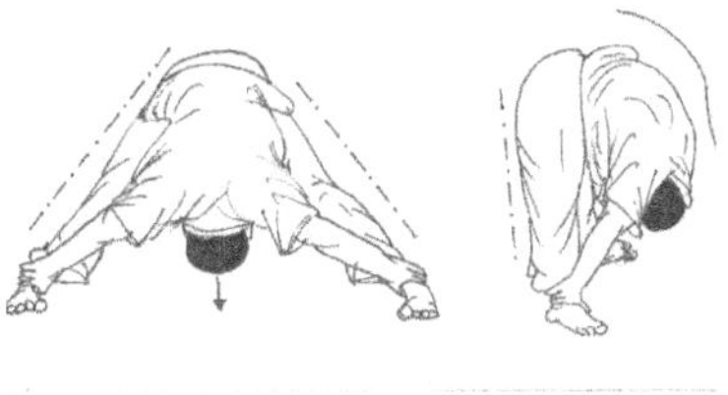

39 Side Splits 9.4.8
1 min

40 Twisting 1-arm Stretch 9.9.14
30 sec each side

41 Advanced Plough Pose 9.8.2
90 sec

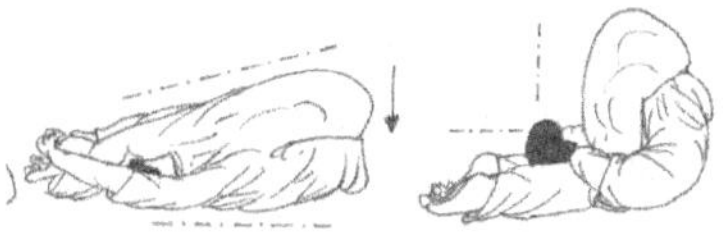

42 Reclining Cobbler 9.4.1
1 min or more...

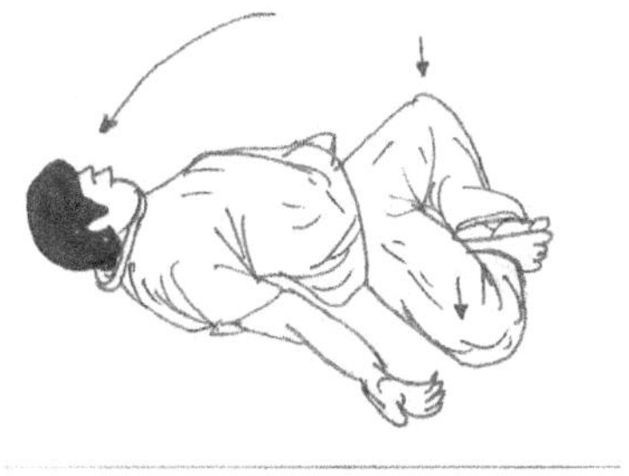

Sweat is the cologne of accomplishment.
~Heywood Hale Broun

PROGRAM 4 DAY 1

12.5.2 DAY 2 — *Plyo and Lower body*

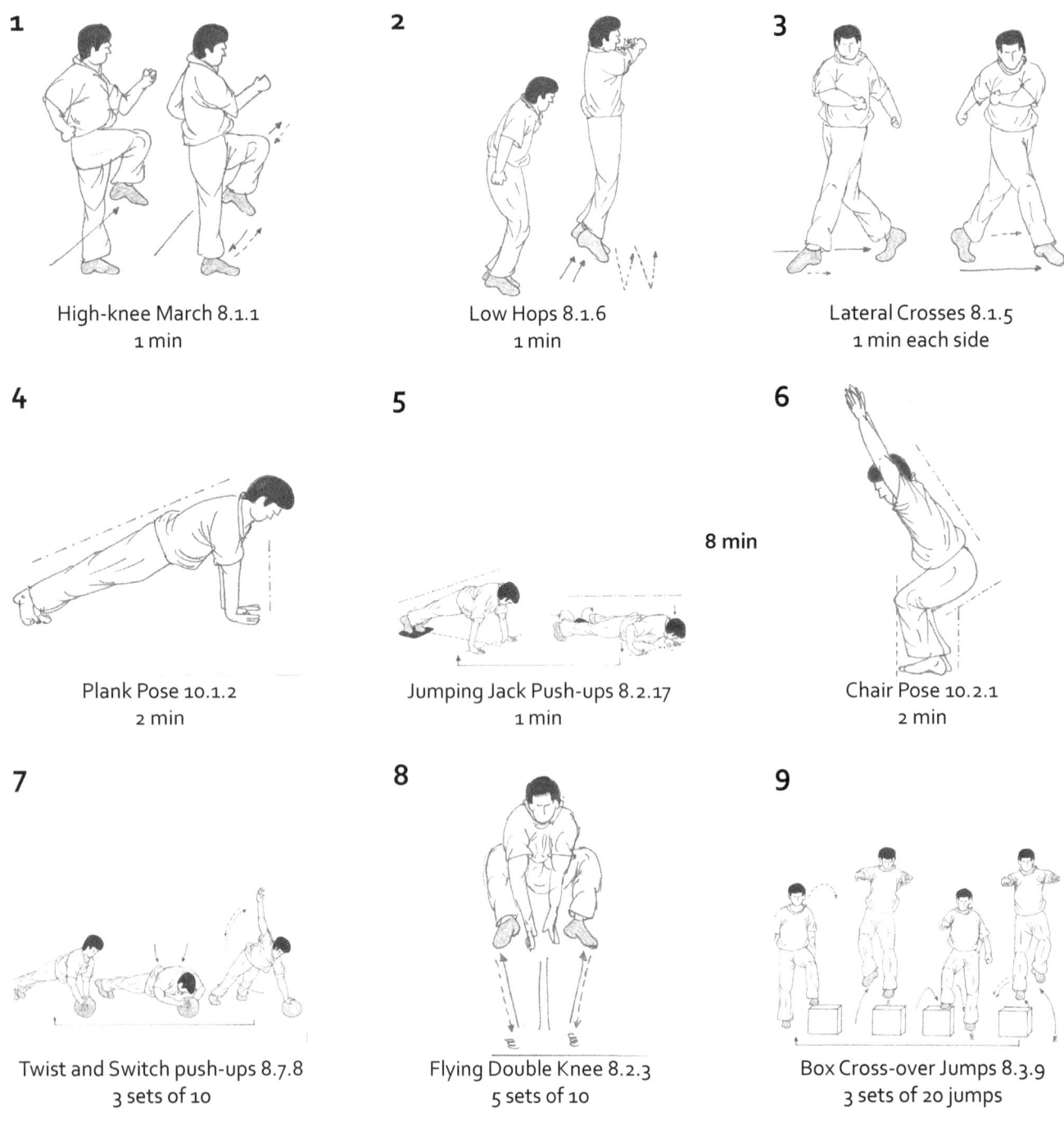

232 **THE ISOPLEX METHOD**

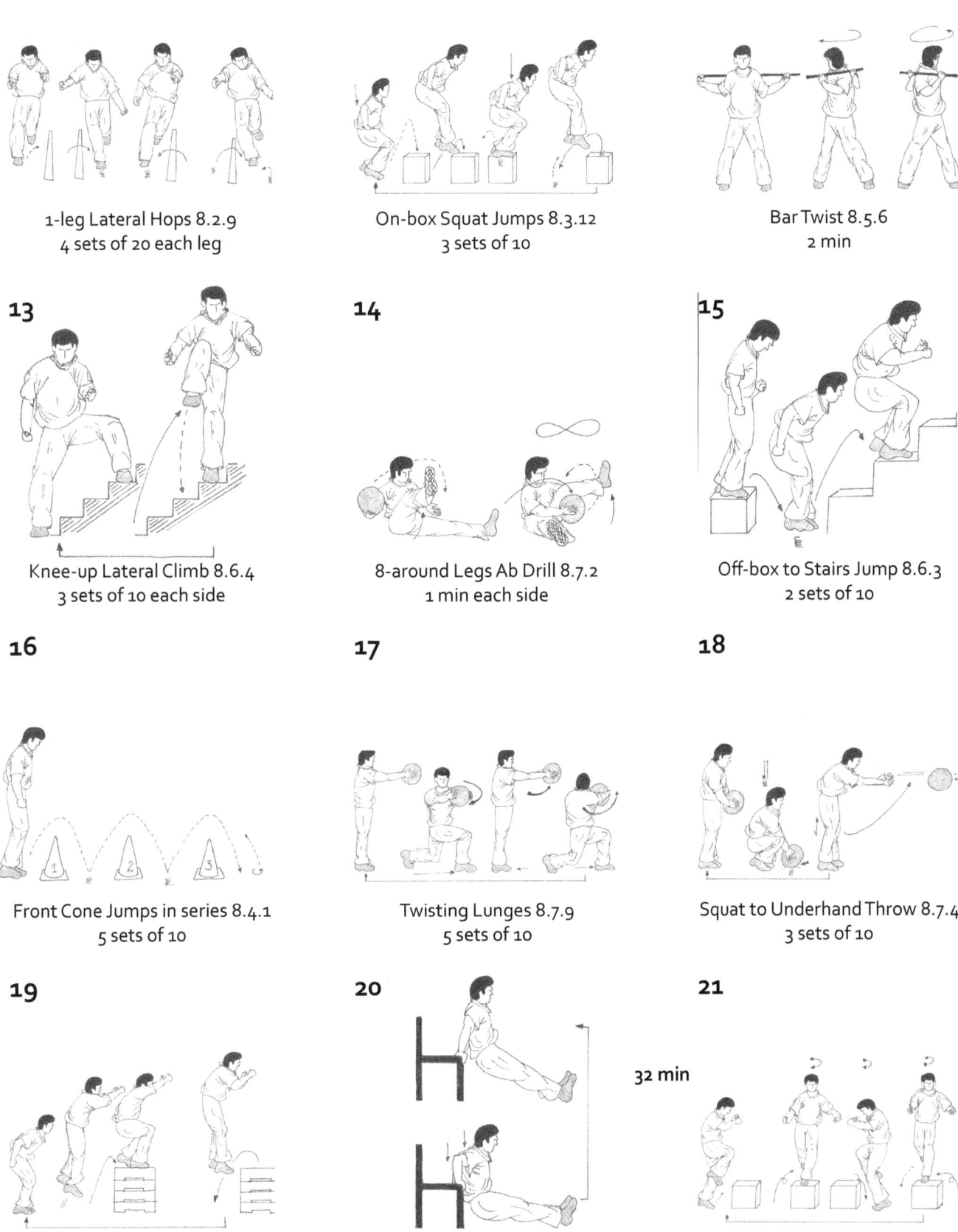

10 1-leg Lateral Hops 8.2.9 — 4 sets of 20 each leg
11 On-box Squat Jumps 8.3.12 — 3 sets of 10
12 Bar Twist 8.5.6 — 2 min
13 Knee-up Lateral Climb 8.6.4 — 3 sets of 10 each side
14 8-around Legs Ab Drill 8.7.2 — 1 min each side
15 Off-box to Stairs Jump 8.6.3 — 2 sets of 10
16 Front Cone Jumps in series 8.4.1 — 5 sets of 10
17 Twisting Lunges 8.7.9 — 5 sets of 10
18 Squat to Underhand Throw 8.7.4 — 3 sets of 10
19 On-box High Jumps 8.3.2 — 3 sets of 10 jumps
20 Triceps Dips 8.3.19 — 3 sets of 15
21 On-box 1-leg Twisted 8.3.5 — 3 sets of 10 jumps

32 min

PROGRAM 4 DAY 2

22
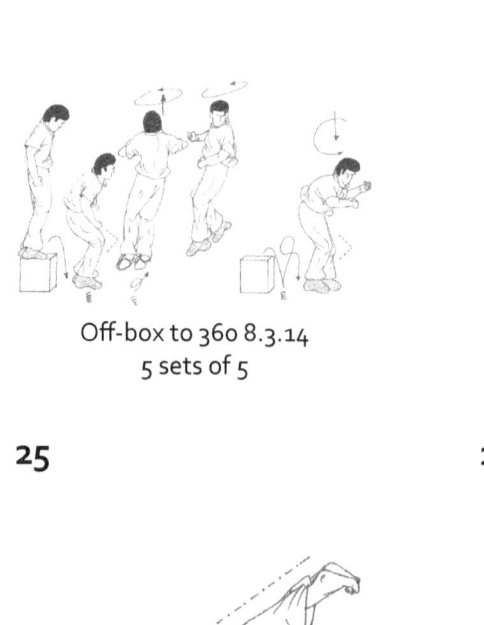
Off-box to 360 8.3.14
5 sets of 5

23
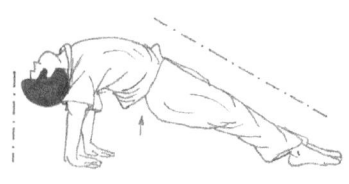
Upward Plank Pose 10.1.4
90 sec

24
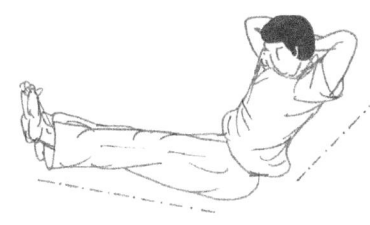
Low Boat Pose 10.1.10
90 sec

25
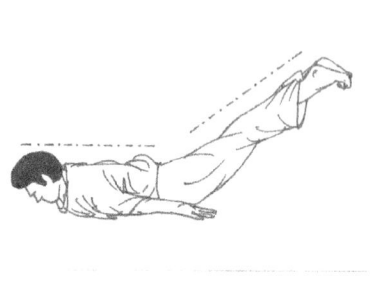
Locust pose 10.2.6
1 min

26

Box-on and Up 8.3.6
3 sets of 10

27
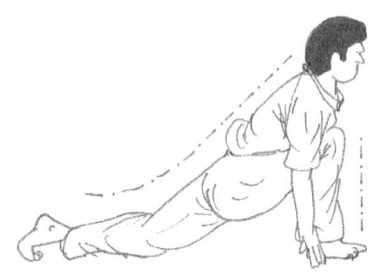
Low Lunge 10.2.7
1 min each side

28

Crossed-legs Bends 9.2.6
30 sec each side

29
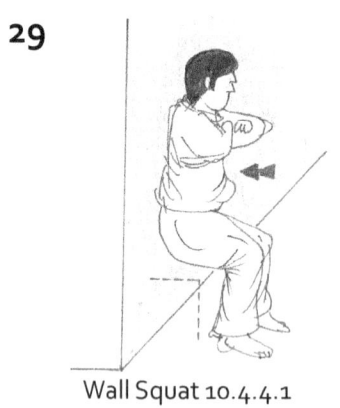
Wall Squat 10.4.4.1
2 sets

30

Lateral Stairs Jumps 8.6.2
3 sets of 5 each side

31
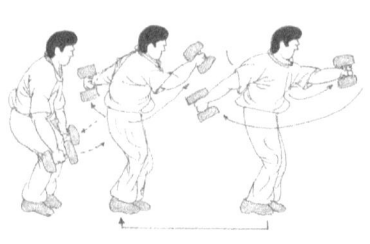
Dumbell Arm Swings 8.5.8
1 min

32
49 min

Incremental Height Jumps 8.4.5
3 sets of 10

33

Double-box Jumps 8.3.11
3 sets of 20 jumps

THE ISOPLEX METHOD

34

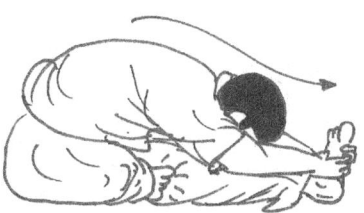

Sitting Bends 9.3.1
1 min

35

Open-legs Sitting Bends 9.3.2
1 min

36

Wide Side Stretch 9.4.3
1 min each side

37

Wide Front Stretch 9.4.4
1 min each side

38

Advanced Quad Stretch 9.5.1
1 min each side

39

Seated Twists 9.8.4
1 min each side

**If you spend too much time thinking about a thing, you'll never get it done.
~Bruce Lee**

PROGRAM 4 DAY 2

12.5.3 DAY 3 — Iso and Flexio

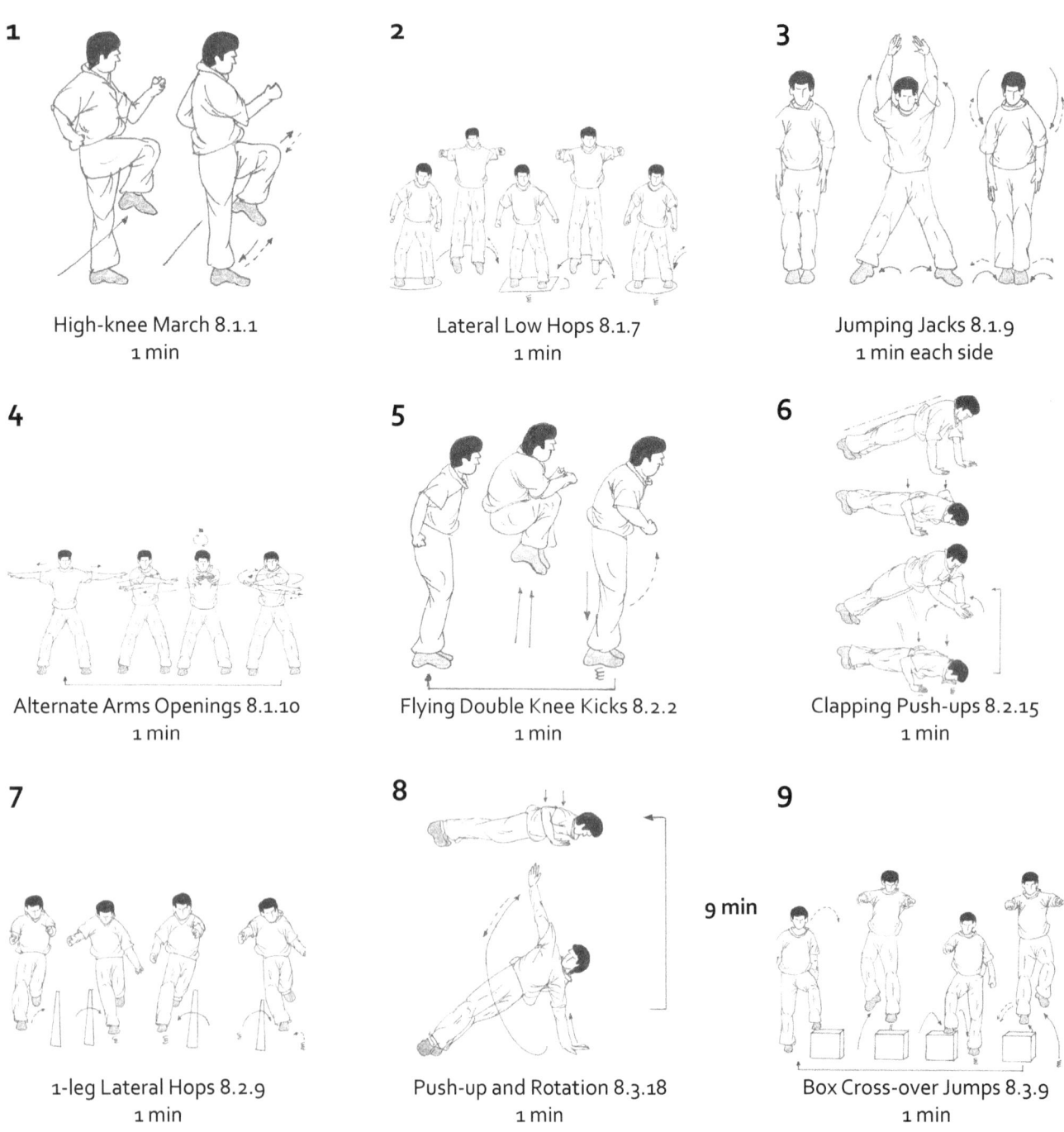

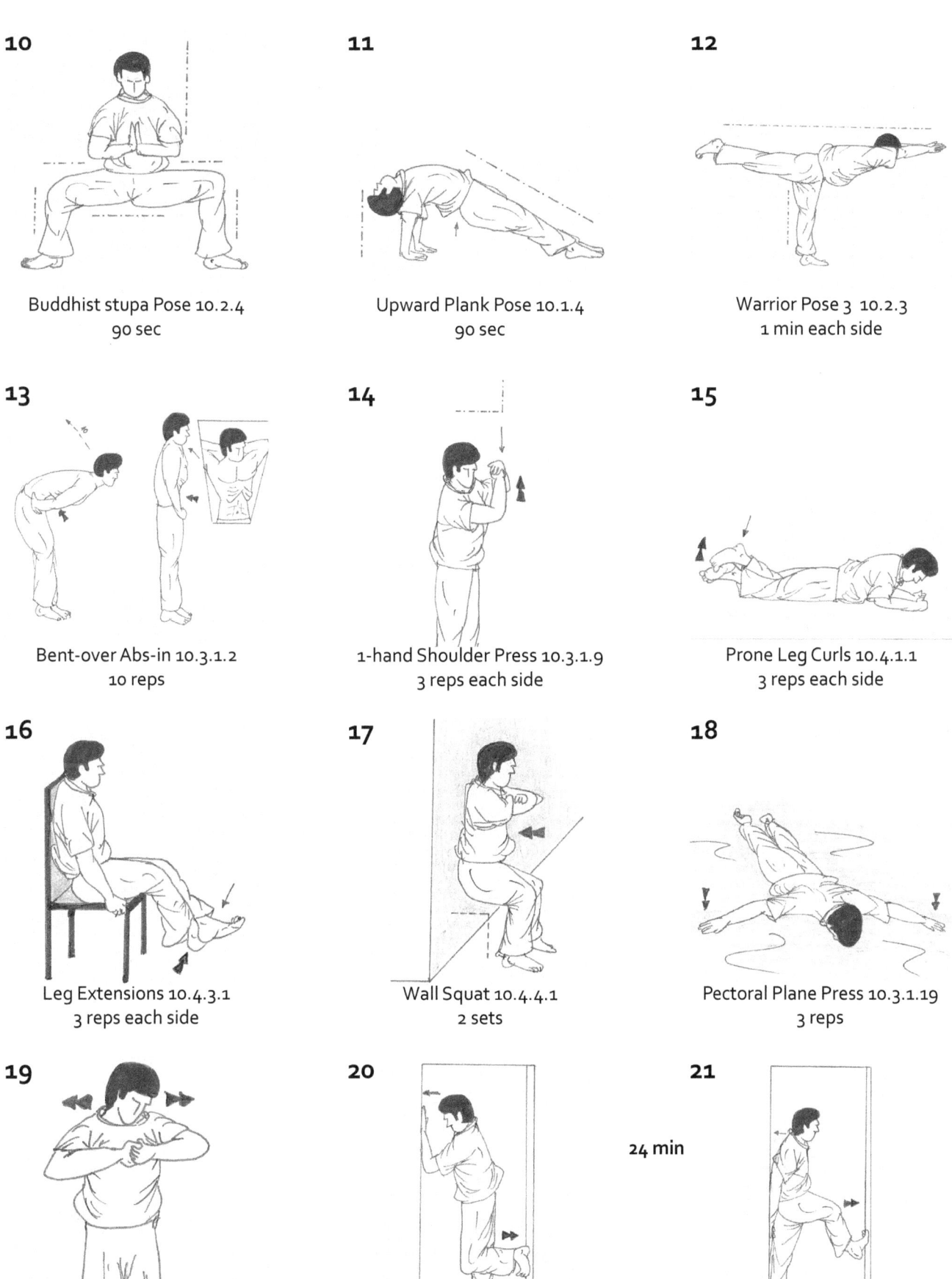

34
Wide Front Stretch 9.4.4
1 min each side

35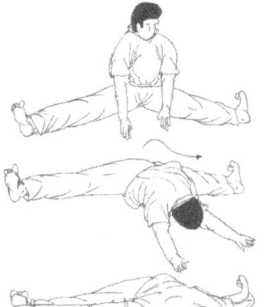
Wide Middle Stretch 9.4.5
90 sec

36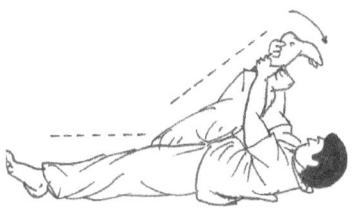
Lying Leg Pull 9.3.3
1 min each side

37
Bent-leg Pulls 9.6.6
1 min each side

38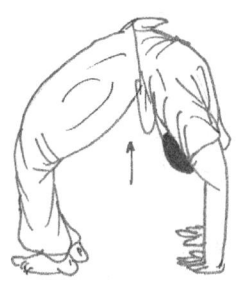
Bridge Pose 9.7.4
1 min

39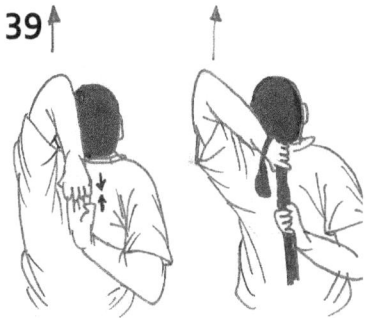
Cow's Face Grips 9.9.8
1 min each side

12.5.4 DAY 4 — *Plyos and Upper Body*

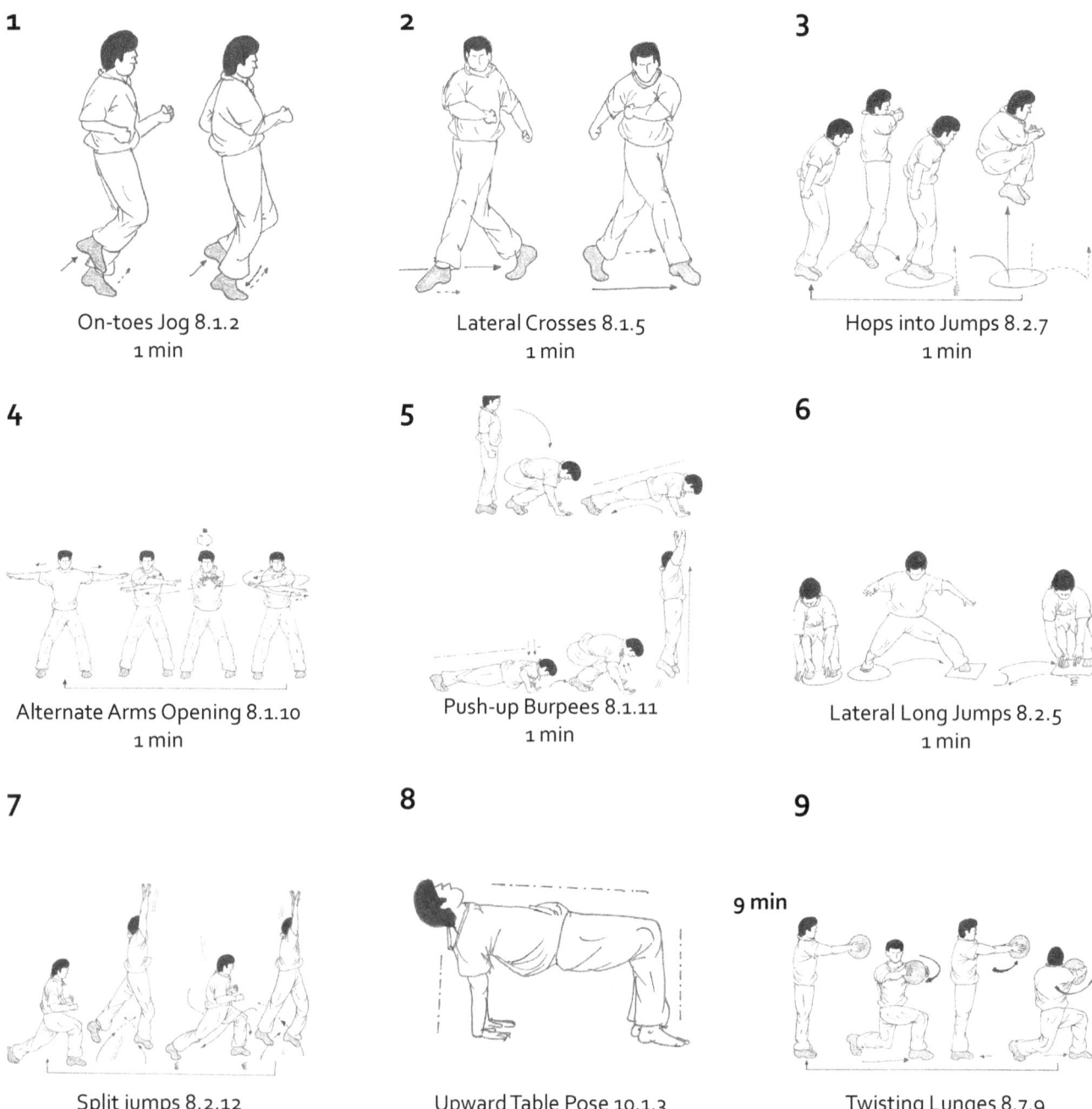

1. On-toes Jog 8.1.2 — 1 min
2. Lateral Crosses 8.1.5 — 1 min
3. Hops into Jumps 8.2.7 — 1 min
4. Alternate Arms Opening 8.1.10 — 1 min
5. Push-up Burpees 8.1.11 — 1 min
6. Lateral Long Jumps 8.2.5 — 1 min
7. Split jumps 8.2.12 — 1 min
8. Upward Table Pose 10.1.3 — 1 min
9. Twisting Lunges 8.7.9 — 1 min

9 min

10

1-arm Push-up Down Dog 8.2.16
2 sets of 10 each side

11

Bar Twist 8.5.6
1 min

12

Dumbell Arm Swings 8.5.8
2 min

13

Half Boat Pose 10.1.5
2 min

14

Triceps Dips 8.3.19
4 sets of 20

15

Pectoral Table Stretch 9.9.2
1 min

16

Biceps-Triceps Drill 10.3.1.15
3 reps each side

17

Front Cone Jumps in series 8.4.1
1 min

18

Sitting Trunk Rotation 8.7.3
1 min each direction

19

Squat to Underhand Throw 8.7.4
90 sec

20

Lateral Wall Throw 8.7.6
1 min each side

21

30 min

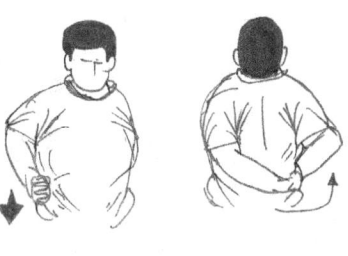

Side Praying Grips 9.9.10
30 sec each side

PROGRAM 4 DAY 4

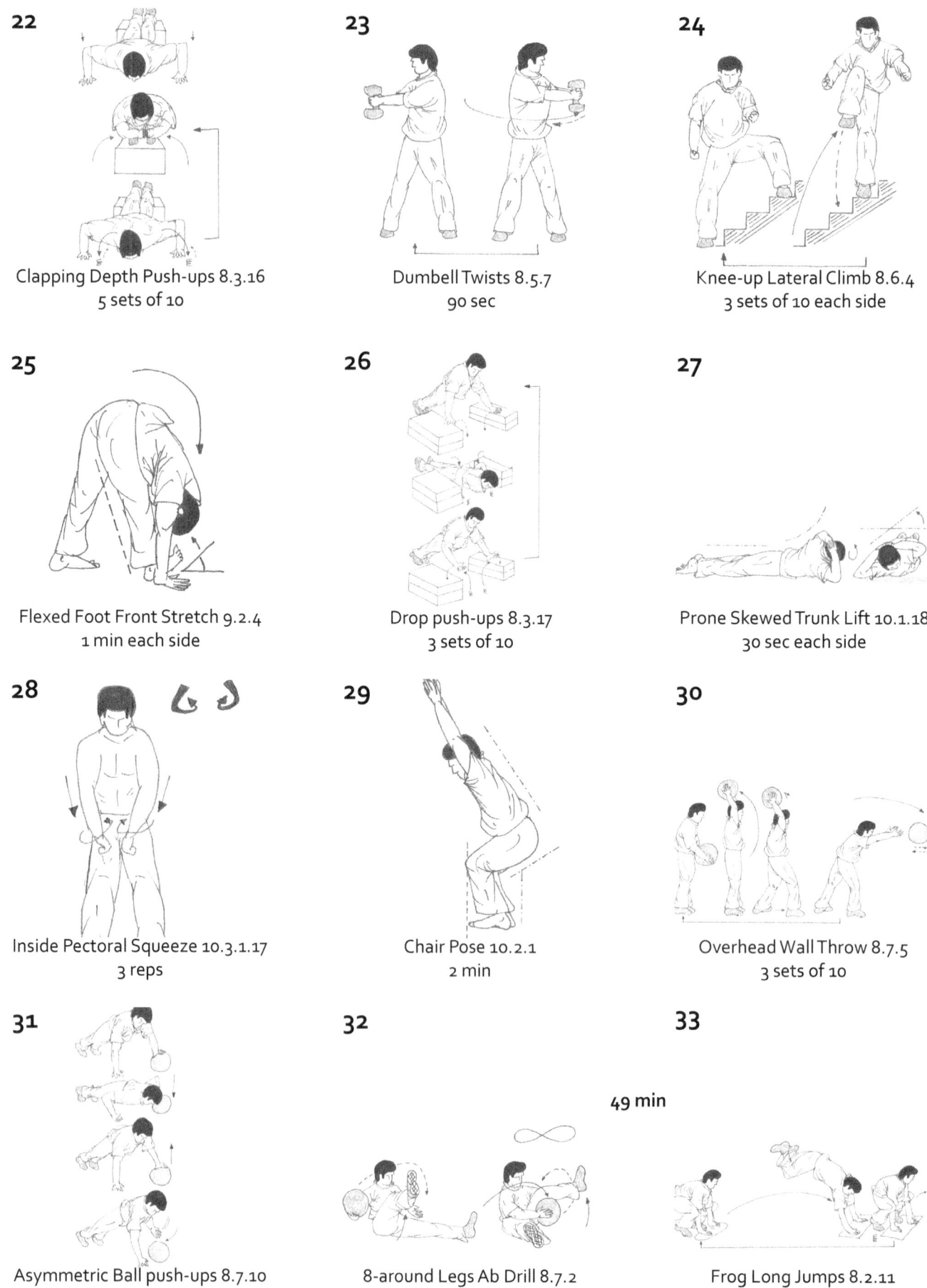

242 **THE ISOPLEX METHOD**

34

Downward Dog Pose 9.9.9
2 min

35

Inverted Triangle Pose 9.8.6
1 min each side

36

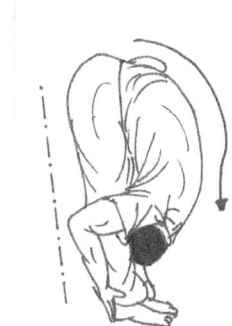

Standing Bend 9.8.1
1 min

37

Elbow's Vise 9.9.11
1 min

38

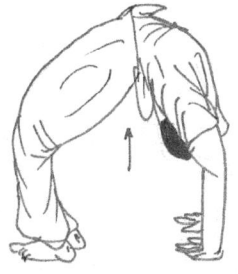

Bridge Pose 9.7.4
1 min

39

Runner's Stretches 9.6.7
1 min each side

40

Reclining Cobbler 9.4.1
30 sec

PROGRAM 4 DAY 4   243

12.5.5 DAY 5 — Iso and Lower Body

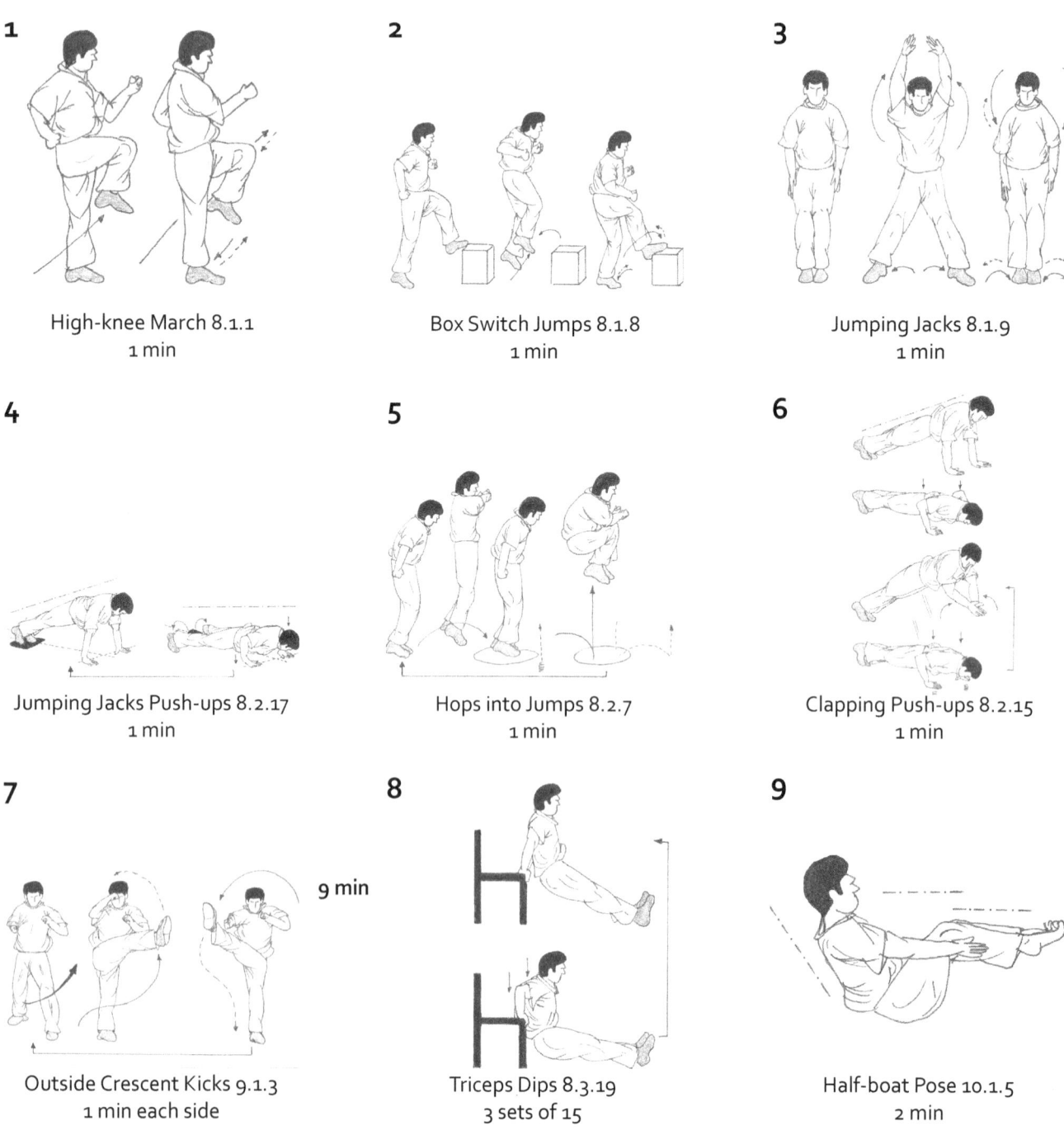

1. High-knee March 8.1.1 — 1 min
2. Box Switch Jumps 8.1.8 — 1 min
3. Jumping Jacks 8.1.9 — 1 min
4. Jumping Jacks Push-ups 8.2.17 — 1 min
5. Hops into Jumps 8.2.7 — 1 min
6. Clapping Push-ups 8.2.15 — 1 min
7. Outside Crescent Kicks 9.1.3 — 1 min each side
8. Triceps Dips 8.3.19 — 3 sets of 15
9. Half-boat Pose 10.1.5 — 2 min

9 min

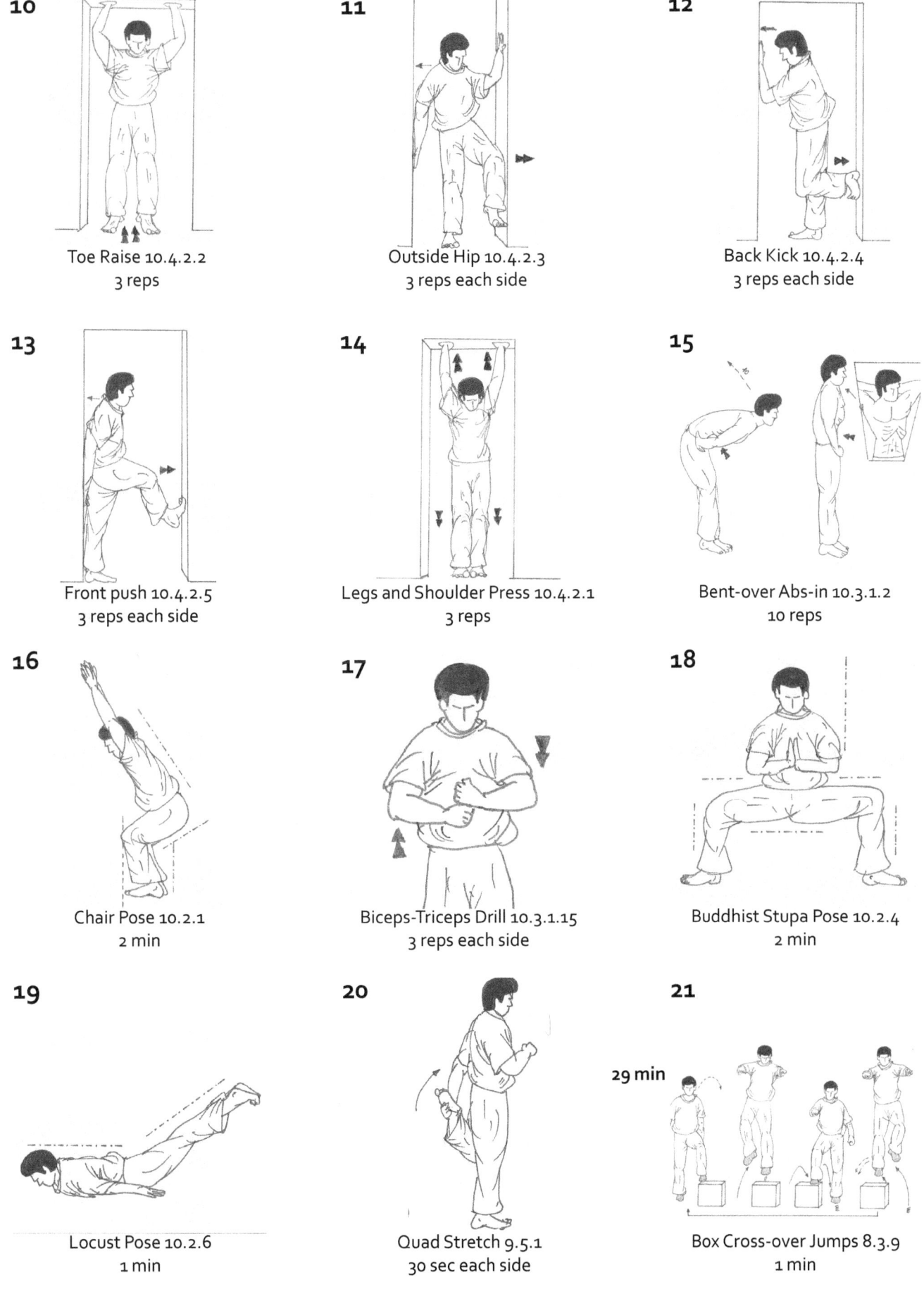

PROGRAM 4 DAY 5

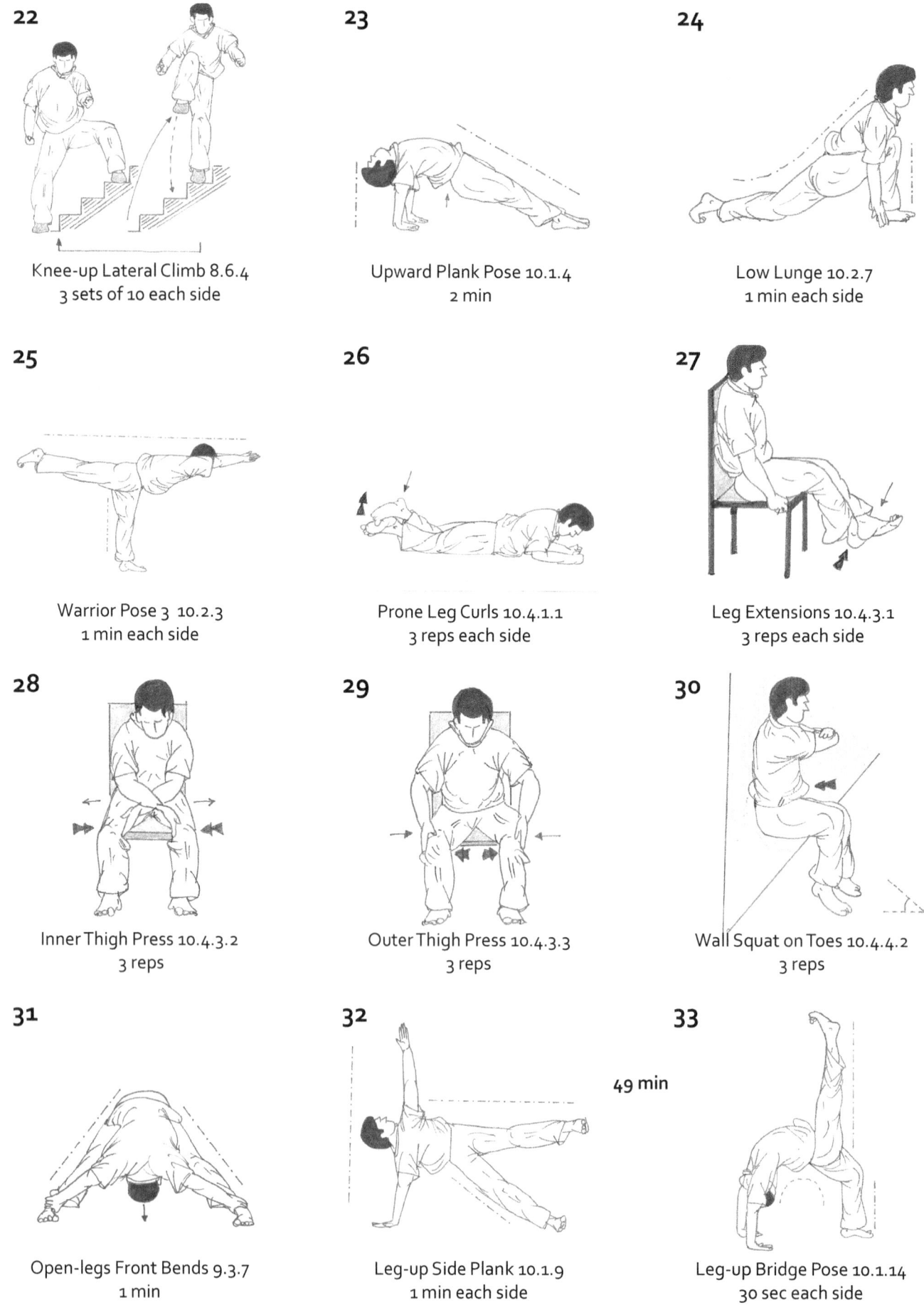

246 **THE ISOPLEX METHOD**

He who stops being better, stops being good.
~Oliver Cromwell

12.5.6 DAY 6 *Plyo and Flexio*

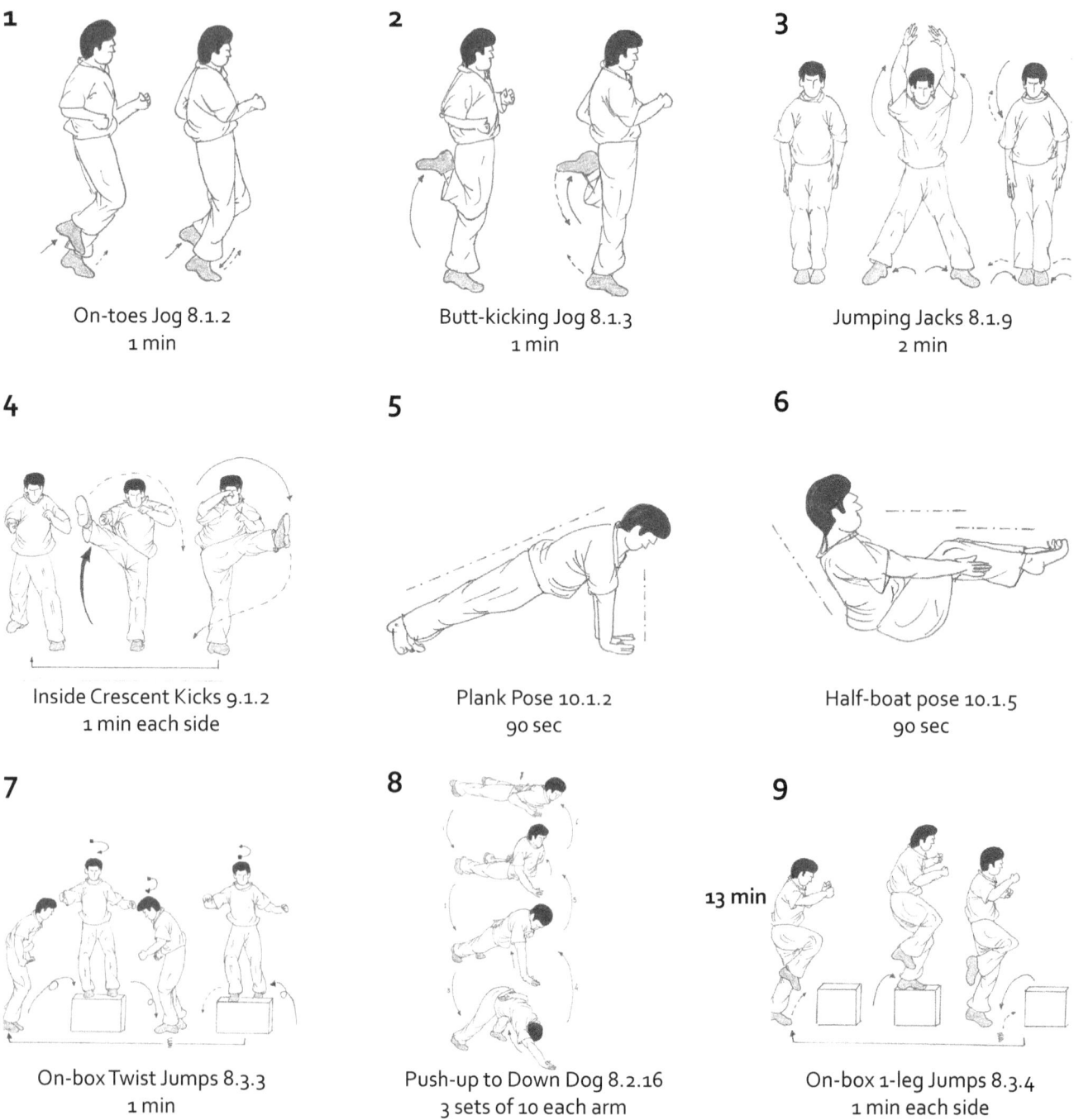

248 **THE ISOPLEX METHOD**

10

Medicine Ball Push ups 8.7.7
3 sets of 10

11

Dumbell Twists 8.5.7
2 min

12

On-box High Jumps 8.3.2
1 min

13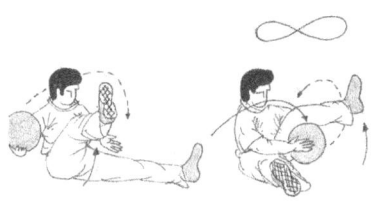

8-around Legs Abs drill 8.7.2
1 min each side

14

Squat to Underhand Throw 8.7.4
1 min

15

Overhead Wall Throw 8.7.5
1 min

16

Biceps-Triceps Drill 10.3.1.15
3 reps each side

17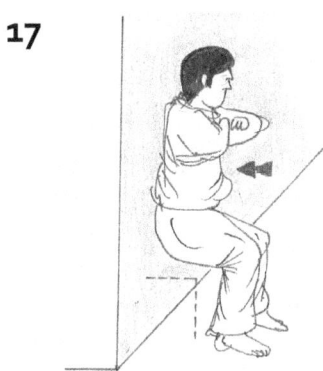

Wall Squat 10.4.4.1
3 reps

18

Box-off and High 8.3.7
2 min

19

Twisting Lunges 8.7.9
2 min

20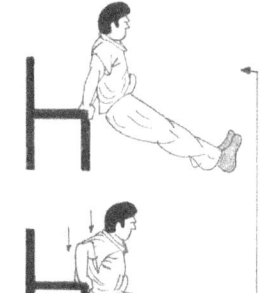

Triceps Dips 8.3.19
4 sets of 15

21

35 min

Lateral Stairs jumps 8.6.2
3 sets of 5 each side

PROGRAM 4 DAY 6

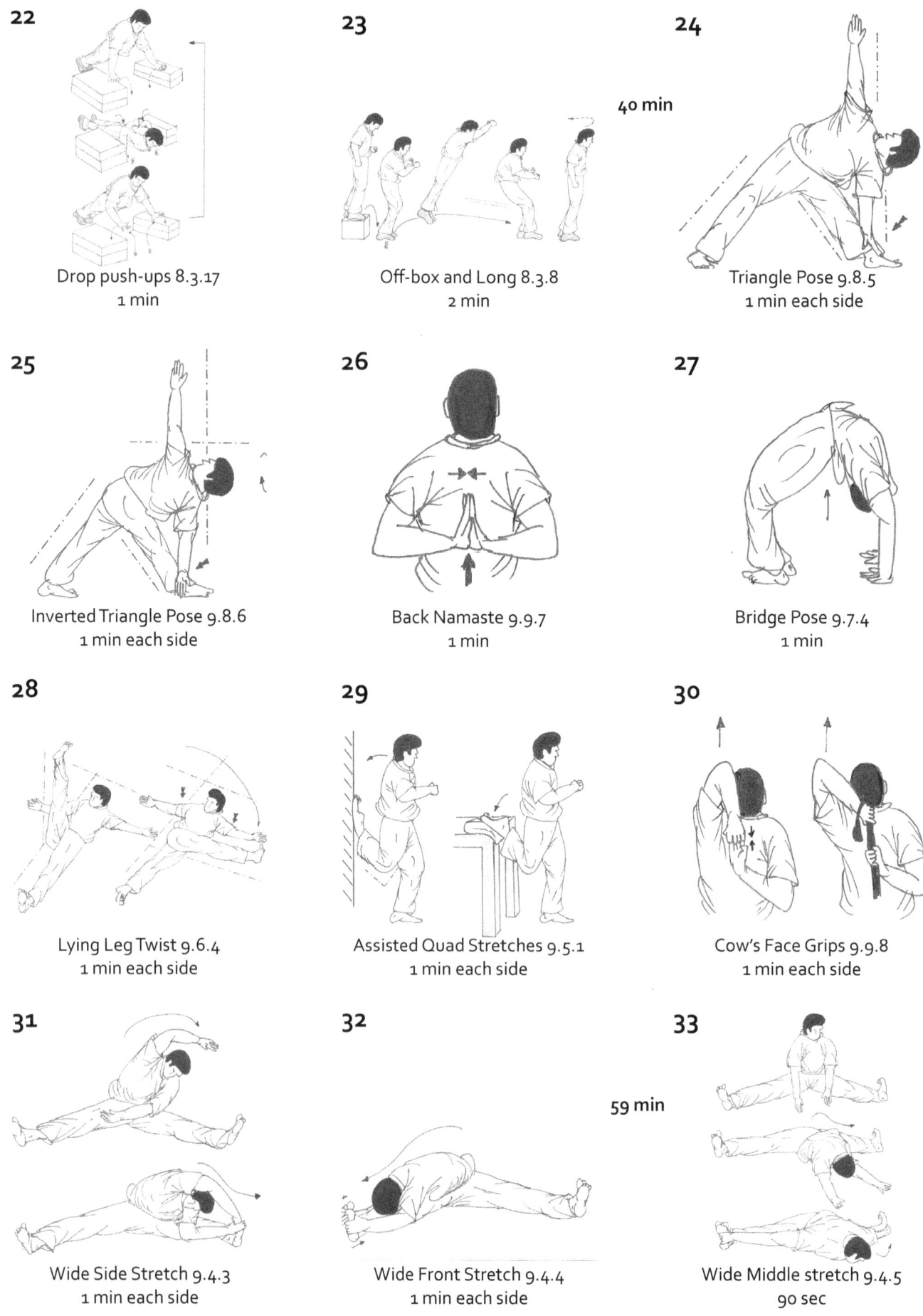

12.6 FIFTH PROGRAM: The Partner

Working out with a partner is fun. It helps motivate you and push yourself a little more. Training with a partner can make the session longer, for the same amount of drilling, but the more intense drills possible make it really worth. You will also be less inclined to skip a session, if you know that your partner is waiting.

12.6.1 DAY 1   *Iso and Upper body*

1 High-knee March 8.1.1
1 min

2 Low Hops 8.1.6
1 min

3 Burpee Push-ups 8.1.11
1 min

4 Clapping Push-ups 8.2.15
1 min

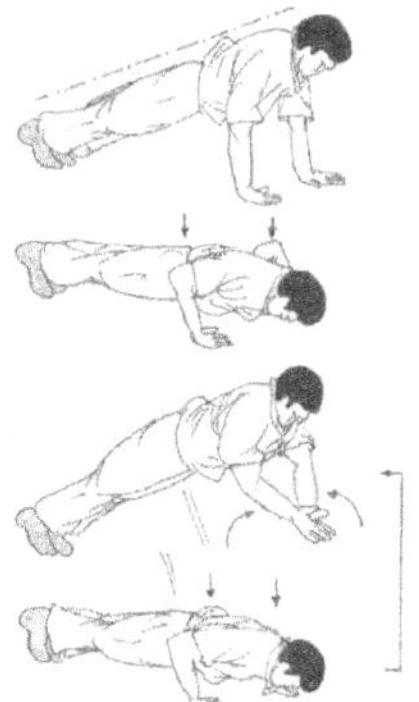

5 Dynamic Crescent Kicks 9.10.1
1 min each leg

6 Basketball Passes 8.8.14
1 min

7 Medicine Ball Twists 8.8.6
1 min each direction

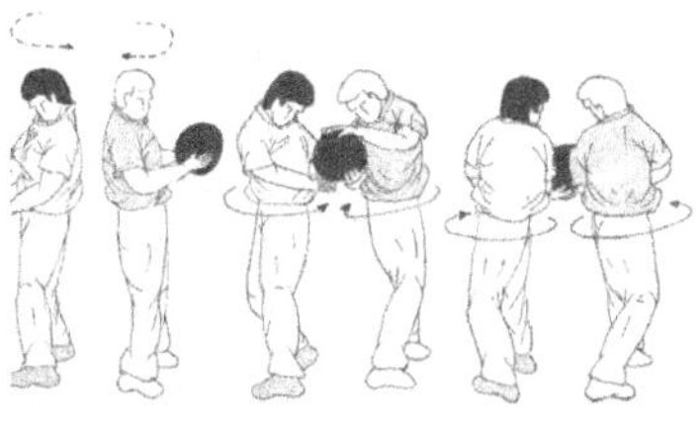

8 10 min 
Plank Pose 10.1.2
2 min

9 Prone Trunk Lift 10.1.17
1 min

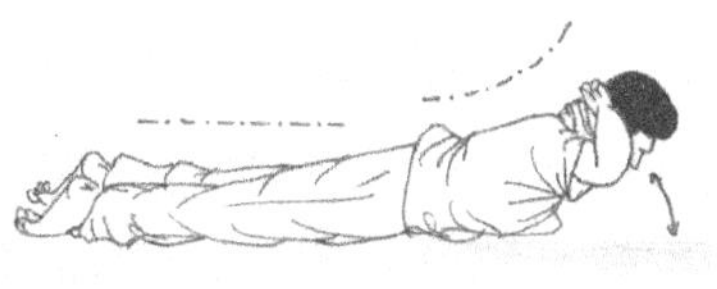

PROGRAM 5 DAY 1

10

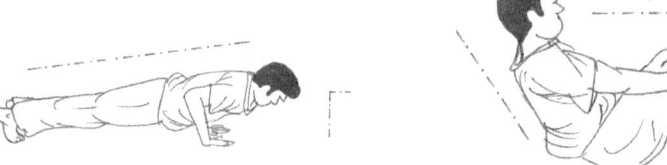

4-limbed Staff pose 10.1.12
90 sec

11

Half-boat Pose 10.1.5
90 sec

12

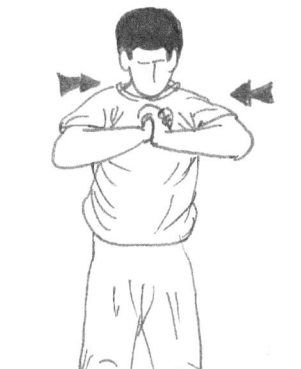

Classic Pectoral Press 10.3.1.16
3 reps

13

Classic Dorsal Pull 10.3.1.18
3 reps

14

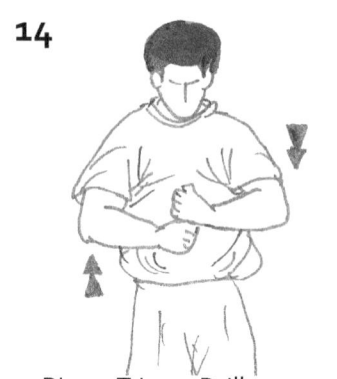

Biceps Triceps Drill 10.3.1.15
3 reps each side

15

Pectoral Plane Press 10.3.1.19
3 reps

16

Warrior Pose 10.2.2
90 sec each side

17

Leg-up Side Plank 10.1.9
1 min each side

18

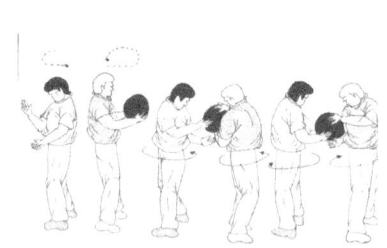

Ball Extended Twists 8.8.7
1 min each direction

19

Shoulders Ball Throw 8.8.9
1 min

20

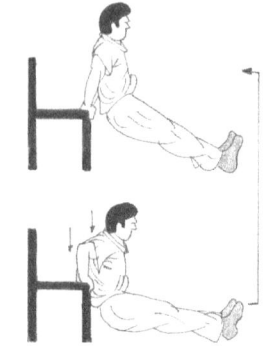

Triceps Dips 8.3.19
4 sets of 20

31 min

21

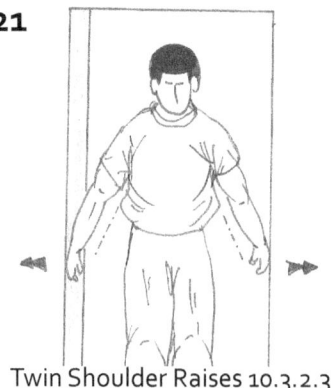

Twin Shoulder Raises 10.3.2.3
3 reps

THE ISOPLEX METHOD

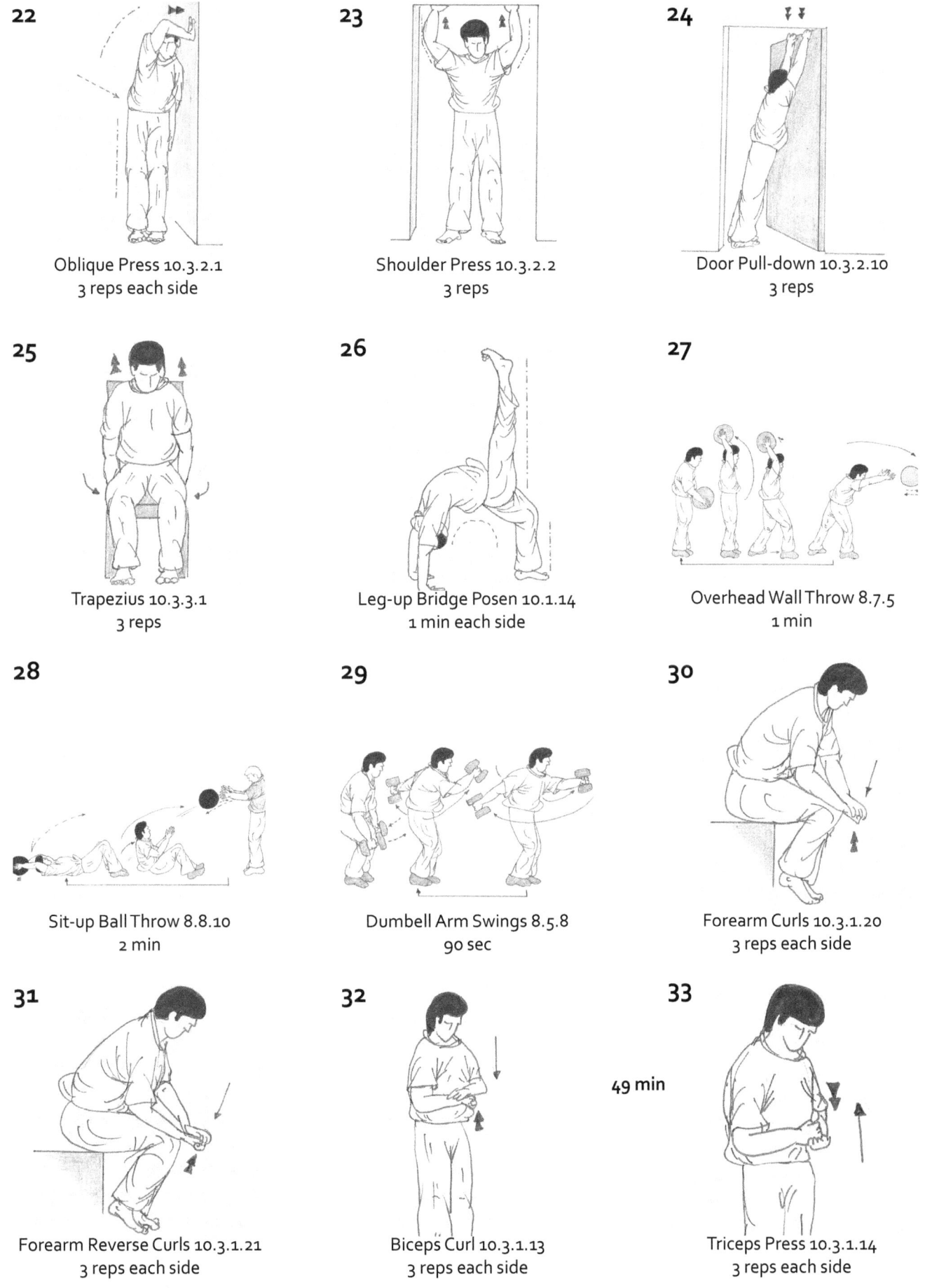

PROGRAM 5 DAY 1

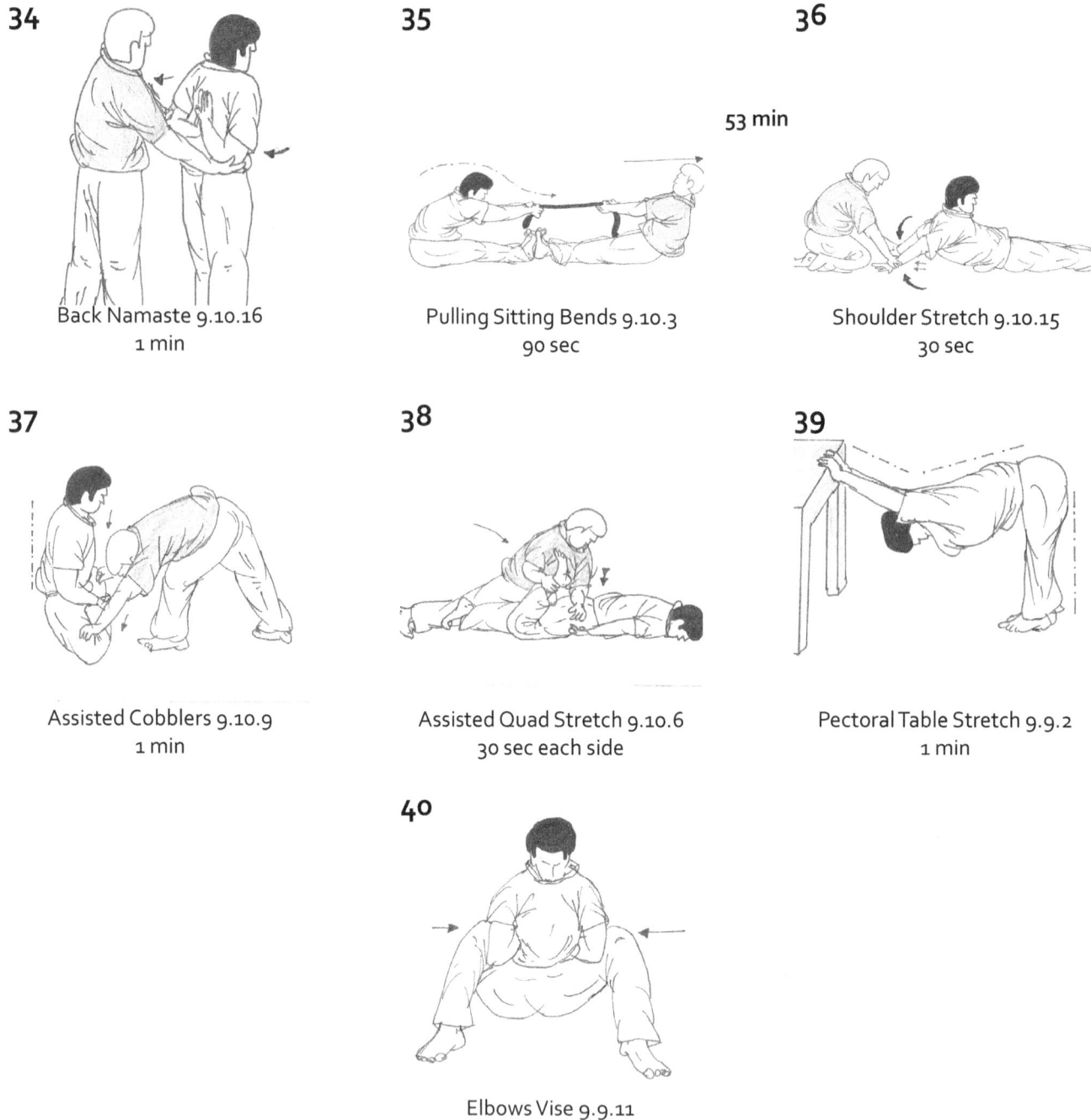

> **Success is the sum of small efforts, repeated day-in and day-out.**
> **~Robert Collier**

12.6.2 DAY 2

Plyo and Lower body

PROGRAM 5 DAY 2

10

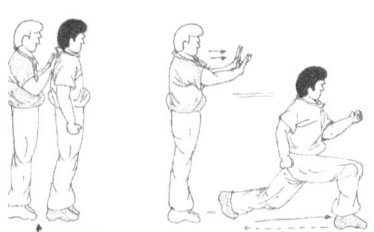

Pushed Lunges 8.8.1
3 sets of 10 each side

11

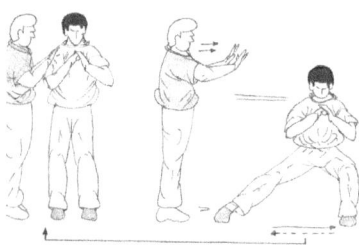

Lateral Pushed Lunges 8.8.2
3 sets of 10 each side

12

Abdominal Leg Throws 8.8.3
3 sets of 20

13

Box-off and High 8.3.7
1 min

14

Box-off and Long 8.3.8
1 min

15

Squat to Underhand Throw 8.7.4
1 min

16

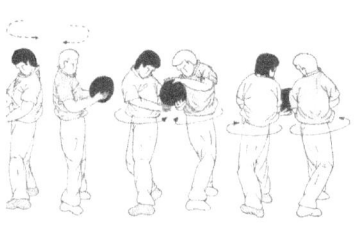

Medicine Ball Twists 8.8.6
1 min each direction

17

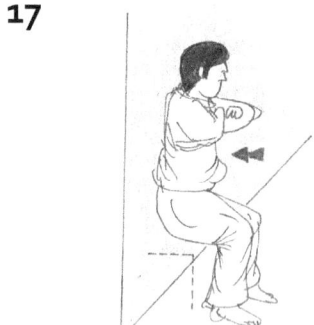

Wall Squat 10.4.4.1
3 reps

18

Sit-up Ball Throw 8.8.10
2 min

19

Elastic Band Sprints 8.8.4
3 times 10 sec

20

32 min

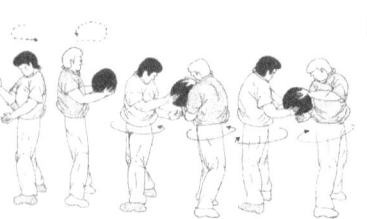

Ball extended Twists 8.8.7
30 sec each direction

21

Overhead Rear Throw 8.8.12
1 min

22

Twisting Lunges 8.7.9
2 min

23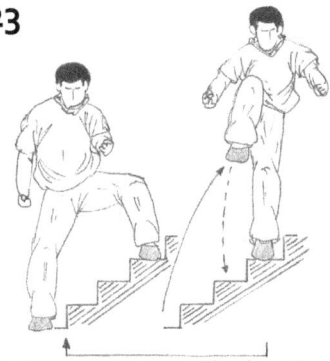

Knee-up Lateral Climb 8.6.4
3 sets of 10 each side

24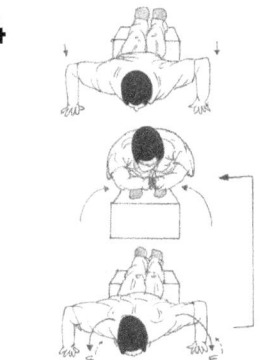

Clapping Depth Push-ups 8.3.16
3 sets of 10

25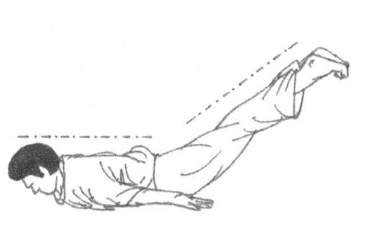

Locust Pose 10.2.6
1 min

26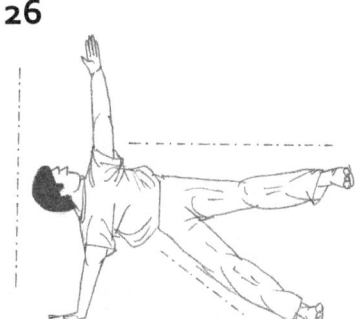

Leg-up Side plank 10.1.9
1 min each side

27

Cone Jumps in series 8.4.1
1 min

28

On-box High Jumps 8.3.2
1 min

29

Triceps Dips 8.3.19
3 sets of 20

30

48 min

On-box and Up 8.3.6
2 min

31

Crossed-legs Bend 9.2.6
1 min each side

32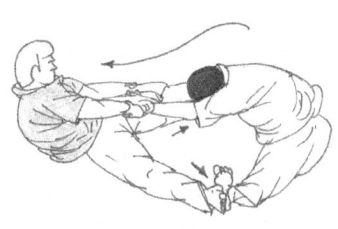

Wide Middle Stretch 9.10.10
1 min

33

Pulling Sitting Bends 9.10.3
1 min

PROGRAM 5 DAY 2

34

Assisted Cobra 9.10.13
1 min

35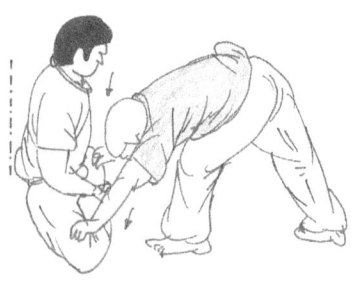

Assisted Cobblers 9.10.9
1 min

36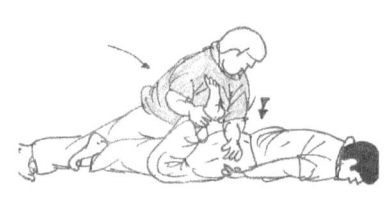

Assisted Quad Stretch 9.10.6
1 min each side

37

Bridge Pose 9.7.4
1 min

**You have to push past your perceived limits, push past that point you thought was as far as you can go.
~Drew Brees**

12.6.3 DAY 3

Iso and Flexio

1

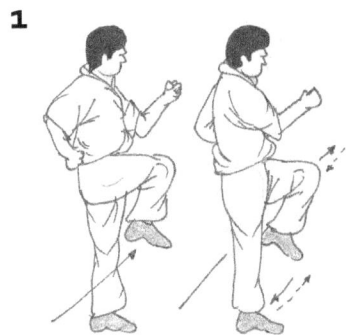

High-knee March 8.1.1
1 min

2

Skipping Jog 8.1.4
1 min

3

Box Switch Jumps 8.1.8
1 min

4

Sit-up Ball Throw 8.8.10
1 min

5

Basketball Pass 8.8.14
1 min

6

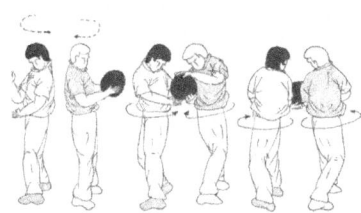

Medicine Ball Twists 8.8.6
1 min

7

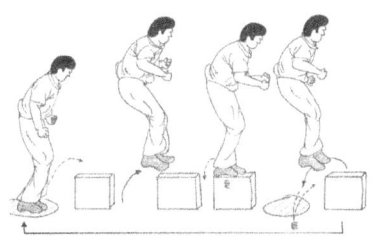

On-box Jumps 8.3.1
1 min

8

Box Cross-over Jumps 8.3.9
1 min

9

10 min

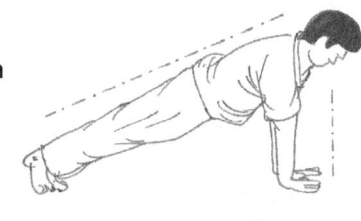

Plank Pose 10.1.2
2 min

PROGRAM 5 DAY 3 259

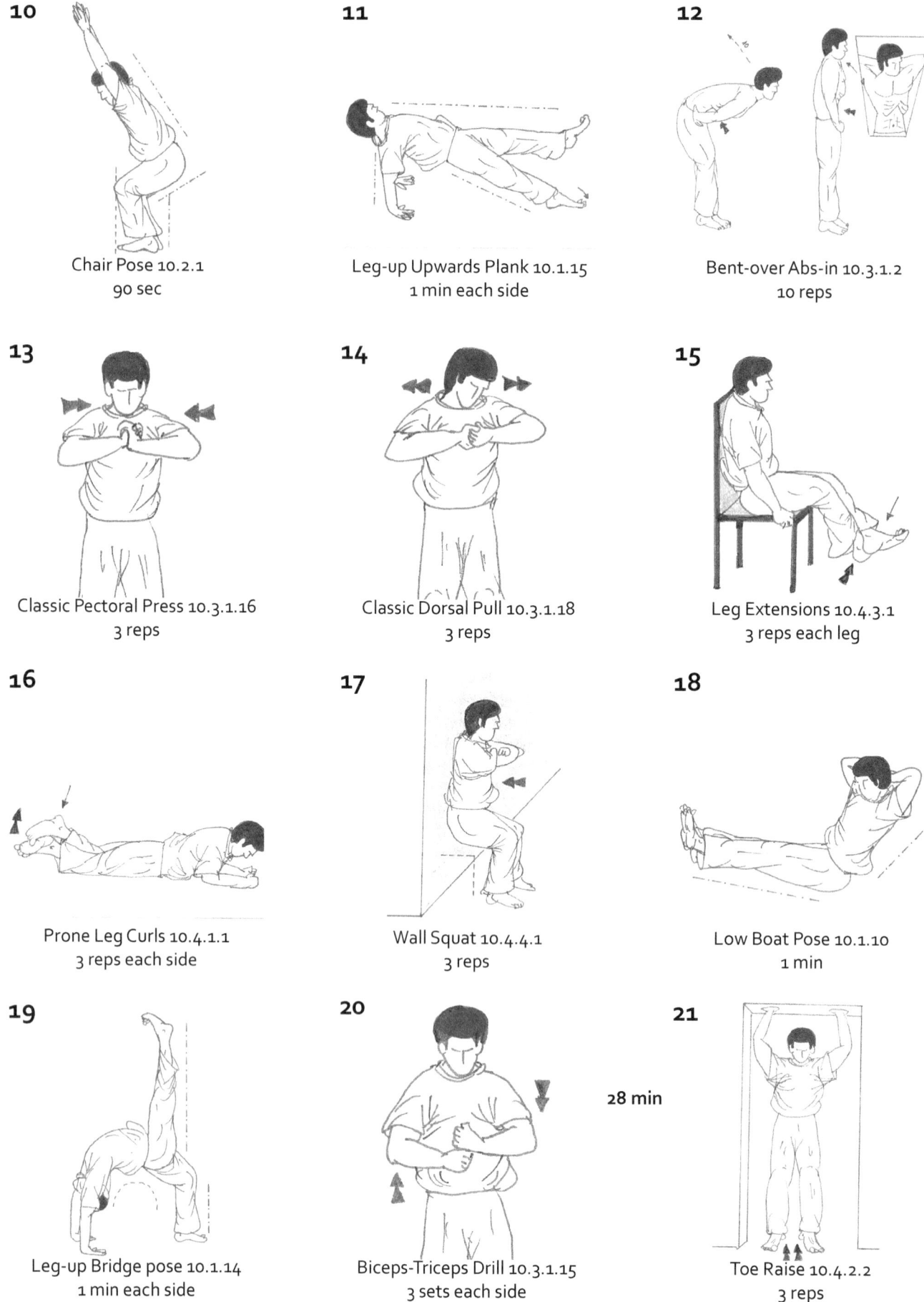

34 Upper Back Stretch 9.10.14
1 min

51 min

35 Assisted Lying Cobbler 9.10.9
1 min

36 Bridge pose 9.7.4
1 min

37 Lying Leg pulls 9.10.5
1 min each side

38 Standing Hip Stretch 9.10.8
1 min each side

39 Reclining Hero 9.5.3
90 sec

Things do not happen. Things are made to happen.
~John F. Kennedy

12.6.4 DAY 4 — Plyos and Upper Body

1. Lateral Crosses 8.1.5 — 1 min
2. Hops into Jumps 8.2.7 — 1 min
3. Push-up Burpees 8.1.11 — 1 min
4. Dynamic Crescent Kicks 9.10.1 — 1 min each side
5. Elbows Staff Pose 10.1.16 — 90 sec
6. High Boat pose 10.1.13 — 1 min
7. Prone Trunk Lift 10.1.17 — 1 min
8. Twist & Switch Push-ups 8.7.8 — 1 min
9. Abdominal Leg Throws 8.8.3 — 2 min

10 min

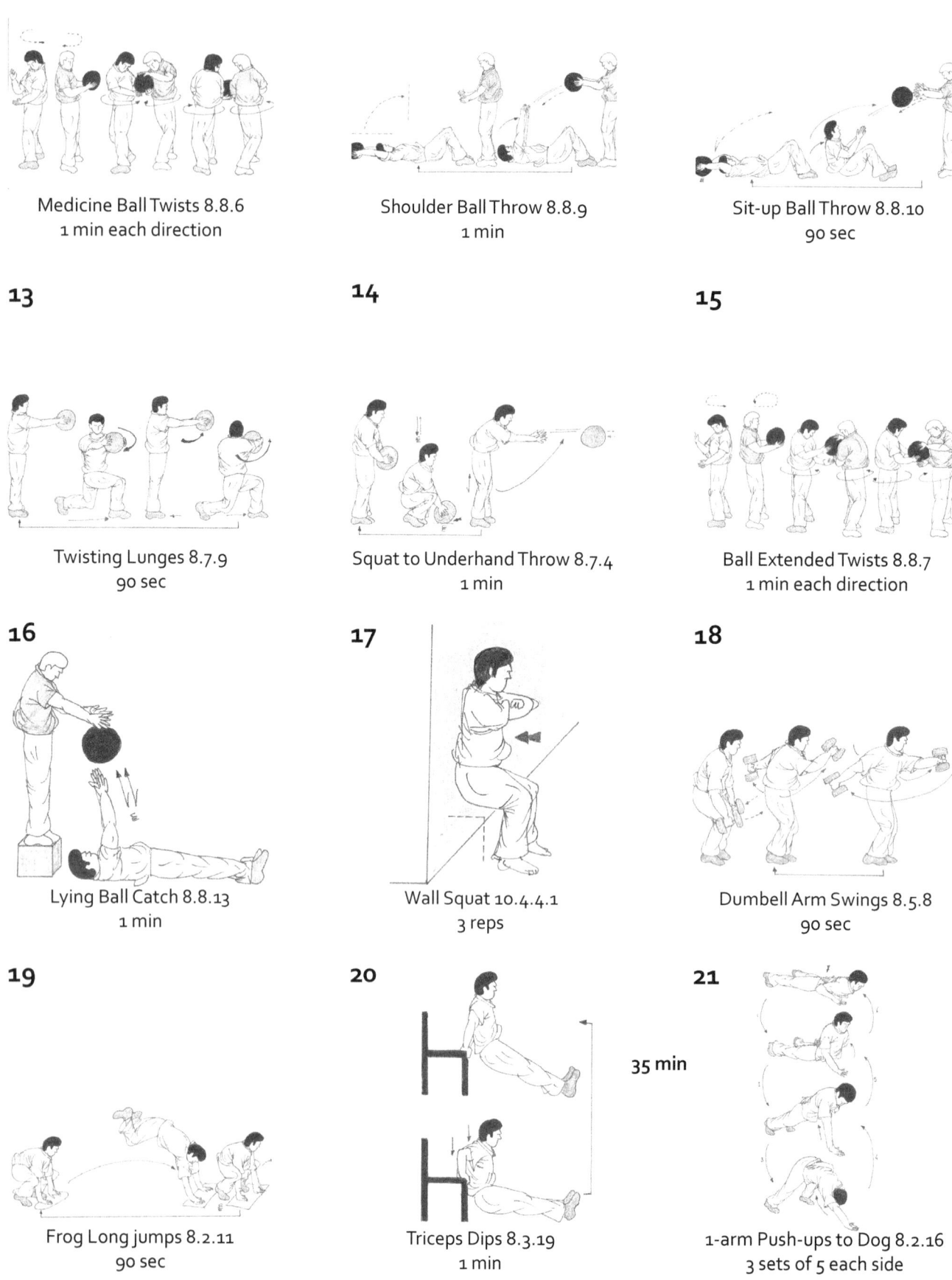

22

Medicine Ball Push ups 8.7.7
1 min

23

Lateral Throws on Knees 8.8.11
1 min each side

24

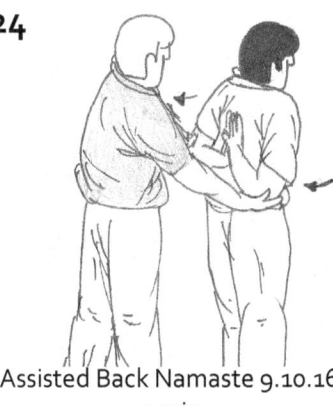

Assisted Back Namaste 9.10.16
1 min

25

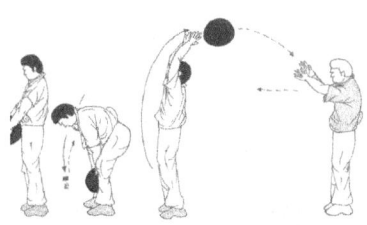

Overhead Rear Throws 8.8.12
1 min

26

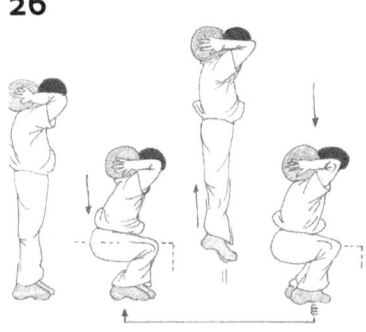

Squat jumps with Ball 8.7.1
1 min

27

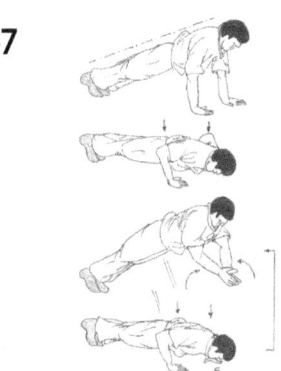

Clapping Push-ups 8.2.15
1 min

28

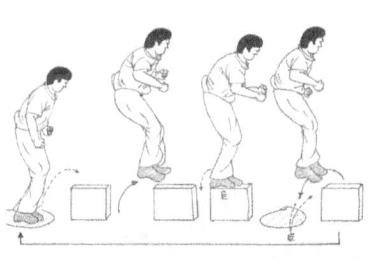

On-box Jumps 8.3.1
1 min

29

Leg-up Side Plank 10.1.9
1 min each side

50 min

30

Assisted Cobra 9.10.13
1 min

31

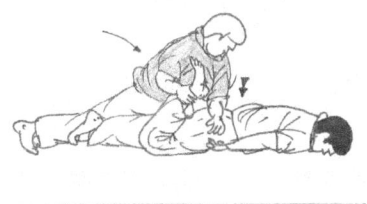

Assisted Quad Stretch 9.10.6
1 min each side

32

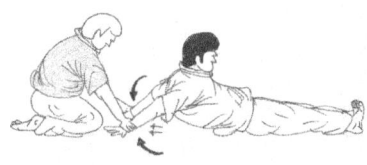

Shoulder Stretch 9.10.15
1 min

33

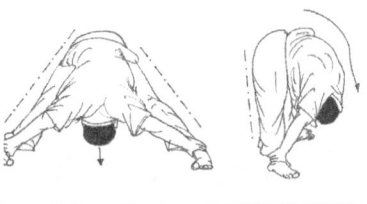

Open-legs Front Bends 9.3.7
1 min

PROGRAM 5 DAY 4

34

Sitting Side Bends 9.8.3
1 min each side

35

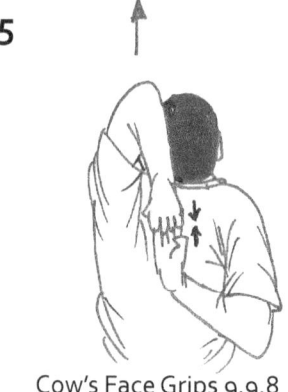

Cow's Face Grips 9.9.8
1 min each side

36

Hero's Pose 9.2.2
1 min

Note that the stiffest tree is most easily cracked, while the bamboo or willow survive by bending with the wind.
~Bruce Lee

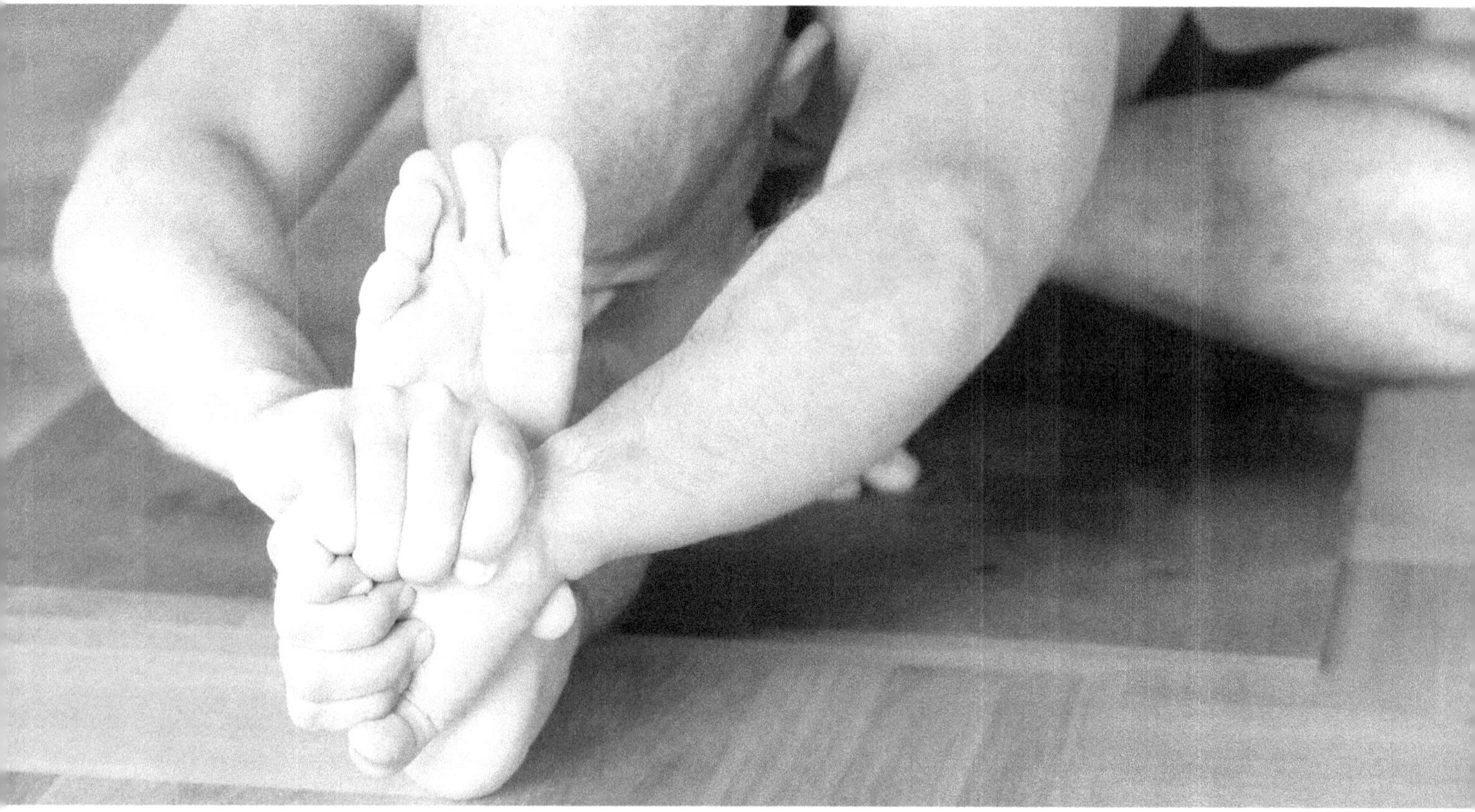

12.6.5 DAY 5

Iso and Lower Body

1. On-toes Jog 8.1.2 — 1 min
2. Butt-kicking Jog 8.1.3 — 1 min
3. Jumping Jacks 8.1.9 — 1 min
4. Alternate Arms Opening 8.1.10 — 1 min
5. Plank Pose 10.1.2 — 1 min
6. Box Cross-over Jumps 8.3.9 — 1 min
7. Push-up and Rotation 8.3.18 — 1 min
8. Front Cone Jumps in series 8.4.1 — 1 min
9. Warrior Pose 10.2.2 — 90 sec each side

10 min

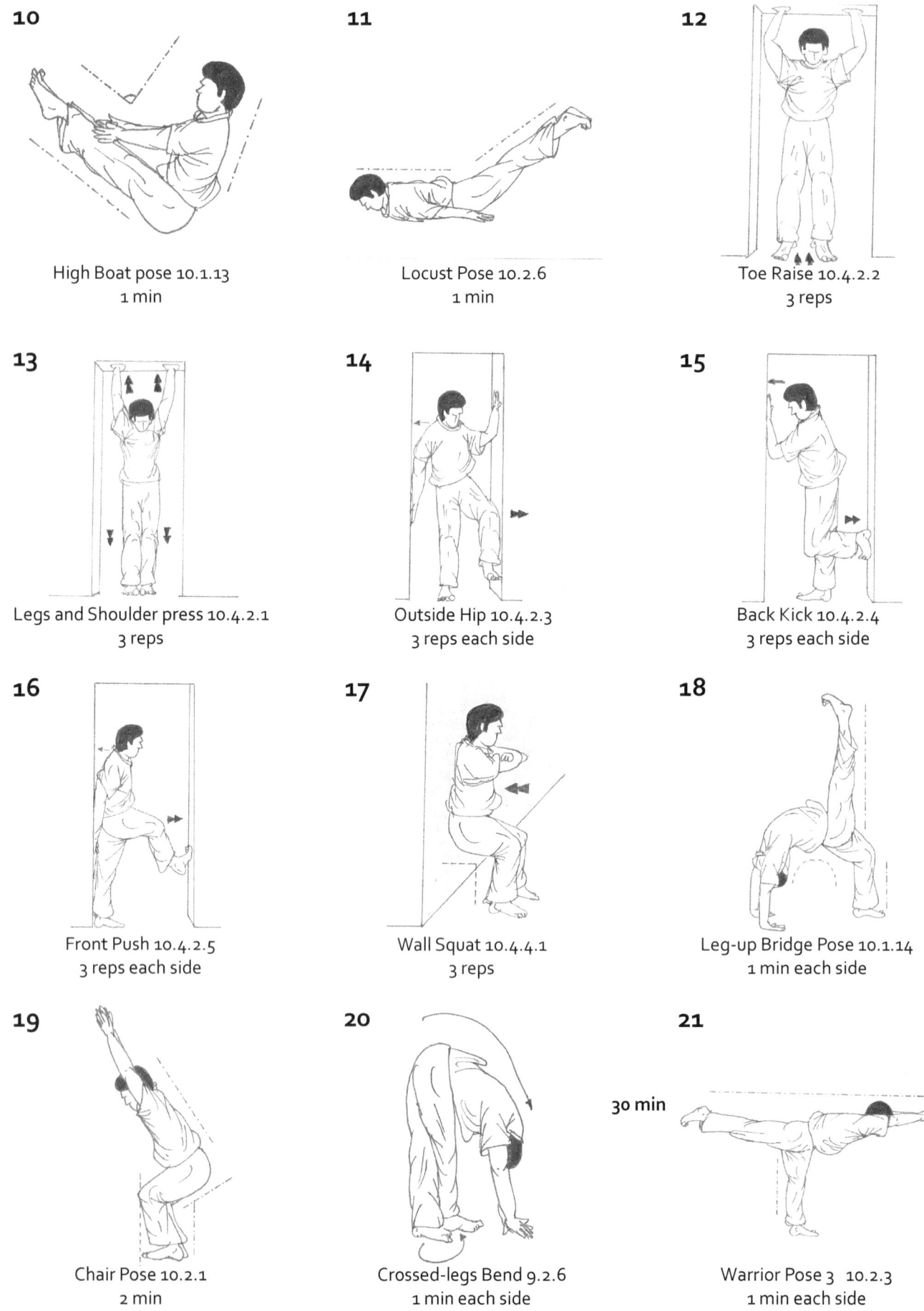

22

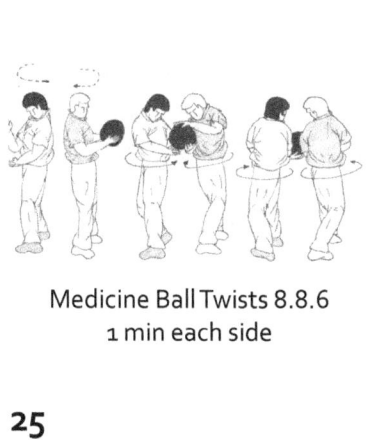

Medicine Ball Twists 8.8.6
1 min each side

23

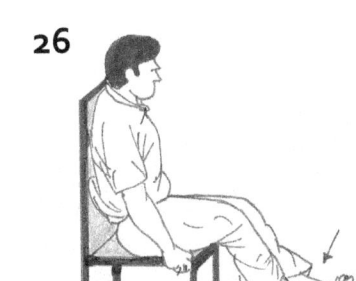
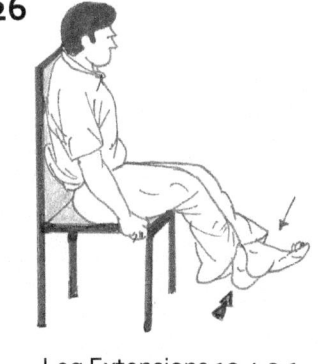

Sit-up Ball Throw 8.8.10
90 sec

24

Powerful Basketball Pass 8.8.14
2 min

25

Prone Leg Curls 10.4.1.1
3 reps each side

26

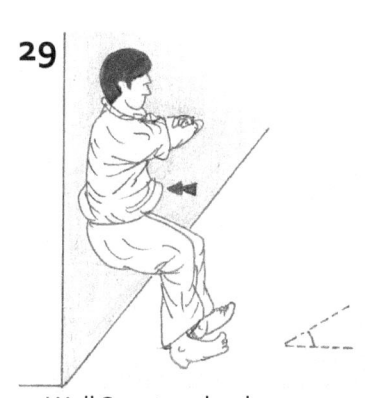

Leg Extensions 10.4.3.1
3 reps each side

27

Inner Thigh Press 10.4.3.2
3 reps

28

Outer Thigh Press 10.4.3.3
3 reps

29

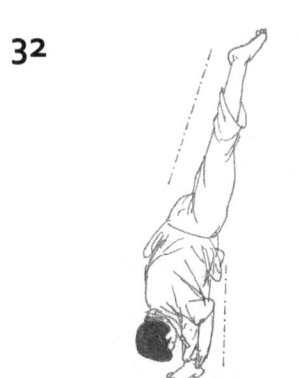

Wall Squat on heels 10.4.4.3
3 reps

30

Squat 10.4.5.1
3 reps

31

Standing Bend 9.3.6
90 sec

32

Leg-up Bend 10.2.9
1 min each side

33

50 min

Assisted Side Splits 9.10.11
1 min each side

PROGRAM 5 DAY 5

34

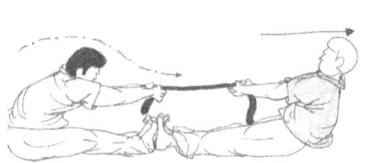

Pulling Sitting Bends 9.10.3
1 min

35

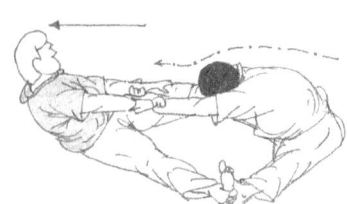

Pulling Wide Bends 9.10.4
1 min

36

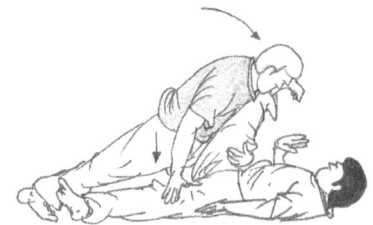

Assisted Leg Pulls 9.10.5
1 min each side

37

Assisted Quad Stretch 9.10.6
1 min each side

38

Bow Pose 9.7.3
1 min

39

Lying Cobbler 9.10.9
1 min

**Perseverance is the hard work you do after you get tired of doing the hard work you already did.
~Newt Gingrich**

12.6.6 DAY 6 — *Plyo and Flexio*

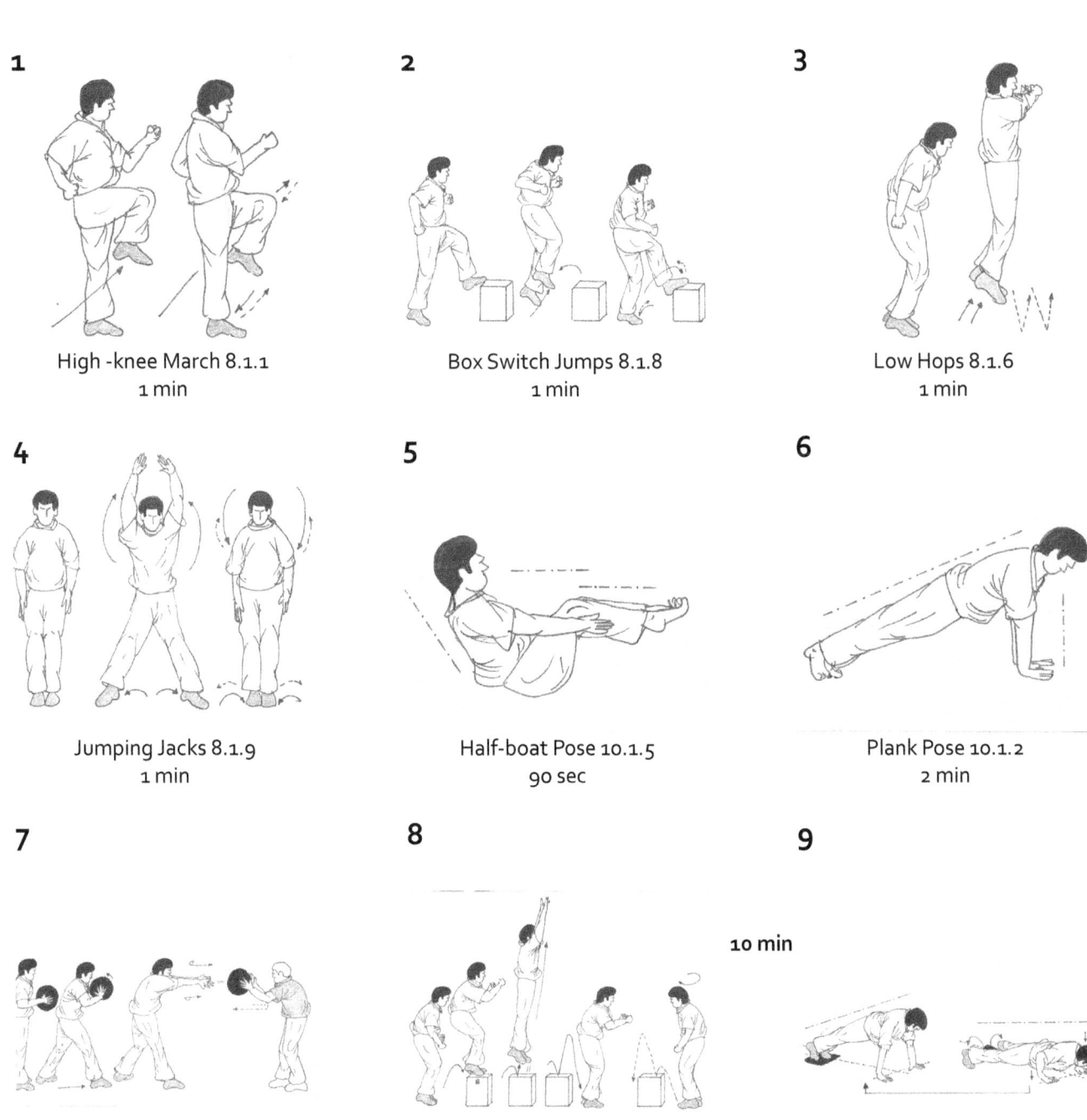

1. High-knee March 8.1.1 — 1 min
2. Box Switch Jumps 8.1.8 — 1 min
3. Low Hops 8.1.6 — 1 min
4. Jumping Jacks 8.1.9 — 1 min
5. Half-boat Pose 10.1.5 — 90 sec
6. Plank Pose 10.1.2 — 2 min
7. Basketball Passes 8.8.14 — 1 min
8. Box-on and Up 8.3.6 — 1 min
9. Jumping Jacks Push-ups 8.2.17 — 1 min

10 min

10

Box-off and Long 8.3.8
1 min

11

Box-off and High 8.3.7
1 min

12

On-box High Jumps 8.3.2
1 min

13

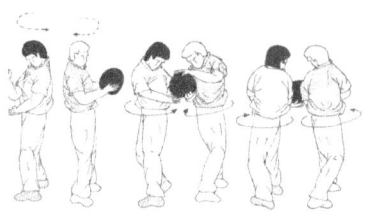

Medicine Ball Twists 8.8.6
1 min each direction

14

Lying Ball Catch 8.8.13
1 min

15

Squat to Underhand Throw 8.7.4
1 min

16

Sit-up Ball Throw 8.8.10
1 min

17

Shoulders Ball Throw 8.8.9
1 min

18

Elastic Band Sprints 8.8.4
3 sprints of 10 sec

19

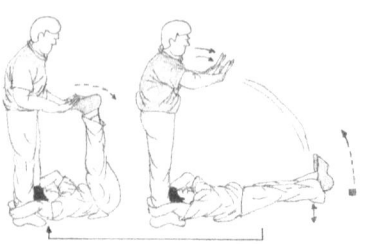

Abdominal Leg Throws 8.8.3
1 min

20

Twisting Lunges 8.7.9
1 min each side

28 min

21

Dumbell Arm Swings 8.5.8
1 min

22

Flying Twists 8.2.4
1 min each direction

23

Extended Ball Twists 8.8.7
1 min each direction

24

Overhead Rear Ball Throw 8.8.12
1 min

25

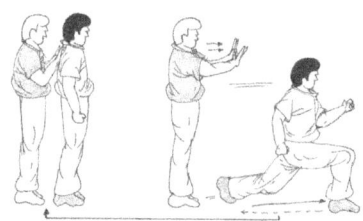

Forward Pushed Lunges 8.8.1
3 sets of 10 each side

26

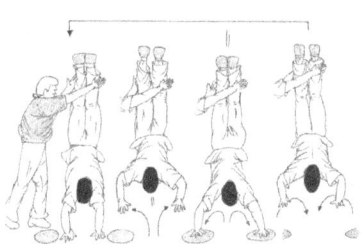

Handstand Plyo Push-ups 8.8.15
2 sets of 10

27

39 min

Incremental Height jumps 8.8.16
1 min

28

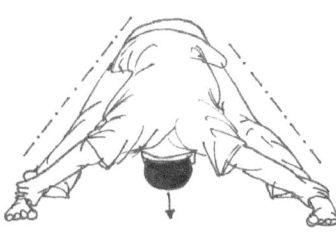

Open-legs Front Bends 9.3.7
1 min

29

Crossed-legs Bends 9.2.6
1 min each side

30

Cross Side Bends 9.6.8
1 min each side

31

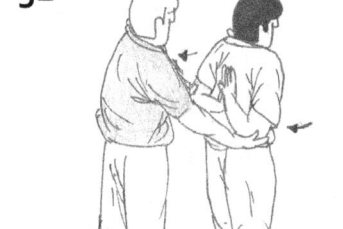

Assisted Back Namaste 9.10.16
1 min

32

Assisted Leg Pulls 9.10.5
1 min each leg

33

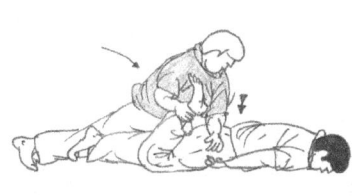

Assisted Quad Stretch 9.10.6
1 min each leg

PROGRAM 5 DAY 6

34

Bridge Pose 9.7.4
1 min

35

Dog Pose 9.9.9
2 min

36

Pulling Sitting Bends 9.10.3
1 min

37

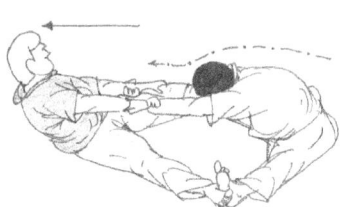

Pulling Wide Bends 9.10.4
1 min

38

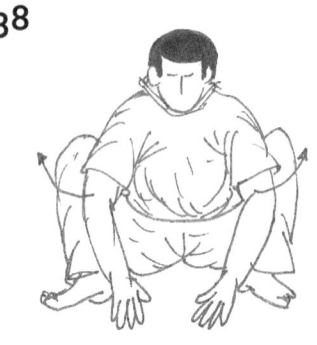

Frog 9.4.7
1 min

39

Hero's Pose 9.2.2
1 min

When you reach the end of your rope, tie a knot in it and hang on.
~Franklin D. Roosevelt

Afterword

We have now covered the proposed drills and their organization into 5 illustrative programs. If you start with the first Program and make your way gradually towards the Advanced one, according to your abilities and according to your progress, you will notice tremendous changes in your body and in your athletic ability.

You will notice, at the beginning, that you need more than one hour to complete a session and that you do not have enough rest time between the prescribed drills. This is normal and only practice will make you better at it. The 'lack' of rest time between the drills is intended to build in parallel your endurance and your aerobic abilities, both important tennets of athletic ability.
Once you have mastered all programs and can execute them fast and well, you certainly are at a level where you can build-up your own programs under the basic principles of Isoplex. You can use the numerous Drills presented in the book, or even research for more complex and sophisticated ones. Just keep the basic synergistic principles in mind.

According to the equipment and the time at your disposal, you may already have had to replace a few of the drills of a specific program by others from the book. Or you may have had to skip some for lack of free time. This is perfectly fine.
The important thing will be to respect the general way in which the Isoplex Method is built, to strive to set aside a daily slot for training, and to persevere. If you can only set half-an-hour a day, and not a full hour, so be it; it is perfectly fine. If you have to skip a session from time to time because of the pressure of modern life, do not feel bad. Do the best you can, but keep at it! Regular exercise and perserverance are the secret of success. It will work, even if it takes longer. Go for it.

If you have any comment or any query, please feel free to email me at martialartkicks@gmail.com

GOOD LUCK!

OTHER WORKS BY THE AUTHOR FOR FONS SAPIENTIAE PUBLISHING:

STOP KICKS are probably the most effective and sophisticated kicks a fighter can use: they are the safest as they are delivered as your opponent is at his most vulnerable. **STOP KICKS** are delivered just as your opponent is fully committed, physically or mentally, to his own attack and as he is starting execution of his attack based on your relative position and his expectation that you can only block in place or retreat. Stop Kicks are executed when your opponent cannot change his mind any more, and they will also use to their advantage the additional power of his attacking momentum.

To paraphrase a well-known author: the most dangerous fighter, the one you should fear, is the one who waits patiently for you to make a mistake...

**Only one who devotes himself to a cause with his whole strength and soul can be a true master. For this reason mastery demands all of a person.
~Albert Einstein**

Low Kicks are powerful, fast, and effective exactly what you need to defend yourself in a real life confrontation. And because they are seldom used in sport fighting, they can be a surprising and valuable addition to your free fighting arsenal. While they may seem easy to execute, not all low kicks are simply low versions of the basic kicks. There are specific attributes and principles that make low kicks work. Marc de Bremaeker has collected the most effective low kicking techniques from Martial Arts like *Krav Maga, Karatedo, Capoeira, Wing-Chun Kung-Fu, MMA*, and *Muay Thai*. In this book, he analyzes each kick in depth, explaining the proper execution and outlining applications and variations from self-defense, sport fighting and traditional practice: Hundreds of examples in over one thousand photographs and drawings.

Plyometrics and Flexibility Training for Explosive Martial Arts Kicks and Performance Sports Plyo-Flex is a system of plyometric exercises and intensive flexibility training designed to increase your kicking power, speed, flexibility and skill level. Based on scientific principles, Plyo-Flex exercises will boost your muscles, joints and nervous system interfaces to the next performance level. After only a few weeks of training, you should see a marked improvement in the speed of your kicks and footwork, the power of your kicks, the height of your jumps, your stamina and your overall flexibility. Hundreds of illustrations and photographs will guide you through the basic plyometric and stretching exercises. Once you've mastered the basics, add the kicking-oriented variations to your workout for an extra challenge.

'Sacrifice Kicks' will comprehensively present the most important Martial Arts Airborne Kicks: Flying Kicks, Hopping Kicks, Jumping Kicks and Suicide Kicks. They have been dubbed 'Sacrifice' in the spirit of Judo's redoubtable Sutemi Takedowns in which one sacrifices his balance in order to throw his opponent down. *Flying Kicks* are not about showmanship, they are very effective techniques when used judiciously. They need not be necessarily high and spectacular; they can be surprising *Jumping Kicks* and *Hopping Kicks* executed long and low. And *Suicide Kicks* take the Sacrifice principles a little further: they are extremely unexpected techniques delivered airborne, but with little hope of landing on one's feet, unlike classic Flying Kicks. All these realistic maneuvers, coming from Karate, Krav Maga, Kung Fu, TaeKwonDo, MMA, Capoeira, Muay Thai and more, are described with applications and training tips. Over 1000 Photos and Illustrations.

Whether you are on the ground by choice or you have been taken down, whether your opponent is standing or is on the ground with you, whether you are a good grappler or you are trying to keep a good grappler at bay, whether you were caught unawares sitting on the floor or you have evaded down on purpose, whether you are a beginner or an experienced martial artist...this book has the right kick for the situation. In **Ground Kicks**: Advanced Martial Arts Kicks for Ground-fighting from Karate, Krav Maga, MMA, Capoeira, Kung Fu and more, Marc De Bremaeker has created a comprehensive collection of Ground Kicks, with hundreds of applications for sport fighting and self-defense situation. Packed with over 1200 photographs and illustrations, Ground Kicks also includes specific training tips for practicing each kick effectively.

Stealth Kicks will introduce you to the Art of executing Kicks that your opponent will not see coming. This subject has never been treated comprehensively before. Whether you are a beginner or an experienced Artist, you will find suitable Kicks or tips to modify your current techniques to give them stealth. It will help you to score in Sport confrontations or make sure to come on top in real life Self-Defense situations. The *Feint Kicks* presented are based on misdirection: they will aim at provoking a misguided reaction that will open your adversary to the real kick intended. The *Ghost Kicks* presented are based on dissimulation and will travel out of your opponent's range of vision to catch him unawares.
Together with general feinting techniques and specific training tips, hundreds of applications will introduce you to the sneaky Art of stealth kicking and will make you a better and unpredictable fighter. Crammed with over 2300 photos and drawings for an easy understanding of the concept of Stealth.

Perfection is not attainable, but if we chase perfection we can catch excellence.
~Vince Lombardi

Other genres from Fons Sapientiae

AVAILABLE IN PAPERBACK AND KINDLE FORMATS ON AMAZON

The Manual is the definitive guide to Enhanced Concentration, Super Memory, Speed Reading, Note-Taking, Rapid Mental Arithmetic, and the *Ultimate Study Method* (USM).

The techniques presented are the culmination of decades of practical experience combined with the latest scientific research and time-tested practices. The system described herewith will allow the practitioner to:

- Read faster with higher comprehension.
- Remember any type of information instantly.
- Store information in long-term memory.
- Enhance concentration and focus.
- Access deeper levels of the mind.
- Induce relaxation.
- Rapidly perform complex mental arithmetic.
- Master the Ultimate Study Method (USM).

USM is a synergistic combination of established techniques for Concentration, Long-Term Memory, Speed Reading, and Note-Taking. It involves a systematic procedure that allows the practitioner to study any topic fast, efficiently and effectively. USM can be applied to all areas of educational study, academic research, business endeavours, as well as professional life in general.

Rain Fund: A riveting thriller

"…For the safety of the readers, this book ought to come with the disclaimer: leave this book read half-way at your own risk. Unless you are Superman, you won't be able to concentrate on much else until you have read the last page of "Rain Fund". The time has come for Patterson, Ludlum, Dan Brown et al to slide over and make space at the top for Marc Brem." - Shweta Shankar for Readers' Favorite

"…In the good tradition of Ludlum and Grisham. Five Stars" Aldo Levy

"Autistic geniuses charting financial markets; Mobster-fuelled Ponzi schemes; sophisticated hardware viruses; spies; and a rising superpower that strives for dominance – so realistic it is frightening."